CU00305071

'Xolela Mangcu is one of a handfu
sustained the best of the black intelle
honesty he strips Mbeki of the robes or tne pnuosopher-king
by seeking deeper truths that shape our political and social reality.
To the Brink is an antidote to the pedestrian commentary that
masquerades as political analysis.'

Sipho Seepe, president of
the South African Institute of Race Relations

'This book is a powerful statement to South Africans to recapture
the language and vision of the non-racial nationalism that
animated our struggle for liberation. Xolela Mangcu writes with
authority and feeling, providing hope for those who fear a post-
Polokwane South Africa.'

Edward Webster, professor of sociology,
University of the Witwatersrand

'Xolela Mangcu writes with courage, erudition and clarity. *To the
Brink* will further his mission to create a climate within
which independent thinkers can feel free to state their opinions,
brilliantly challenging establishment views of race, power and
culture in South Africa today.'

Belinda Bozzoli, author of
Theatres of Struggle and the End of Apartheid

'A crucial post-1994 development is the flowering of a small but
vigorous black intelligentsia, rooted in the dialogue of race but
not bound by it. In *To the Brink*, South Africa's leading public
intellectual, Xolela Mangcu, advances what one might call a New
Africanism – a vision for our society which moves beyond racial
exclusivity and the aggregation of political and moral legitimacy
to an anointed few within the ANC.'

William Saunderson-Meyer,
Jaundiced Eye newspaper columnist

To the Brink

The State of Democracy in South Africa

XOLELA MANGCU

UNIVERSITY OF KwaZulu-Natal Press

Published in 2008 by University of KwaZulu-Natal Press
Private Bag X01, Scottsville, 3209
South Africa
Email: books@ukzn.ac.za
Website: www.ukznpress.co.za

ISBN: 978-1-86914-137-0

Editor: Andrea Nattrass
Typesetter: Patricia Comrie
Indexer: Brenda Williams-Wynn
Cover designer: Flying Ant Designs
Photographer: Russell Roberts

Printed and bound by Intrepid Printers - 5200

Contents

For my mother, Nonji, in whom everything came together.

'I never fail to derive pleasure from Xolela Mangcu's columns. He alternately infuriates, educates, and entertains me, but his views are consistently insightful, erudite, and most of all represent an intellectually rigorous tradition that is such a fundamental part of a free society. Xolela, keep telling it like it is – independent intellectuals like you are worth your weight in gold.'

Bryan Watson, 'Gold Weight', *Business Day*,
28 November 2005

Acknowledgements

MANY PEOPLE HAVE contributed to my personal and intellectual development, first among whom is my wife Phelisa. I would also like to acknowledge my intellectual soulmates: Carolyn Hamilton, for her unyielding thoughtfulness and generosity and for always pushing me to the limits of my thinking; Mcebisi Ndletyana, for being my intellectual interlocutor; Mikki Xayiya and Oyama Mabandla, for rich discussions on the history of the ANC; the distinguished American academic and activist Harry Boyte, whose incisive and encyclopaedic mind has taken me to many a library and a bookstore; and the young men and women of Ginsberg for whom I became an inspiration – Lindani Ntenteni, Andile Jack, Mfundo Ngele, Mandisi Aplom and Tabisa Bata.

Those who have been extremely supportive during my time at Wits University include Lenore Longwe and Oliver Barstow, for providing administrative and strategic support; Wits Council Chairperson Edwin Cameron, Vice-Chancellor Loyiso Nongxa, and Deputy Vice-Chancellors

Yunus Ballim, Rob Moore and Belinda Bozzoli, as well as Dean of the Humanities Tawana Kupe.

I would also like to acknowledge the support of my editor Andrea Nattrass, for her meticulous attention to detail, and my publisher Glenn Cowley, for his free and generous spirit.

However, none of this work would have been possible without the space I was provided by John Battersby, former editor of the *Sunday Independent*, and Peter Bruce, editor of *Business Day* and *The Weekender*.

My former Ph.D. adviser Pierre Clavel always remains in my mind, as does my good friend Sandile Dikeni.

Abbreviations

AIDS	Acquired Immunodeficiency Syndrome
ANC	African National Congress
BPC	Black People's Convention
BSS	Black Students' Society
COSATU	Congress of South African Trade Unions
CIA	Central Intelligence Agency
DA	Democratic Alliance
DBSA	Development Bank of South Africa
GEAR	Growth, Employment and Redistribution
HIV	Human Immunodeficiency Virus
HSRC	Human Sciences Research Council
ICU	Industrial and Commercial Workers' Union
MCC	Medicines Control Council
MDC	Movement for Democratic Change
MEC	Member of the Executive Committee

MIT	Massachusetts Institute of Technology
MP	Member of Parliament
MRC	Medical Research Council
NEDLAC	National Economic Development and Labour Council
NUSAS	National Union of South African Students
PAC	Pan Africanist Congress
SABC	South African Broadcasting Corporation
SADC	Southern African Development Community
SASO	South African Students' Organisation
TAC	Treatment Action Campaign
TRC	Truth and Reconciliation Commission
UDF	United Democratic Front
UDM	United Democratic Movement
ZANU	Zimbabwe African National Union
ZAPU	Zimbabwe African People's Union

Why I Wrote this Book

THIS BOOK COMES out of my urgent sense that South Africa's black political and intellectual tradition is being deeply violated. In brief, and as elaborated on throughout the text, our heritage of racial syncretism is being overwhelmed by the racial nativism that has taken hold of our political culture under President Thabo Mbeki's rule.

What do I mean by these terms? By syncretism I mean the dynamic processes of identity formation that have always underpinned black people's encounter with European modernity. The condition of being native or African or black was always a product of bargaining and contestation of the often derogatory definitions given by colonialists and missionaries alike. There was no essentialised African identity that was pure and untouched by the cultures with which one interacted. Black political and intellectual leaders – from Tiyo Soga to Steve Biko – wrote extensively about the importance of choice, identification, consciousness and values in these processes of identity formation. In particular, Biko's concept of a joint culture comes from black–white or African–European interaction.

Racial nativism, by contrast, harkens to purist, essentialist conceptions of identity. It is enough that one has a black skin or that one participated in the liberation struggle to overthrow apartheid. Those 'qualifications' provide one with exclusive licence to speak or banish those with opposing views. It is as if those who participated in that struggle have a monopoly on wisdom and morality.

In my regular newspaper columns and from other platforms I have been openly critical of this racial nativism – essentially because I have felt something precious slipping away from me and from our political and intellectual landscape. I have spoken out whenever our government has deployed race to show callous indifference to the suffering of people with HIV/AIDS, or the people of Zimbabwe, or victims of crime, or to shut down those who have opposed its policies. I have often felt compelled to say this is not how it was and this is not how it was supposed to be.

I am aware that what I present in this book is but one among many possible interpretations of our encounter with the democratic moment. My interpretation is, however, not based on race or participation in struggle but on a mix of personal observation of everyday life outside the political arena proper, and on years of studying black political and cultural life. In relying on our memories to construct the present and the future we should always bear in mind that we *all* have the right to participate in the telling of the story of our nation.

I start the narrative with my childhood days in the Eastern Cape, not so much to elevate its inhabitants as to assert the opposite, which is that this part of South Africa became home to cosmopolitan institutions such as Lovedale and Fort Hare by bringing together young people from all over the country and the continent. These institutions in turn made possible the forging of syncretic identities in everyday life, which ultimately led to the formation of one of the most syncretic political movements in the world, the African National Congress. It is this syncretism – in both cultural and political life – that I feel is being violated by the racial nativism of our times.

I should also say that this book is not a collection of the newspaper columns I have written over the years – such a project is still to come. I do, however, use text from those columns as a counterpoint to some of the arguments I make. Consequently I have chosen those columns that best serve my purposes here. In some instances I have used abridged versions of the columns and in others the columns do not appear exactly as they did in the published form.

Finally, I have over the years made it my practice to incorporate the opinions of intellectuals whose works I have read to enrich the arguments I make. This is standard academic practice and I have adopted a similar style in writing this book. Readers will hopefully come from all walks of life; there will be those who want to engage with the arguments I make in their esoteric forms and others who are not interested in such academic pursuits. Straddling these 'publics' is never easy. However, I have always seen it as my role and responsibility to bring the world of scholarship into conversation with the public. Scholarship that fails to do this is easily irrelevant, and a public culture that is not engaged with scholarship is diminished. Public scholarship is an important part of an enriched democratic culture, and it is absolutely vital in order to test the political claims of the nativists against the trajectory of our lived experiences in all of their complexity.

The Argument in Brief

ON 14 JUNE 2006 I visited the German embassy in Pretoria to apply for a visa so I could go to the Soccer World Cup finals. As I had expected there was a long line of people waiting with the usual mix of anxiety and anticipation. I sat next to an Indian woman and seated next to her was her daughter. The girl could not have been more than five or six years old. The security guard on duty told the woman that the chairs in the embassy were reserved for visa applicants. The child needed to give up her seat for one of the people standing in line.

It occurred to me that this was patently unfair and unnecessary. Surely the able-bodied men and women in the line could stand on their feet. As is often the case in these matters, the security guard got his way. Feeling a little guilty he then put the girl on his lap. A white woman joined in my protestation. That is when all hell broke loose. A prominent African woman journalist told the white woman that it was 'un-African' for a child to sit while adults stood. 'It is our culture,' she insisted. She

1

then turned to the security guard and instructed him in isiZulu to put the child down: '*Beka phantsi leyonto wena*' (Put down that 'thing').

Surely it was not in African culture to treat children with such lack of feeling? Why then would a fairly prominent, middle class African woman, probably herself a parent, act with such callousness? It seemed to me that her desire to make a political statement to a captive audience trumped any other moral consideration. I would not quibble with the idea that identity is central to the black struggle for freedom. But it seemed like the famous liberation credo 'culture is the weapon' was being subverted for political point scoring. Also interesting is that she chose to explain this aspect of African culture only after the white woman had interjected. The message was unmistakable: white people have no right to speak about how Africans – be they black or Indian – treat their children.

And if you were black the message was that you would cross this woman's line at your own risk. Could she be an official of state, ordering people around and striking fear in their hearts? I knew better. This was the nationalist grandstanding that had come to typify our political culture.

It was a classic example of the racial insider/outsider dynamic at the heart of Thabo Mbeki's strategy of rule. This cultural dynamic goes under the rise of racial nativism. This is the idea that the true custodians of African culture are the natives. The natives are often defined as black Africans because they are indigenous to the country, and within that group the true natives are those who participated in the resistance struggle. And even among those who participated in the liberation, the truest natives are those who are on the side of government. By dint of their authenticity these natives have the right to silence white interlopers or black sell-outs.

The central argument of this book is that racial nativism goes against the long traditions of racial syncretism that have always characterised South African political and intellectual history. In this syncretic approach natives are all the people born in the country, irrespective of their struggle history or where they stand in relation to government. In a democratic society no group of people has greater authenticity or licence than others. Instead, the defining ethos of a syncretic approach to national belonging is captured by the Freedom Charter's opening line: 'South Africa belongs

2

to all who live in it, black and white'. I argue that even the radical Pan Africanist and Black Consciousness movements upheld the ideal of a non-racial democratic society in which all citizens are regarded as equal and therefore entitled to express their views just like everyone else.

To reduce this theory to its most simple form, my argument is that the current, particularly political, trend of condemning anyone who is not black and who is not on the side of the government (what can be called racial nativism) is a negative and destructive one that has developed in the past eight years. This concept stands in stark contrast to the approach that allows all citizens' voices to be heard and welcomes vigorous and open debate on issues (the essence of the syncretic approach).

Oftentimes the nativists invoke Pan Africanist leader Robert Sobukwe or Black Consciousness leader Steve Biko to explain their political behaviour. But neither Sobukwe nor Biko was intolerant. Even though these leaders advocated racial exclusivism as a political strategy to fight white supremacy, they were never racial essentialists. Unlike the woman in the embassy, they did not believe that there is a black essence beyond the access of everyone else. This was clear both in their political writings and in their personal relationships. Sobukwe described his attitude to white South Africans thus:

I know I have been accused of being anti-white, not only by the government but also by others. But there is not one who can quote any statement of mine that bears that out. When I say Africa for the Africans I mean those, of any colour, who accept Africa as their home. Colour does not mean anything to me.[1]

Black Consciousness leader Steve Biko wrote that 'being black is not a matter of pigmentation – being black is a reflection of a mental attitude'.[2] He repeatedly called for the creation of a non-racial, egalitarian society:

We see a completely non-racial society. We don't believe, for instance, in the so-called guarantees for minority rights, because guaranteeing minority rights implies the recognition of portions of the community on a race basis. We believe that in our country there shall be no minority, there shall be no majority, just the people. And those people will have the same status before the law and they will have the same political rights before the law. So in a sense it will be a completely non-racial egalitarian society.[3]

Sobukwe's close relationship with Benjamin Pogrund, the journalist and later deputy editor of the *Rand Daily Mail*, and Biko's relationships with journalist Donald Woods, the academic Francis Wilson and his spiritual friendship with Aelred Stubbs, a monk of the Anglican Community of the Resurrection, are evidence of their non-essentialist, non-nativist approach to politics. Despite leading a breakaway from the multi-racial National Union of South African Students (NUSAS) on account of it being a white-dominated organisation that purported to speak on behalf of black students, Biko continued to maintain close personal relationships with white student leaders such as Neville Curtis, Duncan Innes, Paul Pretorius, Paula Ensor, Geoff Budlender, Horst Kleinschmidt and many others. Without exception all of these leaders attest to Biko's non-racial personality.[4]

But if racial essentialism has no precedence in our history, how has it come to have such a hold on our political imagination in the Mbeki years? The journalist Jonny Steinberg attributes this nativism to a sense of siege in the Mbeki government. He argues that Mbeki's controversial response to HIV/AIDS is an example of a leadership that feels its authority and sovereignty being usurped by *foreign* (my emphasis) forces in cahoots with local civil society organisations: 'What Mbeki coaxed to the surface of SA's political culture was an anxious man's nationalism and a paranoid's nativism.' Steinberg argues that Mbeki 'treated AIDS as a pernicious attack on our sovereignty launched from abroad'. This left us with a shrill and belligerent political culture: 'In diffuse and unhappy ways he has triggered a flurry of trench digging across large strata of SA. It is a troubling legacy to leave behind.'[5]

I will deal with Mbeki's treatment of HIV/AIDS in Chapter 3. Suffice it to say here that the word 'foreign' is not just a geographical reference but has come to be a reference to the foreigner within – the racial outsider, as well as those black critics of government deemed to be in cahoots with those foreigners undermining the authentically 'native' black government. By its very nature racial nativism is exclusionary and inevitably leads to political intolerance, which has manifested through the racial labelling of political critics as traitors on the side of the non-native population. The most ironic deployment of this was when Mbeki accused the black Congress of South African Trade Unions (COSATU), a member of the Tripartite Alliance that also includes the African National Congress (ANC) and the Communist Party, of racism for criticising his economic policies (as elaborated on in Chapter 8).[6] Ultimately, the foreigners are those who exist outside the tradition of the ANC. Indeed, the fact that Mbeki has never met with the head of COSATU shows the disdain with which he views the foreigners in the ANC. It is the ANC and the ANC only that has the prerogative to guide society. This is not just because it has been returned to power with ever-increasing majorities but because this is its historical mandate.

Ultimately, though, any attempt to stifle criticism leads to rebellion. The most significant moments of such rebellion were the ANC's general council in 2005 and the national policy conference in July 2007. In both cases the ANC rank and file moved to signal its dissatisfaction with Mbeki's leadership and indicated that it was time for Mbeki to give way to a new leader. Mbeki has, however, ignored these signs and indicated his availability to lead the ANC for a third term (see Chapters 7 and 8).

This book outlines the deployment of racial nativism in several public policy domains, and the intolerance it has engendered. Chapter 1 reviews how black South Africans have historically dealt with their racial identities. This is done through an examination of black intellectual history and autobiographical reflections of my place in this history. It seeks to demonstrate that the construction of black identity (and all identities for that matter) has always been a matter of what Belinda Bozzoli calls 'syncretic adaptation', and never a form of racial nativism.[7] A related concept is that of transculturation, articulated by Frank Ortiz with respect to Cuba. This incorporates the idea that the oppressed and marginalised select from and subvert the dominant culture through what Ortiz calls 'disadjustment and readjustment'.[8] According to the academic David Attwell, transculturation 'stands in direct opposition to myths of essentialism and uniformity in both colonial and nativist forms of self-representation'.[9]

While racial nativism harkens to purist, essentialist conceptions of what it means to be African, the idea of a joint culture (racial syncretism) looks at African culture and identity as the product of an endless process of adaptation and renewal to meet the challenges of ever changing social and political conditions.

Chapters 2 to 5 take us through the intersection of this racial nativism and public policy. These chapters demonstrate how the racial insider/outsider dynamic has informed Mbeki's approach to the role of black intellectuals, HIV/AIDS, Zimbabwe and corruption.

Thereafter, Chapters 6 to 9 confront the problem of racism by building non-racial constituencies and calling forth non-racial leadership. Ultimately this constitutes a call for the re-imagination of the ANC's relationship with the rest of society. Instead of trying to exert hegemonic influence over society, the ANC should learn more how to lead a complex, differentiated and pluralistic society with constantly shifting alliances, interests and identities. The people whom the ANC has elected at its December 2007 conference will be decisive in determining whether or not the organisation goes back on its promise of building a non-racial culture in which everyone has a sense of belonging or whether it descends further into the racial nativism of the Mbeki years. The nativist siege mentality of the Mbeki era should give way to a new ethos of building bridges with all of the sectors of society.

CHAPTER 1

Bearing Witness
Political and Personal Heritage

THIS CHAPTER IS motivated by one of my favourite passages by the great American sociologist C. Wright Mills. The passage comes from Mills's classic work, *The Sociological Imagination*:

> We have come to know that every individual lives, from one generation to the next, in some society. That he lives out a biography, and that he lives it out within some historical sequence. By the fact of his living he contributes, however minutely, to the shaping of this society and to the course of its history, even as he is made by society and its historical push and shove.[1]

In many ways this passage captures how I was influenced by the political and intellectual history of the communities and families from which I come, and how that history has informed my role as a social critic.

7

I am a child of the Eastern Cape. This region is known for its stunning physical beauty and its rich political and intellectual history. It is in the valleys and mountains of this region that black people resisted colonial occupation to the very end. From the first wars of resistance in 1789 to the last one in 1870, the region's leaders became some of the first prisoners on Robben Island, where one of their grandchildren, Nelson Mandela, would be incarcerated for two decades. Mandela captured the inter-generational influences in the long struggle for freedom in a recollection of how he was influenced by the great Xhosa poet S.E.K. Mqhayi. Mqhayi had been invited to Healdtown College, where Mandela was in high school: 'The day of his arrival was declared a holiday by the authorities. On the appointed morning the entire school, including staff members, both black and white, gathered in the dining hall.'[2] Mqhayi startled the audience with a blistering critique of racism. Mandela recalls:

> I could hardly believe my ears. His boldness in speaking of such delicate matters in the presence of Dr Wellington [the head-master] and other whites seemed utterly astonishing to us. Yet at the same time it aroused and motivated us, and began to alter my perception of men like Dr Wellington, whom I had automatically considered my benefactor.[3]

Leaders such as King Hintsa would be murdered with the same brutality we would witness a hundred years later with the murder of Black Consciousness leader Steve Biko in 1977. British governors such as Benjamin D'Urban and Harry Smith presided over the systematic destruction of Xhosa society, turning otherwise independent people into dependent labourers. They raided their cattle, cut off food production, and sent those who resisted to Robben Island.

Defeated in war, the people of this region became the main focus of missionary proselytising. British missionaries such as William Shaw and John Philip of the London Missionary Society set up mission schools in the region with the express intention of undermining local customs and rituals, which they viewed as heathen and backward.[4] Scholars have long commented on how cultural degradation has always played a central part in the colonisation process. The economic historian Karl Polanyi noted that social calamities were often preceded by and predicated on the destruction of the cultural institutions of the victims, depriving them of vital sources of meaning: 'not economic exploitation, as often assumed, but the disintegration of the cultural environment of the victim is then the cause of the degradation'.[5] The violent cultural contact would be no less devastating for the people of the Eastern Cape throughout the nineteenth century in the so-called 'frontier wars'. I prefer the description 'wars of dispossession', which is both more accurate and more generic. The cultural dispossession happened mainly through the insertion of the Xhosa into missionary schools such as Lovedale and Healdtown College and newly established forms of worship, and ultimately through various processes of proletarianisation.

However, it would be a mistake to present a picture of black people as hapless victims who simply accepted everything that was imposed on them. They improvised by using the very systems of acculturation to bring forth new modern identities. The South African historian Noel Mostert argues that 'all of this together was to set them distinctly apart, in literature, in political and academic life and in their traditions of resistance'.[6] These, I would argue, were the beginnings of the making of a joint culture – forever creating new identities to respond to the emerging political, social and economic reality.

Cultural historian Ntongela Masilela writes about the specifics of this 'syncretic adaptation' through the emergence of what he calls the 'New African Movement'. He argues that the graduates of the missionary schools became increasingly concerned with the historical question of what were 'the political and cultural facilitators of entrance into European modernity'.[7] They concluded that those political and cultural facilitators lay in education, Christianity and modernity. The more they tasted modernity the more they demanded of it, and thereby exposed the hypocrisy at the heart of Christianity. Historian Catherine Higgs notes that these individuals 'wanted to develop the nation by forcing the boundaries of the missionary education which had produced them'.[8] The introduction of these 'political and cultural facilitators' introduced a deep fault-line between those who completely rejected assimilation into the emerging cultural world and those who saw it as a means of collective

9

advancement, and even of outright political resistance. This has often led to descriptions of these groups into social categories: *amaqaba* (the rejectionists) and *amakholwa* (the assimilationists). While accurately depicting the tensions that existed between these groups, we should always be careful not to draw the boundaries too tightly lest we miss out on the solidarity that also existed. This was itself a form of adaptation – a way in which parents facilitated their children's survival in the new world.

Wits University academic Bheki Peterson argues that the response to European modernity was neither complete withdrawal nor complete assimilation: 'It was precisely by occupying the intermediary ground; a diffuse, marginal space that the *kholwa* were compelled to forge profoundly new forms of African identity in response to modernity'. The formation of this identity was not 'univocal' with the masters putting their imprint on the slaves: at the best of times it was 'shot through with complex instances of contestation'. Citing Franz Fanon, Peterson notes how 'the colonized, after encountering the full weight of the colonial culture cannot return to any authentic and unspoilt past; instead they take up the challenge and occupy "a zone of occult instability"'.[9]

And so from Higgs to Masilela to Peterson we are left with an image of the presentation of education and religion as the skills base for the African from the middle to the end of the nineteenth century – but with that very same skills set highly contested. Ultimately, African leaders such as Pambani Mzimba and Elijah Makiwane would play a crucial role in the formation of African independent churches, which was yet another instance of 'syncretic adaptation'. They were taking from the Christian world that which they felt to be useful for their entry into modernity but fusing it with their own cultural and traditional forms of worship.

In yet another instance of this adaptation there were those individuals who, while rejecting the new system of education and worship for themselves, advocated it for their children. Old Man Soga, the father of the first prominent modern African public intellectual Tiyo Soga, is an excellent case in point. He resisted Christian encroachment into his personal life even as he let his son convert to Christianity. Tiyo Soga's own story is instructive as an example of adaptation in black political and intellectual life.

Tiyo Soga: An example of adaptation

Born in 1829, Tiyo Soga entered Lovedale College – the centre of missionary education for Africans for the next 150 years – at the relatively advanced age of fifteen under the tutelage of Scottish missionary William Chalmers. However, his education was interrupted by the wars of resistance that spanned the entire nineteenth century.[10] In 1846 Soga was taken into safety in Glasgow, Scotland, by his colonial minders. He returned to South Africa only in 1849 as a missionary and schoolmaster, but then went back to Scotland at the outbreak of another war in 1851. He was to remain in Scotland until his graduation in 1856 – the first African to graduate from Glasgow University at the time. He returned as the first black ordained minister with his wife, a white Scottish woman, Janet Burnside, to the consternation of both blacks and whites. He denounced African culture as backward and heathen and refused to participate in the all-important custom of circumcision.

However, Soga's experience in Scotland had not been entirely happy, and even after he returned he was not immune to racial taunts, including imprisonment for not carrying a pass, even though he was exempted from doing so because of his elevated status. He was acutely aware that the settler community tolerated him because of his education and missionary standing: 'The Scotch education, not my black face, has been my passport into places where that face would not be permitted to enter.' However, it was when the colonialists raided his father's estate that Soga began to speak openly against the land grabs, albeit in the language of a true missionary convert: 'Warriors of noble spirit disdain to strike a foe without weapons . . . it is beneath the dignity of civilized men to be formidable enemy of naked barbarians, who cannot write and reason like themselves.'[11]

He was outraged after reading a newspaper article by childhood friend and fellow missionary, John Chalmers. Soga's African nationalism was triggered by Chalmers's assertion that black people were indolent and incapable of development and inexorably drawn to extinction. In what is regarded as one of the earliest expositions on a broader African diaspora by a South African, Tiyo Soga drew on the history of African peoples in the diaspora to repudiate Chalmers:

Africa was of God given to the race of Ham. I find the Negro from the days of the Assyrian to downwards, keeping his 'individuality' and his 'distinctiveness', amid the wreck of empires, and the revolution of ages. I find him keeping his place among the nations, and keeping his home and country. I find him opposed by nation after nation and driven from his home. I find him enslaved – exposed to the vices and the brandy of the white man. I find him in this condition for many a day – in the West Indian Islands, in northern and South America, and in the South American colonies of Spain and Portugal. I find him exposed to all these disasters, and yet living, multiplying and 'never extinct.' Yea, I find him now as the prevalence of Christian and philanthropic opinions on the rights of man obtains among civilized nations, returning unmanacled to the land of his forefathers, taking back with him the civilization and Christianity of those nations. (See the Negro Republic of Liberia.) I find the Negro in the present struggle in America looking forward – though still with chains on his hands and chains on his feet – yet looking forward to the dawn of a better day for himself and all his sable brethren in Africa.[12]

Soga's references to Liberia and other African countries suggest he would have most likely been aware of Americo-Liberian intellectuals such as Blyden, Martin Delaney and Alexander Crummel. Soga's biographer Donovan Williams thus describes Soga as the founder of black nationalism and Black Consciousness in South Africa. Williams argues that Soga was caught up in the 'crosstide of cultures'.[13] He avoided both the naive Eurocentrism of his youth and the nativist racial purism of someone like Edward Blyden. He faced his existential dilemma head on by suggesting that African identity was a matter of identification, not biology or skin colour. He thus counselled his mulatto children about their identity with these words:

I want you, for your future comfort, to be very careful on this point. You will ever cherish the memory of your mother as that of an upright, conscientious, thrifty, Christian Scotchwoman. You will ever be thankful for your connection by this tie to the white race. But if you wish to gain credit for yourselves – if you do not wish to feel the taunt of men, which you sometimes may be made to feel – take your place in the world as coloured, not as white men, as kafirs, not as Englishmen. You will be more thought of for this by all good and wise people, than for the other.[14]

According to David Attwell: 'Soga was indeed "a man of two worlds", but he was also a transitional figure *within* Xhosa history, marking a choice that subsequent generations would have to remake for themselves.'[15]

Subsequent generations of African intellectuals – W.B. Rubusana, John Tengo Jabavu, William W. Gqoba and S.E.K. Mqhayi – were to grapple with the question of how to shape their responses to the emerging European modernity. Gqoba, for instance, looked to education as the weapon of struggle. This emphasis on education was famously expressed in I.W.W. Citashe's 1882 poem:

> Your cattle are gone, my countrymen!
> Go rescue them! Go rescue them!
> Leave the breechloader alone
> And turn to the pen.
> Take paper and ink,
> For that is your shield.
> Your rights are going!
> So pick up your pen.
> Load it, load it with ink.
> Sit on a chair.
> Repair not to Hoho.
> But fire with your pen.[16]

However, it was only much later that these individuals were roped, by political notables such as Pixley ka Isaka Seme, into the formation of a much larger nationalist movement, the South African Native National Congress, in 1912, which became the ANC in 1923. What Masilela describes as the transmission lines of the New African Movement began to evolve, both intellectually and politically.[17] The industrial and mining revolution at the end of the nineteenth century had something to do with the evolution of these transmission lines. For example, the diamond mines in Kimberley were accompanied by the development of what we may call the Kimberley intellectuals, the most prominent member of which was Solomon Tshekedi Plaatje, who was also one of the leading lights of the New African Movement in the early twentieth century. Plaatje came under the influence of my great-uncle Gwayi Tyamzashe, who had been a close associate of W.B. Rubusana and moved to Kimberley to establish himself as a priest (see discussion of Tyamzashe in my family history below). Plaatje in turn came down to King William's Town where he edited John Tengo Jabavu's *Imvo Zabantsundu* – even though the two of them were well-known political opponents. Plaatje and many black intellectuals would not forgive Jabavu for his defence of the Land Acts of 1913. Plaatje had had personal experience of land dispossession, and made that a major part of his international campaigns.

The solidarity that existed between *amaqaba* and *amakholwa* was not limited to parents preparing the future of their children; the children themselves began to challenge Western ways of doing things. This happened for the most part in the area of language. Prominent members of the African educated elite – S.E.K. Mqhayi, B.W. Vilakazi and R.R.R. Dhlomo, for example – argued for the use of African languages.[18] The African epistemological revolution contributed to the emergence of the Black Consciousness movement – arguably the most culturalist of black political movements to emerge in South Africa.

Black Consciousness and political adaptation

In his essay 'Negritude: New and Old Perspectives', the South-African born critic and novelist Lewis Nkosi attributes the rise of black militant movements to the general rebellion against the Enlightenment in the West. Nkosi argues that the Romantic rebellion against Western formalism and rationalism suited black militants' desire to liberate themselves from that culture. Black militants – writers, artists, philosophers, etc. – used the same techniques as their white counterparts in their struggle against the Enlightenment. As historian Gianna Pomata argues, the Romantic movement utilised poetry, folklore and a return to ancient custom as the alternative sources of knowledge.[19] Nkosi thus concludes

14

that transgressive as they may seem, black militant movements such as Negritude were in many ways 'the bastard children' of Western modernity, including Romantic modernity:

> that in their efforts to liberate themselves from the 'civilized decorum' of Western culture these black writers were obliged to make use of the weapons which that culture had itself furnished points, of course, to the irony which we are at liberty to enjoy while appreciating the always underlying drama in the dialectic between colonizer and colonized.[20]

The Negritude movement would become the inspiration to the Black Consciousness movement in South Africa. Barney Pityana describes the influence of movements such as Negritude on his colleague, Steve Biko:

> Black Consciousness for him was moulded by a diversity of intellectual forces and fountains: from the liberation history of South Africa, the pan Africanism of Kwame Nkrumah, the African nationalism of Jomo Kenyatta, the negritude of the west African scholars like Leopold Sadar Senghor, Aime Cesaire and others in Paris. Biko taught himself a political understanding of religion in Africa. He devoured John Mbiti, Ali Mazrui, Basil Davidson. He understood the critical writings of Walter Rodney and he interpreted Franz Fanon. He laid his hands on some philosophical writings like Jean Paul Sartre and made ready use of some philosophical concepts like syllogism in logic and dialectical materialism in Marxist political thought. All this by a young medical student.[21]

Biko showed a similar syncretism to the construction of black political and cultural identity. The definition of what it means to be black was very close to that offered by Cesaire. At the founding of the Negritude movement Cesaire had noted that 'black political identity was not biological but historical'.[22] The Black Consciousness movement similarly gave a specifically political as opposed to a biological definition of black people as 'those who are by law or tradition politically, economically and socially discriminated against as a group in the South African society and *identifying* themselves as a unit in the struggle towards the realisation of their aspirations' (emphasis added).[23] Biko emphasised the role that choice plays in identity formation when he was asked about why his movement preferred black over any other definition:

> and when we reject the term non-white and take upon ourselves the right to call ourselves what we think we are, we have got available in front of us a whole number of alternatives starting from natives to Africans to kaffirs to bantu to non-whites and so on, and we choose this one precisely because we feel it is most accommodating.[24]

The impact of this definition on prior understandings of blackness was revolutionary. Before this moment, and even as they joined together in protests against the apartheid government, Africans, coloureds and Indians had understood each other as distinct ethnic groupings mobilising for their own interests. With the intervention of Black Consciousness these groupings began to see themselves as sharing a common political identity. Having provided a political definition of blackness, Biko spoke of the creation of a non-racial society underpinned by what he termed the 'joint culture' made out of black and white cultural experiences.

Biko's exposition of culture came in many forums but one of the most relevant here is the answer he gave when he was cross-examined as a defence witness for his colleagues during the famous South African Students' Organisation/Black People's Convention (SASO/BPC) Trial of 1975–76.[25] His attorney David Soggot asked Biko to comment on his cultural vision for South Africa and his response could not have been more syncretic: 'You know, cultures affect each other, you know, like fashions and you cannot escape rubbing against someone else's culture. But you must have the right to reject or not anything that is given to you.' And then Soggot asked Biko what he foresaw happening on the first day of the open society, saying: 'The question I think which is of greater interest to us is on the first day of the open society, on the following day, is there going to be general destruction – any destruction or proscription of existing culture and cultural values?' To which Biko replied: 'I think a modification all round.'[26]

In his response Biko said the joint culture would 'have European experience, because we have whites here who are descended from Europe. We don't dispute that. But for God's sake it must have African experience as well.'[27] To be sure, it was not enough that the joint culture must just have African experience. The 'joint culture' was not just a value-free enterprise in which we simply adopted an additive or rainbow approach to culture. Particular attention had to be given to African cultural values in a country and continent where the vast majority of people were African. The cultural values of any society would have to reflect the preponderant values of the people of that society without being a threat to others. This is how Biko put it:

> For one cannot escape the fact that the culture shared by the majority group in any given society must ultimately determine the broad direction taken by the joint culture of that society. This need not cramp the style of those who feel differently but on the whole, a country in Africa, in which the majority of the people are African must inevitably exhibit African values and be truly African in style.[28]

Like Tiyo Soga a century before him, Steve Biko rejected the manner in which black identity and therefore black possibilities had been defined by white liberals. He was unyielding in his critique of white leadership of the black liberation struggle: 'I am against the intellectual arrogance of white people that makes them believe that white leadership is a *sine qua non* in this country and that whites are the divinely appointed pace-setters in progress.'[29] However, his critique of white arrogance did not turn him into a racial essentialist. Noel Mostert recalls his first meeting with Biko and how impressed he was by his originality of thinking. Mostert observed that while Biko was missionary educated he was part of a generation that would challenge missionary paternalism over black people.

I am inspired by Tiyo Soga and Steve Biko in two vicarious ways. Tiyo Soga was the progenitor of a great intellectual culture of adaptation in which my own forebears, particularly the Tyamzashes, played a significant part. I see my writings as a continuation of this tradition. Steve

Biko was a larger-than-life presence in my childhood in Ginsberg Township. I also became an active and vocal participant in the Black Consciousness movement.

I grew up with a split identity – split among the Tyamzashe, Mangcu and the Nyamakazi branches of my heritage. There is not much I can say about the Nyamakazi side because I never really spent much time with my father, Syfred Nyamakazi, to whom my mother was not married. As I grow older I feel a deep longing for the relationship with my dad. His picture, showing a dandy man, occupies pride of place in my family living room. Unlike the Tyamzashe and Mangcu sides of my family, the Nyamakazis' reputation came mostly from their wealth. My dad started out as a policeman but through the patronage of his much wealthier brother, Simon, set up business as a general dealer. Simon owned almost every other business in the town of Engcobo: the hotel, the butchery, the boutique, a farm, and on and on. I would often visit during school holidays and really admired them for their entrepreneurship.

But it was with the Tyamzashes that I first identified. There was something about their intellectual history that fascinated me. The greatest influence was Noteya Tyamzashe – we called her Auntie-ntie – who always shared the family's long history of educational achievement.

My Tyamzashe heritage

The story is that in the beginning there was Oya, who gave birth to Mejane, who in turn gave birth to Tyamzashe. Tyamzashe became the head councillor in King Sandile's court and had three sons: Gwayi, Peter and Syfred. Not much is known about Syfred apart from the fact that he did not have children. Family lore thus tends to revolve around the two brothers, Gwayi and Peter. Gwayi was the eldest and more prominent public intellectual. Born in 1844 he was exposed to some of the defining points of Xhosa history, particularly the wars of resistance against the British, as well as the Nongqause cattle killing of 1856/57. He was part of one of the first groups of African students to enter Lovedale College, which had just been established to 'civilise' Africans. After graduating from Lovedale, Gwayi taught at Peelton Mission School. When the headmaster, Robert Birt, went on leave he would ask Gwayi to stand in for him. There Gwayi was joined by a young W.B. Rubusana, a man

18

who would establish a sterling reputation as an intellectual and political leader of the African community.[30]

Gwayi's performance at Lovedale occupies pride of place in early African intellectual history. His intellectual achievements, particularly at Lovedale, are described in T.D. Mweli Skota's *African Yearly Register* as follows:

> Soon Gwayi qualified as a teacher and taught for several years at Gqumahashe – a village just across the Tyumie River. Just at that time Tiyo Soga was reading for theology in Scotland. This caused Gwayi to leave teaching and return to Lovedale for theology. Before doing so, however, he went in for a university entrance examination in which Latin, Greek and Hebrew were essential subjects. This examination was above the ordinary matriculation. It was a red-letter day when Gwayi Tyamzashe passed this examination, flags were hoisted and the day was proclaimed a holiday.[31]

Upon completion of his theological studies Gwayi moved to Kimberley where he played a significant role as a priest and public figure. He would have a great impact on the young Solomon T. Plaatje who was impressed by Gwayi's interest in Xhosa orthography, particularly at a time when Xhosa literary history was in its infancy.[32]

Gwayi also became a columnist for the *Diamond Register* and the Xhosa newspaper *Isigidimi SamaXhosa* (Kaffir Express), chronicling the social conditions on the diamond mines. In addition, he established several mission stations in Zoutpansberg. Gwayi's wife was of mixed race – her father a French Huguenot and her mother a coloured woman. Together they bore several children, the most prominent of whom were Henry and Benjamin.

Henry too graduated from Lovedale and later became a close friend and ally of Clements Kadalie in the formation of the Industrial and Commercial Workers' Union (ICU). Henry became the editor of the ICU's publication, the *Worker's Herald*, and moved with Kadalie when there was a split in the ICU to become the editor of a publication called *New Africa*. A frequent contributor to the press, Henry earned a reputation as 'a critic with an acid pen'.[33] In 1921 Henry published an essay in

Isigidimi SamaXhosa, 'Why Have You Educated Me?', criticising the practice of racial discrimination in South Africa's labour market.

Henry's younger brother, Benjamin (also known as B ka T) became a famous Xhosa musical composer. B ka T composed close to 500 songs. The Eastern Cape provincial capital of Bisho takes its name from his most famous composition, 'I-Bisho Likhaya Lam'.

B ka T is an interesting figure in the context of the major theme of this book, particularly in the construction of a joint culture in African music. His compositions were influenced by both traditional Xhosa music and his training in the music of the West. B ka T composed his first song 'Isithwanda Sam' (My Love) after returning from training in London in 1917. However, the greatest influences in his musical development came when he went to live with his father's younger brother, Peter Tyamzashe, in Mngqesha, which became the main home of the Tyamzashe family – or at least the ancestral home I was exposed to as a young boy.

B ka T's biographer D.D. Hansen described our ancestral home as

> the setting for communal music making, but the musical repertory was a very mixed one: it included hymns and sacred songs, Victorian salon music, 19th century English popular song, works by Bach and Handel, as well as songs of the 'Red People' (*abantu ababomvu*). As Tyamzashe himself put it: 'we sang songs like Rhwa! Rhwa! Rhwa!, Watsh' uNomyayi, Abafana Base Ngqusha, and the Red boys and girls songs'.[34]

In 1964 B ka T was approached by the Catholic and Anglican clergy to compose liturgical music in traditional Xhosa style. To do that, he turned to the music of the great Christian Xhosa prophet and composer Ntsikana. According to Hansen the main difference between Western European and Xhosa concepts of harmonisation is that in the former all parts are subordinate to the soprano, whereas in the latter all parts are considered equal. B ka T's genius was in the manner in which he mixed the two styles:

> Tyamzashe's music is as much African as it is Western European in style because it arises from an African way of harmonising a

main melody (commonly in the soprano), by providing it with three or more counter-melodies which run parallel to it. I often watched Tyamzashe compose in this horizontal way. The chord progressions which resulted from it might resemble the harmonic progressions in Western music, but in fact they are at odds with them, and only incidentally observe Western harmonic 'rules'. Tyamzashe's chordal progressions are *not* a slavish imitation of Western musical technique; they are the result of an African technique of harmonization.[35]

B ka T often came to visit my mother, Nonji, at our home in Ginsberg when I was a little boy. He was particularly fond of my mother who was also a well-known music teacher and choir conductor in King William's Town. Just like the ancestral Tyamzashe home in Mngqesha, the Mangcu home in Ginsberg was a 'setting for communal music making'.

My mother was the direct descendant of Peter Tyamzashe. Peter's history was quite different from Gwayi's. If Gwayi was the public intellectual, Peter was a man of resources and a respected community elder in Mngqesha. He was referred to as i-Nyange (an honorific title reserved for a respected elder in the community). Legend has it that Peter Tyamzashe was the only African who would ride in a horse-drawn carriage into King William's Town – to the utter consternation of locals, both black and white. Peter must have been a man of resources indeed; the house he built in Mngqesha village in 1908 would be comparable to any modern-day mansion. Peter's last born child was Mantondo, my mother's mother.

The Tyamzashe-Mangcu connection was established when Mantondo got married to Rantshi Mangcu, a blind pianist and property owner on John Brownlee's mission station just outside King William's Town. Rantshi and Mantondo had three girls: Nomvula, Tisina and my mother, Nonji. While the other two girls did not advance very much with their education, mainly due to illness, my mother was in the first group of graduates of the newly established Forbes Grant Secondary School in Ginsberg. She then proceeded to qualify as a teacher at St Matthew's College, a prestigious teacher training college set up for girls by the missionaries. After finishing her teacher training programme in 1945, she stayed on to obtain the highly sought after 'red certificate' in music education. My mother never married because to do so would have meant giving up her professional career. Under apartheid legislation, black women teachers lost their jobs if they married and yet as single teachers they were also not allowed to have children. I am told that my mother had to leave our township to give birth to me in Uitenhage. I was then taken to live among the Tyamzashe in Mngqesha for the first few years of my life and came to Ginsberg to start school.

Throughout all of this I had a sense of myself with several identities in competition with one another and yet each rich in its own way. But if truth be told I always saw myself as a child of people who had used education and Christianity as 'the facilitators' of their entry into modernity. This partly explains why my anger towards white people was not only political but also cultural. I was no less an inheritor of modern culture. And I never internalised the idea that we black people were inferior to whites, which probably explains my sense of revulsion to terms such as 'previously disadvantaged'. I was not disadvantaged; I was oppressed. I truly believed we were equal and to be treated in any other way made me furious. By contrast, racial nativists strike me as people who never came to terms with whiteness as a fact of our social life – completely intertwined. They seem to forget Fanon's injunction above, which is that there is no authentic and unspoilt past.

The Mangcus of Brownlee/King William's Town

Brownlee Mission Station was adjacent to King William's Town as a reserve of the London Missionary Society, an organisation founded by William Carey in 1794 to spread the message of 'civilisation' among 'the heathens' of the world. Dyani Tshatshu, one of the first African chiefs to convert to Christianity, welcomed Brownlee to settle among his people along the Buffalo River. Brownlee established a mission church and schools for the local population. The missionaries literally banished people who held on to African cultural customs to a nearby village called Mnqayi. These were the hold-outs – but again even as they encouraged their children to go to school and attend church. The Mangcu family became a prominent landowning family in Brownlee, and took maximum advantage of the 'political and cultural facilitators' into modernity that were then available. Brownlee Mission was, however, demolished in 1939 and its residents were removed to a nearby township known as Ginsberg.

The move was not merely physical. The residents of Brownlee were now moving from the mild treatment of missionary guardianship to the harsh reality of direct colonial/segregationist rule under the control of the King William's Town municipality. Whereas Brownlee Mission was independent of the colonial government, King William's Town became the centre of the missionary expeditions into Xhosa-land.

Ginsberg Township was established in 1901 by the King William's Town municipality, at the instigation of local industrialist and councillor Franz Ginsberg. Local historian Luyanda Msumza argues that 'the idea of a location close to his factory must have appealed to him and he threw every ounce of his energy into it. He worked so hard on this such that when the settlement was finally established it was named after him.'[36] However, a less generous interpretation of Councillor Ginsberg's motives is that the township's establishment was part of an orchestrated series of removals of black people from towns all over the country – a prelude to segregation and apartheid. Councillor Ginsberg's own words seem to give support to the second theory: 'We are going to make it so comfortable for the Natives in the locations and so cheap that I am quite sure in a very short time every native will be glad to go to the location.'[37]

Owing to the exalted position they occupied as educationists, the Mangcus of Ginsberg lived in the better part of the township. My mother's cousin, George Mayile Mangcu, was arguably the most influential person in Ginsberg in the 1950s and 1960s. A young, dandy teacher who had graduated from the prestigious Healdtown College, Mangcu literally took on the role of a missionary do-gooder. He mobilised for the building of the township's first higher primary school, established a self-help community garden in the centre of the township, opened an agricultural co-operative called Masizakhe (Let's Build Ourselves), became the local cricket and boxing coach, and set up a local jazz club, the African Melodies. He was also the leading light in the Ginsberg Civic Association, a group of civic notables who often intervened on behalf of residents facing eviction orders and other apartheid indignities.

Eminent persons such as George Mangcu did not carry ordinary pass books, and were in certain respects spared some of the indignities of apartheid. To separate them from the masses of black people they did not carry the *dompas* (literally, dumb pass) – they were required to carry the 'green book'. George Mangcu wore the patrician badge proudly, and barred his children from mixing with the 'riff-raff' from the other side of the township. In that respect Mangcu was both politically and socially conservative, and brought upon himself the rebellion of an increasingly politically conscious youth, many of whom belonged to the emerging radicals of the ANC and mostly to the newly established Pan Africanist Congress (PAC). Even though it existed as a legal entity for a mere two years before its banning in 1960, the PAC was more influential than the ANC in Ginsberg, which partly explains why Black Consciousness gained a foothold in the township.

Mangcu's conservatism contrasted sharply with that of his neighbour and contemporary, Harry Mjamba, a radical iconoclast and graduate of the University of Fort Hare.[38] The university was a cauldron of radical student politics, the stomping ground for Africa's future leadership. Here Africa's political and intellectual leaders could be found: Z.K. Matthews, Govan and Epainette Mbeki, A.C. Jordan, Phyllis Ntantala, Nelson Mandela, Oliver Tambo, Robert Sobukwe, Robert Mugabe, Joshua Nkomo, Sir Seretse Khama, Quett Masire, Ntsu Mokhele, and many others. While Mangcu ran the primary school, Mjamba was the headmaster of the local secondary school in Ginsberg. He was outspoken about the iniquities of the apartheid system, and even recruited into the ANC people such as Steve Tshwete (who later became a leading member of the ANC and a cabinet member in the Mandela and Mbeki governments).

Growing up in Ginsberg

When I was not in Mngqesha with the Tyamzashes, I was in Ginsberg with the Mangcus. This is the social world I inherited. It was rich in social capital but poor in financial and economic terms, and dominated by a few individuals such as George Mangcu and Harry Mjamba.[39] I was always aware of my privileged status among my childhood friends.

I can still remember the sense of wonder and fascination among the older boys at my ability to speak and read in English. I would read the newspaper to them and explain international developments in politics and sports. I also became very active in sports, dabbling in rugby and boxing, and was part of a group that for the first time brought soccer to our township in the late 1970s. However, nothing enraged my mother more than the time I spent as a caddy at the King William's Town golf course. Not only did she think it unbecoming but she must have been concerned for my safety. I often hung out with the wrong crowd.

Looking back I explain it as part of my own effort to 'fit in' with the rest of the youth. I was determined to stake out an identity separate from my family and my siblings, all of whom were university graduates long before anyone else in our township. It was a rough and precarious existence. My best friends died predictable deaths. They were knifed to death in the shebeens in the rough part of town. I survived because I had a supportive and protective, middle-class family environment.

Ginsberg became a hub for a number of people who are now national leaders. This was partly due to the popularity of the local secondary school, the Forbes Grant Secondary School.[40] My brother Mthobi Tyamzashe became the first director-general of sports in the Mandela government, while his friend Smuts Ngonyama became head of the presidency in the ANC. The senior ANC leader and Deputy Minister of Defence Mluleki George went to school here, as did the late Minister for Safety and Security Steve Tshwete and other prominent ANC leaders such as Griffiths Mxenge and Victoria Mxenge, both of whom were assassinated by the apartheid government in the 1980s. Sindisile Maclean became the first executive mayor of Buffalo City, and cabinet minister Charles Nqakula worked closely with young ANC cadres from our township.

In sport the township produced five rugby Springboks – this was during the days of segregated sport – two national boxing champions, a golf professional and a member of the South African Amateur Golf Country Districts.

In addition, Ginsberg would become a centre of political activity because it was Steve Biko's home.

Getting to know Steve Biko

I was too young to know Steve Biko with any degree of intimacy. I often joke that 'he knew me better than I did'. In small communities such as Ginsberg adults take more interest in the children than the other way round. Children spend the better part of their time running away from parents. It was different with Biko. We followed him around because we suspected he was doing something important. Sometimes we would jump on the back of his van and visit the projects he was running in the rural areas. Our favourite spot was the clinic he ran with Mamphela Ramphele. Biko and Ramphele had a son, Hlumelo, and Ramphele later came into prominence as the first black and female vice-chancellor of the University of Cape Town as well as the managing director for human development at the World Bank. The clinic she ran with Biko has been celebrated as one of the early examples of public health in South Africa. At the end of each day we would simply wait for him to return from work, and chase his car shouting, '*Amandla! Amandla!*' On other occasions we would come out of school and file out of the township to sit in front of the Black Consciousness offices in King William's Town. We particularly enjoyed the confrontations between the Black Consciousness activists and the police. There was a certain fearlessness about Biko and his men. They wore colourful dashikis and left their hair long and un-combed.

One of Biko's closest associates, Mzwandile Mbilini, lived opposite my home on Zaula Street. Mbilini would give a defiant black power salute each time the police came to arrest him. Biko visited the Mbilini home often. It was one of the favourite *shebeens* (the Gaelic word for a speakeasy or illegal informal place for drinks) for the Black Consciousness activists. The last time I saw Biko he was walking across the local public square to visit this *shebeen*, wearing his favourite velvet jacket. He passed my house and went in. There was nothing significant about that – except that it would haunt me for many years as the last moment I saw someone who had been an important part of my upbringing.

Many people remember where they were when they heard of Steve Biko's death on that fateful 12 September 1977. I had just arrived back from school when a relative of the Biko family, Forbes Nyathi, came by our house to see my mother. I suspected something was wrong and so

I hung around to eavesdrop. My mom hurriedly sent me back to our regular after-school classes. When I arrived at school one of Biko's nieces, Nompumezo, who was also my classmate, was crying uncontrollably. There was commotion all over the place, as the older students started singing freedom songs. School was dismissed, and we all rushed back home. A sense of foreboding engulfed the whole community.

Initially I watched everything through the window. My mother had said it was too dangerous to venture out. However, I could not always be relied on to obey my parents, and so I stole away to the local square. People were streaming there from all over the township. The story was that Biko and Peter Jones had been travelling back from a political meeting in Cape Town when they were stopped at a roadblock near Grahamstown. It had been a dangerous and risky trip because Biko was restricted to King William's Town. Then they were transported to the notorious security branch offices in Port Elizabeth where they were viciously assaulted by the police.[41] As the story was recounted, the more impatient youth started calling for revenge. They insisted that the fight should be taken to the whites in town. Caution and reason prevailed. The discussion then turned on who might have tipped the police about the trip. The militant youth went on the rampage, setting government buildings on fire. They also targeted the homes of teachers because teachers were increasingly identified with the much-hated Bantu Education system. I was afraid our home would also be torched but I suspect we were spared this ordeal because of our standing in the community.

In 1978 my parents sent me off to an elite school called Phandulwazi Agricultural High School at the foot of the Hogsback Mountains in Alice. The school was set up by the Ciskei homeland leader, Lennox Sebe, as his own answer to the elite St John's College in the Transkei. It was, however, touted as having more of a practical bent, which was an essential requirement for the new Ciskei citizen. However, Phandulwazi turned out to be nothing more than a collection of spoilt brats and political rebels. Unfortunately, that's what happens when you bring children of the elite (many of whom were Sebe's cabinet members) together in one place. It was hard for the teachers to discipline some of these students.

27

Things came to a head when we organised the commemoration of the first anniversary of Steve Biko's death. It was normal practice at Phandulwazi that every morning we would run to the dining hall at the sound of the siren. Failure to make it before the door was closed would often lead to cane lashing. On the night before the anniversary we decided that we would not run. Instead, we would all dress in black and walk in a slow procession to the dining hall. The siren went its full gamut. Some students panicked and ran for the door. But I was part of the group that refused to break rank.

There were about eight of us, ranging in age from twelve to fifteen. We were all brought to the principal's office and summarily dismissed. Other students came out on strike in solidarity. The whole school was closed. We were eventually called back to finish the rest of the year but my mother had other plans. She took me to a school near our township headed by my brother. It was now his job to keep me in line. He had his hands full. I was so out of control that nobody believed it when my high school results came in with a university entrance pass.

The Wits years

My family had their own ideas about which university they wanted me to attend. Tradition had it that everyone went to Fort Hare. And so, at the beginning of 1983, I was sent off to Fort Hare against my will. I spent just one night there. The following day I went back to my mother and asked for the train fare to Johannesburg. I had never been outside of King William's Town but I was determined to go to the University of the Witwatersrand (Wits). My mom gave me the train fare and two red suitcases. They were her best suitcases.

Wits represented a radical encounter with whiteness – and a challenge to it – but again not as an outsider but in the age-old tradition of those who had come before me. Education was the weapon, and like our great-grandparents we were using the very instruments of Western culture to challenge that culture.

There was, however, a big snag. In those days black students needed a government permit to enrol at white universities. The permit was granted only if the degree of study was not available at existing black universities such as Fort Hare for Xhosas, the University of Zululand for Zulus and the University of the North for Sothos. I wanted to study law but it was available at the very University of Fort Hare I had abandoned.

I was aware of the risk involved in coming all the way to Johannesburg on my own. The only instruction I was given was that I should not get off anywhere but the last stop. I remember alighting at Johannesburg's Park Station to find a group of young men playing with a ball on the platform. My red suitcases might have given everything away but I was dressed like a 'clever', and walked just like one as I hailed a taxi to the university.

I remember the day I arrived at Wits like it was yesterday. I had never seen so many white people gathered in one place. And then there was the opulence of it all. However, even though I had been admitted by the university, I did not have the requisite ministerial consent. Every week I would take the train from Johannesburg to the ministry of education in Pretoria to beg for the 'ministerial consent' to study at Wits. It was a humiliating experience as I was constantly abused and insulted by the white Afrikaner officials. Who did I think I was to want to study with whites, they would ask? My hopes were dashed and I was on the verge of returning home when I was advised by members of the law faculty to stay on because there was a real possibility that legislation governing the attendance of blacks at white universities would change the following year.

The new legislation provided for white universities to register a limited number of black students under a new quota system. I came back in 1984 to register officially for a law degree. I have no doubt that this harrowing experience contributed to the radical role I would assume in the following years.

The making of a radical
My political activism at Wits started as a poet at student gatherings at Glyn Thomas House just outside of Soweto. This was the main residence for black students at Wits. As a result, it became a haven of political discussions, debates and activism. I was not very good at the poetry and instead concentrated on giving fiery speeches at student political rallies. My childhood in Ginsberg and my political apprenticeship at high school

served me rather well. My militancy earned me the nickname Qaddafi (after the Libyan leader Muammar Qaddafi), and I had to live up to the image by carrying around Qaddafi's *Green Book* – his book of policy and political thought – not that I now remember anything in it.

I instantly became the torchbearer of Steve Biko's Black Consciousness philosophy. I suppose I felt a sense of loyalty and obligation to my homeboy. I publicly challenged white academics at every turn, especially those who were considered experts on the liberation struggle.[42] On one occasion at a public rally I criticised the noted political scientist Tom Lodge for leaving out the Black Consciousness movement in a speech on black politics in South Africa. I forever endeared myself to the small group of black students on campus. To this day I still meet people who say what that moment meant for them personally. I did this throughout my stay at Wits – challenging this great liberal university's symbols of authority.

I also spent a great deal of time proselytising and arguing with rival student leaders, many of whom espoused the ANC's philosophy of non-racialism. Tiego Moseneke was by far the most articulate, refined, and charismatic student leader at Wits. He had crowds eating out of his hand and women adored him – to our greatest envy and resentment. Many of my political rivals went on to occupy senior leadership positions in government: Dali Mpofu became the head of the South African Broadcasting Corporation (SABC); Pascal Moloi became the city manager of Johannesburg; Chris Ngcobo, the head of Johannesburg Metro Police; Firoz Cachalia, the Member of the Executive Committee (MEC) for Safety and Security in Gauteng; Phindi Nzimande, the chief executive officer of the National Electricity Regulator; Nthabiseng Mogale, a well-known human rights activist; Mpoti Ralephata, a senior executive at BHP Billiton; Khehla Shubane, a well-known policy analyst, and so on.

On the Black Consciousness side we boasted people such as Mojanku Gumbi, who went on to become President Thabo Mbeki's legal adviser; Saths Cooper, a veteran Black Consciousness activist; Enos Banda, a well-known businessman; Hale Qangule of the auditing firm Sizwe Ntsaluba VSP; and my dear friend, the late Linda Mtshizana. This was arguably the most radical moment in the history of the university. For the first time Wits had a critical mass of black students who did not come from the polite culture of private schools. Many of the students who came from 1985 onwards had been expelled from black universities such as the University of the North and Fort Hare. They brought their militant political culture with them. For them the university was another battleground in the fight against apartheid. Wits proved to be a relatively free political space that allowed student leaders to prepare themselves for the leadership roles that would be thrust on them in the transition to democracy.[43]

Unfortunately, the ideological battles between the Black Consciousness movement and the ANC-aligned non-racial formations turned frighteningly violent in the mid-1980s, especially in places such as Soweto and Port Elizabeth. I maintained a posture of bravado throughout these ideological wars but the whole thing scared me hugely. My childhood friends kept on urging me to get out of politics. They argued that I was more likely to die in the hands of my own black brothers and sisters than in the hands of the enemy. I resisted their warnings for a little while but my interest in active politics had also begun to wane.

From the political battleground to public policy: A guerrilla in the bureaucracy

Towards the end of 1986 political activists on campus began to have debates about new career paths. The main argument was that we needed to enter the policy domain, and even join apartheid institutions, to prepare ourselves for our future role as governors of the country. The Black Consciousness radicals among us initially resisted these ideas, completely oblivious to the fact that the ANC was at that time already having talks with the enemy. We also had to convince ourselves that we were not going to be simply co-opted in what could end up being a 'whitewash' of our struggle.

The argument for engagement was strong enough to convince me to switch from legal studies to policy planning. I ultimately found myself working as an urban specialist in a creation of the apartheid state, the Development Bank of Southern Africa (DBSA). I literally saw my role as that of pushing the boundaries of the institution, getting it to interact with community organisations it would never have imagined working

31

with. From my new position I initiated negotiations between local activists and municipalities on the need for joint local government forums, including the much celebrated Stutterheim experiment of 1989. I knew some of the local activists in Stutterheim and became the go-between in their dealings with the Development Bank and the progressive mayor of the town, Nico Ferreira, in negotiating one integrated local government structure in the town. The community was boycotting local businesses in support of its demands, and Ferreira was not entirely unsympathetic to their cause. He was well connected in the National Party government but had come to realise that the present system of apartheid-based planning was a dead-end. Moreover, local businesses were reeling under the consumer boycott. This was happening throughout the country with many of these forums prefiguring the collapse of the segregated local government structures in the townships. By the time a new local government dispensation came into being a few movement activists had had at least some exposure to policy and administrative processes.

I did not last at the DBSA, and accepted a fellowship to the Massachusetts Institute of Technology (MIT) in Boston in 1991, and later enrolled at Cornell University for a Ph.D. in City and Regional Planning. I did not come back to South Africa until the end of the decade, with the specific intention of contributing further to the processes of change going on in the country. But I also could not resist going back to the public domain. I chose the role of a public intellectual partly to fulfil my own personal goals and partly to continue a family and community tradition that has been my source of inspiration.

I recall all of this social history to highlight a point made by the British philosopher John Stuart Mill more than a century ago: individual citizens acquire leadership skills at the local level and later generalise those skills to the broader society.[44] I have always understood my role as an extension of this early history of the Eastern Cape, of my community in Ginsberg, and of my own family heritage.

CHAPTER 2

The Enemy Within
Mbeki's Assault on Black Intellectuals

THABO MVUYELWA MBEKI walked on to the South African political stage championing the themes of cultural reclamation and self-reliance that were central to the Black Consciousness movement of my youth. Here was a black intellectual whose posture and message reminded me so much of my own family history, the self-assured black person who had mastered 'the political and cultural facilitators' into modernity. He was suave, urbane and sophisticated. I was a visiting scholar at Harvard at the time, and watched events back home with great interest. From a distance I heard that there had been a tussle between Cyril Ramaphosa and Thabo Mbeki for the leadership of the ANC. I was for Thabo Mbeki. There was something about his cultural nationalism that made me proud. Besides, I was one of those black radicals who felt Nelson Mandela was doing too much to assure white people.

Mandela's biographer Anthony Sampson captured the mood of my generation as follows:

> In his first months as President, he [Mandela] enjoyed a brilliant honeymoon, particularly with white South Africans, to whom this tolerant old man came as a wondrous relief . . . at the end of the first hundred days in office the *Financial Times* could find no whites who had a bad word for him. It was a normality which carried its own dangers, as black militants saw the revolution betrayed, and younger ANC leaders including Thabo Mbeki knew they must make reforms which would offend the whites.[1]

Mbeki felt like the right man for the moment – a radical cosmopolitan intellectual in the mould of nationalist leaders such as Robert Sobukwe and Steve Biko. I would liken him to people such as the third president of the United States, Thomas Jefferson, or India's first prime minister, Jawaharlal Nehru. I compared Mbeki's 8 May 1996 speech, 'I am an African', to Nehru's 'Midnight to Millennium' speech and to Jefferson's Declaration of Independence. This was the equivalent of what the eighteenth-century philosopher Jean Jacques Rousseau called the civil religion.

It so happened that at the time I had shifted from my studies in city planning to a greater focus on leadership and nation building. I spent a great deal of time studying early American history, and how the Americans, through a process of syncretic adaptation, had created a new republic with what Gunnar Myrdal, Swedish intellectual and keen observer of American politics, would call the American creed.[2] This creed was captured in Jefferson's Declaration of Independence: the idea that all men are created equal. (Jefferson did not make references to women as equals but such exclusion would be offensive today.)

To be sure, Americans were not always true to this ideal of equality. The American republic was created on the ashes of the Native American population and on the blood, sweat and toil of African slaves. But as the Columbia University historian Eric Foner argues, it was the existence of the creed that became the language of mobilisation for the civil rights movement.[3] Benedict Anderson, one of the world's leading scholars of nationalism, makes a similar point: 'It is the fact of being of the same place – the nation – with its set of values that gives the language to appeal against human rights abuses in our countries. The Declaration of Independence provided that set of values for Americans.'[4]

I also travelled to India to try to understand the biggest and most diverse nation in the world. India, too, was born through the bloodshed of secession in Pakistan. But as authors such as Shashi Tharoor and Sunil Khilnani have argued, speeches such as Nehru's 'Midnight to Millennium' speech on Independence Day formalised the idea of India as a place for all.[5] Mbeki's 'I am an African' speech gave South Africans a similar feeling.

I wrote an op-ed article in the *Mail & Guardian*, the weekly newspaper established as the *Weekly Mail* in the 1980s by Anton Harber and Irwin Manoim to provide the most audacious exposés of the apartheid government. In this article I celebrated the dawning of a new nationalist era under Mbeki. I argued that South Africa's transition to democracy had been framed almost exclusively in political and economistic terms, with very little attention to public values and public culture. Mbeki was well placed to articulate a set of national values that would guide a new process of public purpose building. The African Renaissance was an excellent example of how to achieve this national consensus. I suggested four principles to guide such a process.

First, the development of any national consensus would have to recognise the pluralistic nature of our society. Second, public intellectuals could play a leading role in the articulation of such a consensus, and at times they could be supportive and at times critical of the national leadership. I argued that black intellectuals were particularly suited to play this role because of their organic proximity to the experience of black people. In other words, black intellectuals represented a set of values and world experiences that have historically been locked out of what I called the knowledge–ideas complex in South Africa. It was indeed worrisome that the subject of black intellectual empowerment had not received the same level of national attention and visibility that political and economic empowerment had received. Third, I suggested that the media, public policy institutes and community forums were the vehicles through which the debates about the national consensus should take place. I also called for private funding of new policy institutes by the

new black millionaires. This would not be just a matter of social responsibility but a pragmatic investment in the generation of new ideas.
Fourth, all of this could be one way of fostering a deliberative culture,
and in the process could cultivate the next generation of public intellectuals.[6]

No sooner had I published that article than appeared a warning in
the form of a letter to the editor from a University of the Western Cape
academic, Suren Pillay. He warned that I would live to regret my praise-
singing for Thabo Mbeki. It is worth reproducing Pillay's response at
length, if only for the manner in which it exposed my own *naïveté* and
for how accurately he predicted what would happen once the nationalists
gained hold of power:

As I read Xolela Mangcu's heartfelt ode (Crossfire, 5–11 June)
to the need for national values, I see the jets roaring over the
Union Buildings, leaving behind in their thundering blur a
rainbow of colours. Presidents, ministers and generals stand stony-
faced, with hand on heart, framed by the deafening adulation of
people waving a new flag. It is this aspect of nationalism that
creates the lump in the throat and tear in the eye. It is also this
nationalism that deadens the senses, obfuscates the problems and
creates the us-and-them mentality that sends nations to war. His
[Mangcu's] implicit and disturbing assumption seems to be that
we need another cult of the individual through which to establish
a democracy. Around this national leader are 'public intellectuals'
who carry forth the message 'through multiple institutions like
the media, policy institutes and community forums', who will
paternalistically encourage the public to air their views and then
stamp on the debate 'a common morality' and consensus . . .

While I do not necessarily have a problem with trying to
construct some set of national values, I do have a problem with
making national consensus a national value. 'Public intellectuals',
for Mangcu, are an essential part of his project of building national values. My argument is that the kind of public intellectual
Mangcu is evangelising for is an anti-intellectual.

36

This brings to mind one of the most eloquently written defences of the intellectual, from Palestinian academic and activist Edward Said, when, in the 1993 Edward Reith Lectures, he observed that 'the intellectual, properly speaking, is not a functionary nor an employee completely given up to the policy goals of a government or a large corporation, or even a guild of like-minded professionals.

'In such situations the temptations to turn off one's moral sense, or to think entirely within the speciality, or to curtail scepticism [for national consensus?] in favour of conformity, are far too great to be trusted' . . . Are those involved in intellectual pursuits not being asked, nay, being told, to become 'functionaries' whose task it will be to change themselves into the spin doctors of this or that policy, like Gear and the 'African renaissance', which are the current wisdom?

Are intellectuals, quoting Said, not becoming those who are not being asked to 'lead, but to consolidate government's policy, to spew out propaganda against official enemies, euphemisms, and on a larger scale, whole systems of Orwellian Newspeak, which could disguise the truth of what was occurring in the name of national honour'?[7]

Racial nationalism and its discontents

Pillay was absolutely right. I had allowed myself to be swept away in the euphoria of nationalist pride. At its best nationalism is the desire that people have to belong to a group of people with a shared history and experience. The nationalist feeling often emanates from a despised group's desire to assert itself as an equal member of the general family of humankind. However, what is at the centre of this book is what happens when the same nationalism is no longer an instrument of struggle but an instrument of rule.

Isaiah Berlin, regarded as one of the leading liberal thinkers of the twentieth century, has described nationalism in similar terms: 'To be the object of contempt or patronizing tolerance on the part of proud neighbours is one of the most traumatic experiences that individuals or societies can suffer.' Berlin, however, also warned that 'the response, as often as not, is a pathological exaggeration of one's real or imaginary virtues'.[8] In straightening their bent backs from the humiliation of oppression, nationalist leaders lash out at anyone who might even remotely remind them of previously held stereotypes. As the group's gate-keepers nationalist leaders manipulate their followers' fears by keeping alive the idea that the non-Ruritarians might just return to oppress the Ruritarians again. The Marxist historian Eric Hobsbawm describes the insidious way in which nationalism becomes a state project relationship as follows:

All that was required for the entry of nationalism into modern politics was that groups of men and women who saw themselves, in whatever manner, as Ruritarians, or were so seen by others, should become ready to listen to the argument that their discontents were in some way caused by the inferior treatment of Ruritarians by a non-Ruritarian state or ruling class.[9]

Mugabe used this argument to great and tragic effect in Zimbabwe – about how Britain seeks to recolonise his country – a theme that I shall return to in Chapter 4 on Zimbabwe.

I saw this politics of racial blackmail slowly unfolding at the beginning of 2000, barely six months after Mbeki's inauguration as Mandela's successor. Mbeki started calling on black intellectuals to come to his defence on a number of public policy controversies. 'Where are the black intellectuals?' he would ask. Could we really blame him? After all, we were the people who had celebrated his rise to power as the dawn of a new era.

Business Day columnist Karima Brown wrote that former *Mail & Guardian* editor Howard Barrell had been vindicated when he had said Mbeki was unfit to rule. Barrell, who had known Mbeki for years in exile, was pilloried as racist for this observation. Brown describes those early years of Mbeki rule as:

a dangerous era, which ushered in the cult of the personality around Mbeki, to whom we were told we needed to look to provide all the answers. In line with this twisted logic, the all-knowing president was the only one who could provide leadership, be it in the ANC or the state, even as he patently failed to do so time and again, be it on HIV/AIDS, Zimbabwe, crime or the leadership crisis in his own party.[10]

She recalls how the black bourgeoisie and some black journalists rallied around Mbeki under the guise of a 'misplaced patriotism'. However, the initial celebration increasingly gave way to disenchantment with Mbeki, perhaps sooner than anyone might have anticipated. As president of the country Mbeki had begun to adopt controversial public policies on HIV/AIDS, Zimbabwe, corruption, crime and economic policy. Having initially sung Mbeki songs of praise I increasingly became disenchanted and angry with myself for having so blindly hoped that 'political and cultural facilitators' into modernity were sufficient for the exercise of leadership.

The most courageous role was played by Sipho Seepe through his 'no-holds barred' column in the *Mail & Guardian*. Seepe's strategy was to cut right through Mbeki's intellectual façade – a façade that had prevented many people from speaking out against the president. Individual scholars and journalists were afraid of the Mbeki put down. But Seepe was suggesting that beyond the façade was an insecure and intolerant individual. I did not always agree with Seepe's personal approach but I admired the man for his courage at a time when no one dared to speak out. To criticise government was not only described as unpatriotic but was portrayed as an act of collusion with the enemies of the revolution. In August 2000 Mbeki delivered the Oliver Tambo Memorial Lecture hosted by the National Institute of Economic Policy. Drawing on a range of historical figures, from the Guinean revolutionary Amilcar Cabral to the Kenyan playwright and novelist Ngũgĩ wa Thiong'o, Mbeki asked the rhetorical question about black intellectuals:

What then of our own petite bourgeoisie which emerged out of foreign domination and which aspires to a way of life which is similar if not identical with that of the foreign minority... where is the black intelligentsia now given that the victory over white minority domination, scored through their joint action with the native masses, has created the conditions for them to pursue their class interests, without let or hindrance?[11]

Initially a culture of fear and conformity began to grow within the black community in response to Mbeki's increasingly vituperative language. This was especially the case among a black intellectual class that stood to enhance its reputation through its close proximity to power. There was also the matter of government contracts and assignments that awaited those who sang the president's praises. A group of business leaders, clearly aligned to Mbeki, took out a full-page advertisement in the biggest weekend newspaper in the country, the *Sunday Times*, remonstrating with black intellectuals and writers whom they castigated as 'uncle toms' in the service of the white establishment.

I remember being interviewed by then *City Press* journalist Sandile Memela who argued that no matter how much independence I claimed, I was beholden to the owners of the newspaper I wrote for, which was then the *Sunday Independent*. This was preposterous as my own public writings sometimes criticised the newspaper and I ultimately left it. What Memela had forgotten was that the very newspaper he worked for was owned by Afrikaners. It was all so disingenuous. In this formulation critical voices were spending our time colluding with our liberal white bosses. We had no moral autonomy of our own. In response I wrote a satirical/tongue-in-cheek piece in which I sought to assure Mbeki's thought-police that:

> *I, Xolela Mangcu, being of sound mind do solemnly swear that I have not now or at any time in the past colluded with rightwing forces or white liberals to undermine the democratically elected government of President Thabo Mbeki. I also swear that, as far as I can recall, I do not have any puppet-master pulling the strings behind every thought or word that originates from my pen ... I fully recognize that being black demands that I denounce any claim to independent expression and democratic citizenship. This is an irony by which I pledge to live, so that I may remain authentically black!*

The advertisement in the *Sunday Times* was relying on the same nativism that Mbeki's supporters were utilising. It used racial oppression as a form of political blackmail. At the heart of it is the politics of racial authenticity:

black people are urged to put solidarity with their leaders or heroes above everything else. The writer Mothobi Mutloatse describes this as 'the liberation handcuffs that have given us Mugabe, Nujoma, and Chiluba',[12] and I continued in my column:

> *The distinguished African American scholar Cornel West, like Steve Biko before him, defines blackness as a political and ethical construct: 'appeals to black authenticity ignore this fact; such appeals hide and conceal the political and ethical dimensions of blackness.' Indeed, throughout our history political solidarity was always tied to moral reasoning. That is why we denounced barbaric acts such as 'the necklace.' What is troubling now is that political solidarity is being separated from, and supersedes, moral reasoning. As black intellectuals we are asked to be party to that separation, but only on the side of political solidarity . . . But what about the sense of fairness that has always informed our political struggle. Aren't we entitled to our own autonomous sense of right and wrong about such matters without being manipulated by white people? And why should those who speak in the name of black authenticity predicate the moral integrity of black people on the actions of whites?*[13]

In his book *Do South Africans Really Exist*, Ivor Chipkin demonstrates how the concept of blackness has changed under Mbeki's leadership. In this new incarnation 'Blackness is no longer a social position (in the racial capitalist relations of production) or a psychological condition [as it was with Biko]. It designates an authentic national subject who is loyal to the state because that state is controlled by other blacks like it. The facts are irrelevant to the proof.' Chipkin describes how easy the slide is from the politics of authenticity to mysticism. The mysticism goes something like this:

> Blacks, because of their very blackness, are reversing the legacy of apartheid. Anyone who disputes that is against blacks, and therefore against the reversal of apartheid, whether that reversal is actually happening or not. And thus there is a certain form of

41

knowing through belief that is accessible only to black people: belief (that the government is authentically Black) does not derive from the facts (data collected, sorted and interrogated by reason). Rather the facts are revealed through belief.

Chipkin concludes:

The facts by which we measure the merit of President Mbeki (as a Black) are those of a mysterious and sublime quality. Blackness here is attached to a spiritual knowing . . . and this knowledge is accessible only to authentic Blacks because they alone are true believers. What this kind of nation building does is transform the presidency and the government into quasi-religious objects that endure all torments and survive with immaculate beauty.[14]

Taking their cue from their leader, government spokespeople started openly insulting black intellectuals who were critical of Mbeki's government. Sandile Memela who by 2006 had made the transition from *City Press* columnist to spokesman for the ministry of arts and culture, wrote an op-ed article for the *Mail & Guardian* in which he described me and several other commentators as 'coconuts' and 'celebrity in-tellectuals' who had made their way to the top by criticising a black government.[15] Included in this list were individual journalists such as Barney Mthombothi and Vuyo Mbuli as well as radio presenter Tim Modise. A coconut is allegedly someone who is black on the outside but really white on the inside. We were 'celebrity intellectuals' because of the amount of publicity/space we received from a predominantly white media industry. Following the same line of argument Ronald Suresh Roberts gave a speech at Wits University at which he called me *Business Day* editor Peter Bruce's native assistant.

One of Mbeki's most ardent defenders and deputy chairperson of the SABC Christine Qunta increased the volume of the rhetoric to new levels when she criticised black critics of government as '*askaris*' – the much hated black operatives of the apartheid government in the 1980s. In an article in the *Star* newspaper, Qunta argued that South Africa was not entirely liberated. She suggested that the country was under the kind of indirect rule that Britain practised in the colonies or that prevailed in the Belgian Congo. Just as black people had been the instruments of indirect rule, and just as *askaris* viciously defended apartheid rule, black critics worked to serve white interests in the new dispensation.[16] In other words, we were criticising the government because it was black – and not because it was messing up.

Then Roberts wrote a paean to Mbeki that was simply unreadable – mostly for the invective and insults he throws at everyone who disagrees with Mbeki. His targets were white liberals and imperialists, and their black 'lackeys'. Roberts is of course unsympathetic and unapologetic that this was a collaborative project with Mbeki himself: 'In the end, however, these are my thoughts, informed by the president's suggestions and reactions.'[17] Even someone as sympathetic to Mbeki as the SABC board member, journalist and publisher Thami Mazwai lamented that a book marketed as a study of Mbeki revealed nothing about the subject. Mazwai wrote that Roberts 'could have given readers a more comprehensive picture of Thabo Mbeki as this is what many most desire'. Mazwai continued: 'This is the next challenge for Roberts and for the Native Club. An intellectual discourse around Mbeki the visionary, leader and manager would do much for the intellectual edification of African pride.'[18]

It is this sense of being tormented that has led to Mbeki representing himself – or being represented by Roberts – as misunderstood. It is never really clear where this perpetual misunderstanding comes from. His praise singers will argue that he is being deliberately misunderstood by a racist white media, and sometimes he is misunderstood because he is too intelligent for ordinary mortals, and sometimes he is misunderstood because he is ahead of his time.

He appears to be the most misunderstood individual in the world, which begs the question of why he does not do more to be understood. I suspect he does not do so because there is a certain psychological appeal to being inscrutable and a cut above the rest.

The SABC has also played its part as Mbeki's propaganda machine. For a long time there had been complaints by opposition parties, civil society organisations and trade unions that the public broadcaster was biased in its reporting and had become nothing more than a public relations agency for Mbeki's political ambitions. This has been particularly the case under the leadership of Snuki Zikalala, the head of SABC news and a long-time ANC apparatchik.

Zikalala has made no bones about his ANC loyalties and his intention to tell the government's story. News bulletins are thus literally a nightly parade of cabinet ministers. One of the most painful things to watch on television is an interview with Mbeki. The whole thing is so stage managed you wonder why any self-respecting journalist agrees to be part of it. But still with all of that protection the much misunderstood Mbeki will say something embarrassing or downright self-defeating, and this is usually in an effort to be clever. On one occasion he tried to ridicule the seriousness of the crime situation in the country by saying no one was likely to walk into the studio brandishing a weapon.

In June 2006 *Business Day* revealed that Zikalala had a 'blacklist' of individuals who were no longer going to be used on the SABC's news bulletins. When the SABC was caught out it gave a flimsy argument about how important it is to give different people an opportunity to provide commentary, and how important it is to get experts to comment. Instead of getting a political analyst to comment on HIV/AIDS, the broadcaster would get a medical researcher. Instead of getting someone such as Moeletsi Mbeki (the president's younger brother and sometimes most trenchant critic of his government policies) to comment on Zimbabwe, the SABC might select a sympathetic foreign policy analyst from one of the government-funded institutions.

SABC spokesperson Kaiser Kganyago denied the allegations of a blacklist on the radio show hosted by the popular presenter John Perlman. But Perlman refused to go along with the cover-up and rebutted denials. He said that he had been instructed not to interview certain individuals. Perlman was immediately charged with bringing the SABC into disrepute. It is still not clear what happened after that but both Perlman and his co-host Nikiwe Bikitsha resigned from their popular morning pro-gramme. Since then a number of SABC reporters have resigned from the public broadcaster as it lurches from crisis to crisis. It is as if the ship has no rudder.

When the blacklist controversy first flared, SABC group chief executive officer Dali Mpofu established a Commission of Inquiry and promised that heads would roll if there were evidence of any wrongdoing. The Commission was headed by two respected South Africans, former SABC chief and struggle veteran Zwelakhe Sisulu and lawyer Gilbert Marcus. The Commission confirmed the existence of the blacklist and reprimanded Snuki Zikalala for his part in it. However, instead of acting on his promises Mpofu sought to prevent the publication of the report, and insisted that the Commission had established no such wrongdoing. Unfortunately for Mpofu, the *Mail & Guardian* had already obtained a copy of the Commission's report, and the newspaper published it in its entirety on its website. It was an embarrassing moment for Mpofu. What was he to do other than play what the African American newspaper columnist Stanley Crouch (whose politics I abhor) has called the racial blame-game?

I had known Mpofu since our years as student leaders in the liberation movement. He was a leader of the Black Students' Society (BSS) at Wits. I was a rival of sorts – representing the Black Consciousness camp. Mpofu always patronisingly said that I would one day come to appreciate the virtues of non-racialism. I was therefore shocked to read his rather indigestible article in the *City Press* using race as a way out. In essence Mpofu was arguing that whites wanted to determine the SABC's agenda. Over his dead body, he asserted. He concluded his article with a rather petulant utterance unbecoming of the head of the SABC: '*Ag sies, bayasinyanyisa*' (They make us wanna puke, the whites that is). What this had to do with the SABC's blacklisting of black commentators was not clear.

I knew then that the game was over for Mpofu. Here was a man who had established a Commission, and was now going against its re-commendations and his own word. He had lost all manner of public respectability and, contrary to the formidable character I had known in my student days, had become angry and bellicose. So I wrote a column in which I asked: 'So Dali please tell me this: what do I now do with the memories of your non-racial teachings and your generous tempera-ment at varsity?'[19]

45

Mpofu's reversal is an example of the great U-turn in the politics of the ANC. It is indeed an irony that I should now be the one reminding Mpofu and the ANC of their patronising lectures about non-racialism, and that they should be the purveyors of the worst kind of racial politics.

After five years spent working for the Steve Biko Foundation I took up the position of executive director at the Human Sciences Research Council (HSRC). It was here that I experienced first-hand the tension between power and freedom of expression. The issue of my public writings came up during my job interview: how did I plan to balance my public intellectual role with the work of the HSRC? I made it clear that I had absolutely no intention of disappearing from the public domain. I had all of that inserted as an addendum to my employment contract.

I established a healthy modus vivendi with my boss, Mark Orkin, an academic who had taught me in my first year sociology class at Wits. Orkin was, however, in the last year of his contract, and Olive Shisana, who had done stellar research on HIV/AIDS, was appointed. However, scientists do not always make the best democrats. No sooner was Shisana appointed than she introduced what she called a media policy for the organisation. This policy was meant to guide our public writings in the media. The new policy recommended that our public commentary be limited to our research findings.

Where did that leave me as a columnist? Columns are not research reports, and if they were, no one would read them. Besides, this restriction went against both the spirit and the letter of my employment contract. However, it became clear to me that this was a form of censorship by stealth. My fears were confirmed when Shisana informed me, in the presence of other senior executives in the organisation, that Thabo Mbeki's wife, Zanele Mbeki, and some cabinet ministers were unhappy with my public writings. When I told her to tell the politicians to back off she simply said she could not do that because 'they give us work'. There and then I knew it was time to quit but not without first stirring up a storm about it both within the HSRC and in the general public. Soon thereafter a number of senior colleagues also left, citing the same kind of censorship.

It was clear to me that what was happening at the HSRC was also happening at other public institutions – from the SABC to the Medical Research Council (MRC), where Mbeki was putting pressure on Malegapuru Makgoba to go along with his denialist approach to HIV/ AIDS (more about that in Chapter 3). Michael Walzer captures the intensity of these individual commentators: 'Their own lives, I suppose are emotionally intense, but in relation to society and economy this is a dangerously free-floating intensity. In time of trouble it can be turned against the internal others: minorities, aliens, strangers.'[20]

However, in order to understand the relationship between Mbeki and these individuals we have to place it in the context of the relationship between African rulers and intellectuals over the past six decades of post-colonial independence. The African scholar Thandika Mkandawire, argues that African rulers saw themselves as the lead intellectuals, mainly because many of them had received higher education, and often in some of the best universities in the West. Leaders such as Kwame Nkrumah (Ghana), Jomo Kenyatta (Kenya), Kenneth Kaunda (Zambia) and Mwalimu Julius Nyerere (Tanganyika, later Tanzania) developed a penchant for assuming the role of the philosopher-king and reducing intellectual work to the incantation of the thought of the leader.[21]

African leaders saw this as a way of constructing and imposing their own political hegemony over their societies. In the process they became as defensive and then as brutally dictatorial as their past masters. Alternative ideas were suddenly seen as subversive or undermining the nationalist revolution or standing in the way of development. Mkandawire argues that part of the problem is in the different logics by which intellectuals and politicians function. The intellectual function, by definition, requires critical autonomy. The political function is to enforce uniformity: 'African states were apparently never in greater need of any social category other than that of disposable sycophants, and few African leaders bothered to curry favour with intellectuals qua [as] intellectuals.'[22] And thus for the six decades since independence African nationalist leaders have been on a collision course with their countries' intellectuals.

As Suren Pillay cautioned in his letter to the *Mail & Guardian*, I should have known better. There was no reason Thabo Mbeki would be any different. Mbeki's defining self-perception is that of an intellectual leader – a philosopher-king. He is also the leader of a government and a political party brandishing a new national philosophy in much the same way that people such as Nkrumah, Kenyatta, Kaunda and Nyerere did. These leaders are characterised by an 'I know best' paternalism. Only Nyerere ever spoke frankly about the dangers of his leadership style.

In 1997 I had occasion to host Nyerere at the Bellagio Centre in northern Italy. It was one of the greatest times of my life – spending four full days talking about leadership with Nyerere. He reflected critically on his tenure and warned our group about the dangers of the big man syndrome in Africa: 'You either supported me or you shut up. No one could come out and oppose me, because he would be a traitor. If you were working for government, you did not want to lose your job and so you shut up. Occasionally you might even secretly come to me and give me some facts.'[23]

Mbeki's behaviour thus fits in a long line of behaviour by leaders who had come to power with a great deal of promise, only to betray their people's expectations. That is at least how I analyse Mbeki. The more he sought to cling onto power – a topic I shall deal with later – the more convinced I became that he had been another wolf in sheep's skin. I had been fooled by the promise of his rhetoric.

Chapter 3 demonstrates how this culture of fear and silence saw our country watch silently as its philosopher-king took it down a path of self-destruction on the most lethal health challenge it had ever faced: HIV/AIDS.

The Unkindest Cut of All
How HIV/AIDS Became Mbeki's
Achilles Heel

THABO MBEKI'S LEGACY will largely be defined by his intransigence
on the greatest public health threat facing South Africa – HIV/AIDS. In
order to understand the gravity and sheer irresponsibility of Mbeki's
apparent denialism we need only look at the evolution of a potentially
manageable disease into a pandemic that has claimed the lives of millions
of South Africans. It is also important to document Mbeki's record on
HIV/AIDS in the light of attempts by his supporters to revise history.
James Myburgh has detailed Mbeki's utterances and actions in what is
probably the most authoritative time-line of our president's dalliance with
denialism. Myburgh warns about 'the power of forgetting, the determination of the presidency to rewrite the historical record and the
capacity of such propaganda – endlessly repeated – to distort the memory
of historical reality'.[1]

The earliest indications of the threat of HIV/AIDS came in the 1980s. The apartheid government dismissed HIV/AIDS as a disease affecting homosexuals. With all the stereotypes and prejudices surrounding homosexuals the government saw the disease as a matter of just deserts for people it regarded as wayward. In addition, antenatal studies done in the late 1980s showed no prevalence of the disease among heterosexual couples. Even under Nelson Mandela's government HIV/AIDS did not receive as much attention as it warranted. This is attributable mainly to the fact that Mandela found it awkward to talk about sexual issues, and was apparently discouraged from doing so by members of his own party. This cultural conservatism was compounded by the challenges of setting up a new health system in the recently democratised country. However, scientists argue that even under the best of conditions there was no way the Mandela government could have prevented the rise in HIV prevalence. This is because of the high levels of migration from the rest of the continent at the time, and the different strains of the virus that came with this migration.[2]

By the time Mandela handed over to Mbeki in 1999 about 7 per cent of the population was HIV positive. Undoubtedly then, Mbeki inherited an increasingly serious situation. It is the manner of his response that shocked the world. Instead of confronting the challenge head on, Mbeki did everything to obfuscate the problem, and ultimately deny its existence.

South African economist and social scientist Nicoli Nattrass traces the origins of Mbeki's denialism to the Virodene scandal that took place towards the end of the Mandela administration. Two University of Pretoria scientists, Ziggy and Olga Visser, came to the government to suggest they had found a cure for the disease. They were given an audience with the cabinet by the then Health Minister Nkosazana Dlamini-Zuma. The then Deputy President Thabo Mbeki waxed lyrical about 'the moving testimonies of AIDS sufferers who had been treated with Virodene, with seemingly very encouraging results'. Nattrass observes: 'It does appear that it was through his connection with the Vissers that Mbeki took the first steps down the road to AIDS denialism – or at least to adopting the rhetoric that marked him as an AIDS denialist in the public eye.'[3] However, Nattrass points to the oddity of the Vissers presenting a drug to the cabinet, and not to the Medicines Control Council (MCC), the statutory body set up to conduct clinical trials and register drugs in the country. Instead, Mbeki and the Minister of Health Dlamini-Zuma continued to do everything in their power to castigate, undermine and ultimately threaten to close the MCC down for, in Mbeki's words, refusing AIDS patients 'the possibility of mercy treatment'.[4] However, the MCC stood its ground, and the testing of the drug had to be taken outside the country (with the assistance, it has been recently alleged, of the presidency).

I firmly believe that Mbeki must have taken this slight personally. He had spent a great deal of time cultivating the image of an intellectual, and had in fact staked his presidency on this intellectual image. His language became more strident, and he introduced the language of racism in the debate about HIV/AIDS. When members of the opposition took the government to task for undermining its own MCC to adopt a fake cure, they were criticised as racist. The use of words such as quackery or fakery could only reveal the largely white opposition's racist stereotypes about Africa.

Mbeki launched one of his first salvos against the 'AIDS establishment' in a speech he gave to the National Council of Provinces shortly after his inauguration. He insisted that the government would never authorise the use of AZT to prevent mother-to-child transmission because the drug was toxic. He urged his colleagues in government to join him in following the debates about HIV/AIDS on the Internet. He found ammunition in these debates to fight back against those who had humiliated him in the Virodene saga. So deep was his anger that he totally gave up his sense of judgement. He set up a Presidential AIDS Advisory Panel consisting of some of the most notorious AIDS denialists in the world: Roberto Giraldo, Peter Duesberg, Sam Mhlongo and David Rasnick, and a spattering of South African scientists including respected South African immunologist, Malegapuru Makgoba, who was then head of the MRC. Makgoba came under a great deal of pressure to come to Mbeki's side.

It is perhaps worth explaining why Mbeki was so chagrined by Makgoba's refusal to join him in his denialism. Mbeki had stood by Makgoba when the latter came under fire from white academics at Wits

University. Makgoba and Mbeki became comrades in arms and Mbeki even wrote an introduction to Makgoba's book *Mokoko*. Mbeki must have reasoned that it was now Makgoba's turn to support him. Apparently Mbeki wrote Makgoba a 30-page letter raging about his sense of betrayal. In addition to his sense of intellectual pride, Mbeki has an even deeper sense of being betrayed, and thus can be unforgiving to those who have betrayed him.

I say 'apparently' because the letter was not signed by the president, but when Makgoba looked at the document's electronic properties they revealed that it came from Mbeki's computer. However, Makgoba told the president that he was not about to give up his professional career built up over 30 years of hard work simply to ingratiate himself to a politician. Sorry Mr President, not on this one, Makgoba is reputed to have told Mbeki.

Mbeki it appears never forgave him for that. At every opportunity he would make snide remarks about academics who do not read – in reference to Makgoba and Michael Cherry, a zoologist, with whom Mbeki had an exchange of correspondence.[5] As I pointed out in Chapter 2 this was not the first time Mbeki castigated black intellectuals for not reading. Perhaps because he was an outsider to the medical research community, it did not occur to the president that the literature he was praising was on the margins of the scientific community. Nattrass describes how Mbeki got caught up in the arguments of one AIDS denialist, Eleni Papadopulos-Eleopulos, and used those arguments to put down Makgoba and Cherry:

This says several things about Mbeki's approach to scientific authority. Firstly, he was clearly impressed by the scientific credentials of Papadopulos-Eleopulos's article, which was published in a special supplement to the journal *Current Research and Medical Opinion*, describing it as 'a very senior scientific journal'. To put this in perspective, this journal was cited by other journals a total of 1 148 times in 2004. Compare this to the number of times the top medical science journals get cited; for example, the *New England Journal of Medicine*, 159 498 citations; the *Lancet*, 126 002 citations; and the *Journal of Immunology*,

108 602 citations. Cutting-edge AIDS research gets published in these journals, not in minor journals that publish mainly reviews and opinion pieces rather than original research.[6]

Makgoba argued that Mbeki's 'undermining of scientists and the scientific method was especially dangerous in a developing country still in the process of establishing a strong scientific research base'. As head of the MRC Makgoba felt duty-bound

> to tell Mbeki to 'leave science to the scientists'. When, in April 2000, Mbeki wrote to world leaders (including Bill Clinton, Tony Blair and Kofi Annan) defending his support for the denialist scientists, Makgoba took the gloves off entirely by describing the action as 'emotional and irrational' and predicting that Mbeki 'will regret this in his later years . . . [because he] displays things he does not understand'.[7]

However, Mbeki was not about to give in – not with his intellectual reputation and pride at stake. The long letter that was allegedly traced to his computer then reappeared in the form of an ANC paper, now authored by one of his trusted lieutenants, Peter Mokaba, a man whose life is widely believed to have been claimed by HIV/AIDS. The paper rejected as

> . . . illogical the proposition that AIDS is a single disease caused by a singular virus, HIV . . . It accepts that HIV may be one of the causes of this immune deficiency, but cannot be the only cause . . . It rejects as baseless and self-serving the assertion that millions of our people are HIV positive . . . It rejects the claim that AIDS is the single largest cause of death in our country.[8]

Mokaba had now become the HIV/AIDS expert or was it Mbeki? Either way, one cannot help but recall Mkandawire's observation that in many African governments 'even characters adamantly committed to mediocrity and obscurantism promulgated ideologies that were supposed to inform their countries' transformation'.[9] I wrote a satirical piece in response to 'Mokaba's' (or Mbeki's) attack on Makgoba:

Mr Loyal Cadre is a senior member of the ANC's National Executive Committee. He receives notice of a special meeting to debate the government's position on HIV/AIDS. Arguing the government's position that there is no demonstrable link between HIV and AIDS is the revolutionary Peter Mokaba of 'Kill the Boer, Kill the Farmer' fame. Representing the mainstream view that HIV causes AIDS is the distinguished Oxford-educated immunologist Professor Malegapuru William Makgoba.

Mokaba brings the roof down with a foot-stomping, chest-beating, fire-eating oration titled 'Castro Hlongwane, Caravans, Cats, Geese, Foot and Mouth and Statistics: HIV/AIDS and the Struggle for the Humanization of the African.' As someone used to the quiet din of the laboratory Professor Makgoba is visibly shaken by the taunts and jibes from the other side. He nervously stammers through his presentation, 'How HIV Fulfils Koch's Hypothesis as a Causative Agent of AIDS'. The vote is a mere formality, and Mokaba trounces Makgoba by 100– 0. The meeting adjourns and everyone is invited for cocktails, caviar, whisky and wine. A queue forms to congratulate Mokaba: 'umshayile mfowethu, icabanga ukuthi i-clever le-outie' (you fixed him right, he thinks he's clever).

Mr Cadre drives home to find his daughter, Renaissance, elated that she's been admitted to study for her Ph.D. in medicine at Oxford. Now she needs advice about the challenges of Oxford. Comrade Mokaba, his oratory notwithstanding, is not exactly the person Mr Cadre has in mind. So he reluctantly calls Makgoba, who, following the afternoon's events, has decided to return to Oxford. Makgoba graciously agrees to take Renaissance under his wing. Mr Cadre thanks the professor profusely, and then says: 'Please, please, please, prof, this conversation never happened.'

A couple of months later the government appoints Comrade Mokaba as the new minister of health in recognition of his under- standing of 'ama-issues' and 'ama-dynamics.' After all, Thomas Kuhn once said scientific breakthroughs are often brought about by outsiders like Comrade Mokaba. Comrade Mokaba might just be entered in the Guinness Book of Records *for initiating both a militant youth revolution and a medical breakthrough. A first for the African Renaissance!*[10]

By this time I was also thoroughly disgusted by how the ANC had put its backing behind Mbeki. No one escaped the president's admonition, including Nelson Mandela, who was advised by Mbeki to stay out of the debate. In early 2002 Mandela was rapped over the knuckles for speaking out of turn on HIV/AIDS.[11] He was literally paraded by the ANC leadership in front of television cameras to proclaim that our government had the best HIV/AIDS programme in the world. He was for that moment caught up in a dilemma between loyalty to his party in government and his own conscience. However, Mandela soon found his footing and did the right thing. Together with Archbishop Desmond Tutu they started calling on the government to take the lead on HIV/AIDS. The Nelson Mandela Foundation became the biggest sponsor of research on HIV/AIDS, and Mandela launched the now popular 46664 concert (the number being a reference to his prison number) to raise funding for HIV/AIDS programmes.

By this point I was so exasperated and disillusioned that I concluded that there was very little we could expect from Mbeki on this issue. I issued a call to the nation to take the initiative when our leaders fail us on HIV/AIDS, saying:

> *While I applaud former President Nelson Mandela and Archbishop Desmond Tutu's implorations to President Thabo Mbeki to take leadership on this issue, I have personally given up on that possibility. I feel very sad about that conclusion because, as Archbishop Tutu has so often said, the president has so much going for him on other fronts. We should perhaps see the president's failure on this most important front as a challenge to our own understandings of leadership.*

I argued that instead of looking to Mbeki for leadership, 'we should all follow the example set by people like Mandela, Tutu, [Nthato] Motlana, and the Treatment Action Campaign and respect the consensus on HIV/AIDS reached by our people through their own empirical reality of death', and called for, 'more leadership voices from within the ANC's National Executive Committee'. I asked:

> *Or has the NEC become such an elective oligarchy that not a single member, other than Mandela, has the courage and integrity to speak*

out openly on such a defining issue for our children and our nation? Surely, the deaths of our children are more important than political loyalty or fiscal austerity? Or have we all become so callous as to allow bureaucratic power and political self-interest to blunt the moral sensibilities of ubuntu *that have always informed our very identity as a caring and feeling people?*[12]

Mbeki took his denialism to the international stage. It is perhaps here that he met with the greatest rebuke. This became apparent when delegates walked out while he was speaking at the International AIDS Conference in Durban in 2000. This was the largest gathering of scientists and activists from around the world, and they were thoroughly disgusted with Mbeki. It is not clear whether what Mbeki did there was a matter of unbelievable hubris or just outright folly. He told delegates: 'The world's biggest killer and the greatest cause of ill health and suffering across the globe, including South Africa, is extreme poverty.' He continued: 'As I listened and heard the whole story told about our own country, it seemed to me that we could not blame everything on a single virus.'[13] He reiterated this position later that year when he told parliament that a virus could not cause a syndrome: 'How does a virus cause a syndrome? It cannot really, truly. I think it is incorrect from everything I have read to say immune deficiency is acquired exclusively from a single virus.' He also published an article in the *Sunday Times* making pretty much the same argument – to the utter consternation and contempt of the medical community.[14] He went far and wide with his denialist sentiments. He gave an interview with *Time* magazine in which he stated that 'the notion that immune deficiency is only acquired from a single virus cannot be sustained'. When asked if he would acknowledge the link between the virus and the syndrome Mbeki said: 'This is precisely where the problem starts. No, I'm saying that you cannot attribute immune deficiency solely and exclusively to a virus.' It was Mbeki goobledegook at its worst.[15] He told a *Washington Post* reporter in September 2003: 'Personally, I don't know anybody who has died of AIDS. I really honestly don't.'[16] This is notwithstanding that his adviser Peter Mokaba and spokesman Parks Mankahlana are widely believed to have died from the disease.

Mbeki had appointed one of his loyalists, Manto Tshabalala-Msimang, as the minister of health in June 1999. Tshabalala-Msimang subsequently became the butt of jokes, ridicule and outright contempt. This intensified when the *Sunday Times* revealed that she had undeservedly received a liver transplant but continued to drink while she was awaiting the operation. The newspaper also alleged that she was a certified klepto-maniac who had been convicted of theft in Botswana. Apparently she had stolen items such as bed linen and a patient's watch. Mbeki came to Tshabalala-Msimang's defence, arguing that anyone who had evidence of dereliction of duty on the minister's part should come forward. Her handling of HIV/AIDS was lost on Mbeki, precisely because of his own blindness to the disease.

Tshabalala-Msimang's role on HIV/AIDS would become comical, particularly her advocacy of a combination of beetroot, lemon and garlic as the best way to treat the disease. The South African stand at the International AIDS Conference in Toronto (in 2006) had beetroot, lemon and garlic, and initially absolutely no antiretroviral drugs (although some were added later) as if to thumb her nose deliberately at the international community. South Africa came under heavy pressure to relent on its prevarications. Stephen Lewis, the United Nations Special Envoy for HIV/AIDS in Africa, only had harsh words for the government at the end of that conference:

South Africa is the unkindest cut of all. It is the only country in Africa, amongst all the countries I have traversed in the last five years, whose government is still obtuse, dilatory and negligent about rolling out treatment. It is the only country in Africa whose government continues to propound theories more worthy of a lunatic fringe than of a concerned and compassionate state. Between six and eight hundred people a day die of AIDS in South Africa. The government has a lot to atone for. I'm of the opinion that they can never achieve redemption.

There are those who will say I have no right, as a United Nations official, to say such things of a member state. I was appointed as Envoy on AIDS in Africa. I see my job as advocating for those who are living with the virus, those who are dying of the virus . . . all of those, in and out of civil society, who are fighting the good fight to achieve social justice. It is not my job to be silenced by a government when I know that what it is doing is wrong, immoral, indefensible.[17]

What the whole HIV/AIDS saga revealed was a leader who had lost his sense of judgement because of his personal hubris. It is indeed implausible that leaders can be right all of the time and the people are wrong and dimwitted all of the time. But Mbeki was somehow convinced that he could stand against the whole world – under the false pretence of being an intellectual. But what he forgot is that democratic leaders allow the citizenry to work out its problems, and only weigh in with their opinions having allowed citizens to achieve their own synthesis of social issues. It is of course not always the case that citizens can be practically involved in the making of public policy. But there will be those who pay enough attention to public affairs to have more than cursory knowledge and interest. There are also the experts on whom public leaders will from time to time rely. This is the socially respected expertise of medical professionals who spend their time through scientifically proven methods working on problems such as HIV/AIDS. It is this expertise that leaders need to respect.

Mbeki's arrogance was not just to dismiss the experience of the citizenry, but also to dismiss the body of science and scientists. By rejecting science he elevated himself above the scientists and the citizenry. I do not believe in rule by experts because experts themselves can only excel through engagement with the public. That is when experts stop purely being experts and become intellectuals engaged with the social challenges of their societies. This requires that leaders have a certain degree of modesty and empathy for the pain and suffering of other people; that they move away from intellectual self-indulgence.

In an interesting observation on his faulty judgement on the Iraq war the former academic turned politician Michael Ignatieff argues that 'acquiring good judgment in politics starts with knowing when to admit your mistakes'. A biographer of the great British intellectual, Isaiah Berlin, Ignatieff points to the distinction Berlin made between political and intellectual judgement. Berlin argued that while intellectuals are often interested in whether their ideas are interesting or not, politicians – or at least good politicians – are interested in the truth and relevance of their ideas. Ignatieff thus argues that 'among intellectuals, judgment is about generalizing and interpreting particular facts as instances of some big idea. In politics, everything is what it is and not another thing. Specifics matter more than generalities. Theory gets in the way.'[18]

I am not here advocating a schizophrenic model of leadership in which leaders are always mere followers of expert opinion. Some of the great leaders of the twentieth century are those who went against the popular view in their countries. The United States would probably not have entered the war against Hitler were it not for Franklin Delano Roosevelt's consistent cultivation of sceptical public opinion. In other words, sometimes the Herculean conception of the leader, often captured in seductive phrases such as 'leaders lead', is necessary to break through social lethargy. But there are really no formulae for how leaders should decide. It is a matter of judgement, or as Berlin puts it:

> If I am driving a car in desperate haste and come to a rickety bridge, and must make up my mind whether it will bear my weight, some principles of engineering would no doubt be useful. But even so I can scarcely afford to stop to survey and calculate. To be useful to me in a crisis such knowledge must have given rise to a semi-instinctive skill.[19]

It is this semi-instinctive skill that Mbeki lacks on HIV/AIDS. The instinctive skill would have been that of erring on the side of people's actual, lived realities. As Ignatieff puts it: 'Roosevelt and Churchill knew how to do wrong, yet they did not demand to be judged by different ethical standards than their fellow citizens did. They accepted that democratic leaders cannot make up their own moral rules . . . They must live and be judged by the same rules as everyone else.' And this demands that leaders do not hold to their ideas like the dogma. They must take the risk to be wrong, and when proven wrong admit so openly. As if with Mbeki in mind Ignatieff argues that 'fixed principle matters . . . But fixed ideas of a dogmatic kind are usually the enemy of good judgment.'[20] Mbeki's failure lay in not making these distinctions. He theorised ad infinitum about something that was affecting people on a daily basis, and suggested that what was happening to them was not what they were actually experiencing but another thing, and that thing lay in the theories of the AIDS denialists. By all indications it seemed at this point that Mbeki's position on HIV/AIDS was increasingly bound up with his own reputation as an intellectual.

Unfortunately, Mbeki was surrounded by people who were just as fascinated by his theories – a reflection perhaps of their own intellectual and theoretical bankruptcy. He acted as if he was posing a political principle when he was in fact nursing a personal slight. His instinctive skill was to deny all rational argument to defend his 'fixed principle'. In the end we are saddled not only with his ill-thought-out intellectual theories and fixed ideas but also with one of the most tragic political (mis)judgements of modern times.

Business Day editor Peter Bruce described Mbeki's approach to people as follows: 'If a peasant in Mpumalanga were to stand up at a presidential *imbizo* and complain about crime, Mbeki would argue with him until he won.'[21] There is something unreal about Mbeki in that respect, or as Justice Malala put it in an article in the *Sowetan* newspaper: 'Nothing in what he says or does suggests that the man lives in the country whose people voted him into power. Mbeki displays signs of being deluded and completely out of touch with what is happening in his country.'[22] Throughout this debacle Mbeki demonstrated an incredibly stubborn streak, which is a terrible trait for anyone who aspires to leadership.

A different kind of instinct

There has been much speculation about why a man who prides himself on rationality should be so irrational on such a critical issue for his nation. Some have suggested that the answer lies in the coincidence of the rise of the disease with the return of the exile community, many of whom came from different countries and possibly brought various strains of the virus with them. They argue that Mbeki did not want the exiles to be associated with the disease. They brought freedom, not death. This defensiveness stands in sharp contrast with the attitude of the late Chris Hani, a man Mbeki is often compared with, to his great personal chagrin. As early as 1990 Hani spoke openly and frankly about the challenge of HIV/AIDS:

Those of us in exile are especially in the unfortunate situation of being in the areas where the incidence of this disease is high. We cannot afford to allow the AIDS epidemic to ruin the realisation of our dreams. Existing statistics indicate that we are still at the beginning of the AIDS epidemic in our country. Unattended, however, this will result in untold damage and suffering by the end of the century.[23]

Indeed, by the end of the twentieth century about 30 per cent of pregnant women were HIV positive, and South Africa had the dubious honour of being ranked the country with the highest number of HIV positive people in the world. As the controversy raged, the president ratcheted up his rhetoric on the racial motivations of his critics. Suddenly, what had started out as the president's questioning of the technical aspects of the disease increasingly turned into racial diatribe. Mbeki started arguing that African people should resist Western orthodoxy – this from a man who swallowed hook, line and sinker the World Bank's austerity programmes.

Such contradictions notwithstanding, Mbeki and his lieutenants gave credence to the idea that HIV/AIDS was a Central Intelligence Agency (CIA) plot to reduce the African population. Another version, also emanating from government leaders, was that the disease was invented by pharmaceutical companies to get black people to buy their drugs.[24] With race as the weapon, Mbeki appealed to African leaders directly. In the appeal he justified his decision to invite dissident scientists to serve on his AIDS Advisory Panel thus:

It is suggested, for instance, that there are some scientists who are 'dangerous and discredited' with whom nobody, including ourselves, should communicate or interact.

In an earlier period in human history, these would be heretics that would be burnt at the stake! . . .

People who otherwise would fight very hard to defend the critically important rights of freedom of thought and speech occupy, with regard to the HIV-AIDS issue, the frontline in the campaign of intellectual intimidation and terrorism which argues that the only freedom we have is to agree with what they decree to be established scientific truths . . .

I am greatly encouraged that all of us, as Africans, can count on your unwavering support in the common fight to save our continent and its peoples from death from AIDS.[25]

Mbeki's most explicit racialisation of HIV/AIDS came in the form of the Z.K. Matthews memorial lecture he delivered at Fort Hare University on 12 October 2001:

Thus does it happen that others who consider themselves to be our leaders take to the streets carrying their placards, to demand that because we [black people] are germ carriers and human beings of a lower order that cannot subject its [sic] passions to reason, we must perforce adopt strange opinions, to save a depraved and diseased people from perishing from self-inflicted disease.[26]

Interestingly, HIV/AIDS was also the one area where Mbeki's nativism met its limits. No one in their right mind was going to buy into his theories. His aides may have gone along with him but the population, especially those who were dying from the disease were going to have none of it. It took the Treatment Action Campaign (TAC) and the extraordinary courage and determination of Zackie Achmat to mobilise people around the country to push for the treatment of HIV positive people.

The TAC emerged in the late 1990s under the leadership of Achmat, a gay activist who advocated openness and disclosure. As Mandisa Mbali of the Centre for Civil Society notes, the TAC framed the problem of HIV/AIDS not simply as a medical problem but as a human rights issue that extended beyond the gay community. As Mbali puts it:

From a mere handful of openly HIV positive white gay activists in the early 1990s, in the first years of the twenty-first century,

AIDS activists would heed Achmat's call and TAC's protests would come to consist of a human sea of thousands of HIV positive and HIV negative activists wearing t-shirts proudly proclaiming 'HIV POSITIVE' . . . The transformation of HIV/AIDS from an unspeakable and invisible epidemic in the early 1990s to one which affects a highly politically vocal and visible constituency in the early 2000s has been absolutely fundamental to the success of TAC as a political movement.[27]

The strength of the TAC as a social and political movement was clear when it took the government to court in 2001 and obtained an important legal victory against it, compelling the government to allow for the use of Nevirapine in mother-to-child transmission prevention and to provide a national plan to roll out mother-to-child transmission prevention.[28]

But in reality there is very little a court can do to compel a reluctant government to enforce its decisions, and so the government found all kinds of reasons to delay the implementation of the court order. The government was reduced to rearguard action. On the face of it Mbeki withdrew from the debates. He was confined to ongoing support for his embattled minister of health, amidst calls for Tshabalala-Msimang to resign. Following the Toronto conference he shifted responsibility for the government's HIV/AIDS programme to Deputy President Phumzile Mlambo-Ngcuka. Commentators suggested that this was a reaction to the embarrassment of the South African government in Toronto.

In his book Ronald Suresh Roberts tries to revise Mbeki's denialism, suggesting that the president had been ahead of everyone in the medical community in speaking out against the toxicity of antiretroviral drugs such as AZT.[29] Added to the mysticism were pedantic defences of his position on HIV/AIDS. Now Mbeki's critics were being asked to go on a wild goose chase in search of the one sentence where Mbeki had said HIV does not cause AIDS. We were now being asked to ignore all of his actions – including his invitation of HIV/AIDS denialists to his AIDS Advisory Panel.

There was a sense of reprieve in February 2007 when Manto Tshabalala-Msimang was relieved of her duties because of illness, and everyone expected Mbeki to replace her with someone else. The Minister of Transport Jeff Radebe was appointed acting minister of health, and Deputy Minister of Health Nozizwe Madlala-Routledge took on a more vocal role. She took an HIV/AIDS test and called on people in leadership positions to do the same. She was part of a growing number of cabinet ministers who were now speaking openly about HIV/AIDS. While the president said he knew no one with HIV/AIDS, one of his cabinet members, Minister of Labour Membathisi Mdladlana spoke openly about how some of his relatives had died from HIV/AIDS. Senior cabinet member Zola Skweyiya was reported to have prevailed on the minister of health to stop her antics.

However, Mbeki reinstated Tshabalala-Msimang to her position as soon as she was back from hospital. Instead, he fired the government's only open HIV/AIDS advocate. He fired Madlala-Routledge after she went to an international AIDS conference. According to government protocol cabinet ministers are not supposed to leave the country without the president's approval. Civil society organisations and opposition parties saw this as a pretext for firing her for her activism on an issue in which the president had been found woefully wanting. Madlala-Routledge said Mbeki had said she had no business being in a meeting of technical experts. Initially Mbeki's office said the president did not owe anyone any explanation for his decision, but perhaps sensing possible fall-out later said he had fired her because she was not a team player. I bet she was not a team player. It must indeed be hard to be a team player in denialism.

Thabo Mbeki had shown us that under his stewardship racial nationalism would trump even the most deadly public health issue of his time. In Mbeki's hands racial nationalism, which had been the source of political adaptation and survival for black people for centuries, had become a weapon of defence for a wounded politician bent on salvaging his personal intellectual reputation. The consequences have been deadly. As the commentator Rhoda Kadalie puts it: 'Fuelled by denial and inaction we sit today with a pandemic that has become the epicenter of the disease in sub-Saharan Africa.'[30]

Mbeki's racial nativism is singularly responsible for all of this. It is a racial nativism that would also inform his approach to Zimbabwe.

CHAPTER 4

Liberation Handcuffs
Zimbabwe and the Zanufication of South African Politics

HOW DID ZIMBABWE, a country that was once regarded as the bread-basket of southern Africa, turn into a basket case of the region? Almost every day we see on television pictures of Zimbabwean shops with no food and long lines of people waiting for petrol, as well as hear about runaway inflation that is in the region of 7 500 per cent, no doubt the highest in the world. We see a government that is one of the most brutal in the world, beating up its official opposition in public. And the South African government continues to maintain that it will say nothing to condemn Zimbabwe.

As with the issue of HIV/AIDS, Thabo Mbeki has shown a remarkable lack of political judgement about the most crucial foreign policy challenge facing South Africa. Mbeki's policy of quiet diplomacy, which is essentially that the South African government should engage behind closed doors instead of standing on rooftops to denounce Mugabe, lies in tatters as millions of Zimbabweans flood South Africa, fleeing their country's political and economic meltdown. For years Mbeki promised that negotiations between the Zimbabwe African National Union (ZANU) and the official opposition would take place. At every turn Mugabe dishonoured any undertakings to negotiate with the opposition, even to the extent of not showing up at meetings – to Mbeki's eternal embarrassment.

When asked about the consequences of the influx of Zimbabwean refugees, Mbeki simply said we would have to get used to them. He would have been thrown out of office for such a statement in any other democracy. But, alas, he has survived his overt and covert support for Mugabe's government because of his manipulation of the politics of racial nationalism.

How did all of this happen? Part of the explanation lies in black South Africans' fascination with Robert Mugabe. Mugabe was a hero for many of us. When I was a young boy I would gather my friends at my home in Ginsberg to discuss the liberation struggle in Zimbabwe. We were divided between Robert Mugabe and Joshua Nkomo sup- porters. A veteran of the nationalist liberation struggle, Nkomo was more aligned with the ANC while Mugabe was aligned to the more radical PAC. Given my sympathies for Black Consciousness I was naturally a Mugabe supporter. With the little money I had I bought books, which included a couple of biographies on Mugabe, and I often discussed politics with an older man in our township who was a radical Black Consciousness activist, Nazibho Hlanganisa.

However, none of us ever seriously thought Mugabe was popular enough to beat Nkomo in the country's first democratic elections in 1980. And so we were all surprised to wake up one day to the news of Mugabe's landslide victory, giving him an unassailable majority in the new parliament. It was one of the defining moments in the global black liberation struggle. A concert was held in Zimbabwe featuring artists such as reggae pioneer Bob Marley. Robert Mugabe was a cult figure among black people all around the world. I was personally impressed by his intellectual achievements – a string of degrees, some of which he had obtained during his long spell in prison. Legend has it that Mugabe had the chutzpah to tell the British Secretary of State for Foreign and Commonwealth Affairs, Lord Carrington, to go to hell during the Lancaster House Conference, which Carrington chaired. The Conference was held from 10 September to 15 December 1979 to settle the terms of an independent constitution and the supervision of elections under British authority.

Throughout the early 1980s Mugabe elevated himself to arguably the emerging senior African leader after the generation of Julius Mwalimu Nyerere and Kenneth Kaunda. The Zimbabwean economy was doing well; the country had a strong military; and Zimbabweans had a reputation for being highly educated. Some of Mugabe's cabinet ministers, particularly Edison Zvobgo, were admired for their intellectual achievements. However, news began to emerge that not all was well in Mugabe's Zimbabwe. There were rumours, which were later confirmed, of government-led massacres in Matabeleland in the mid-1980s. There was growing unhappiness with the pace of land reforms, and the government's embrace of structural adjustment programmes. But still, this was Mugabe, the godfather of the liberation movement.

Twenty-seven years after Mugabe assumed power there was still the idea that he could do no real wrong. The fact that an individual leader could be in power for that long did not even raise any questions from our government or our people. Mugabe spoke at the World Summit on Sustainable Development in Sandton in September 2002. He used the platform to attack British Prime Minister Tony Blair. To rapturous applause he told Blair: 'Blair keep your Britain and I will keep my Zimbabwe.' He received similar applause when he entered Orlando Stadium at the funeral of Walter Sisulu.

However, I saw the cynicism of it all. I suppose I was not the bright-eyed nationalist of my youth any more. I expressed my disgust at someone Wole Soyinka rightly called a monster.[1] I could understand the celebration of Mugabe in my generation's youth – when the ideal of freedom was so tantalising. But why celebrate a brutal dictator 27 years into his rule? Is it because he has really reversed the legacy of colonialism or does the celebration emanate from the belief that because he is black he is reversing that legacy? Is this another case of substituting racial mysticism and solidarity for objective reality and experience?

'If we are incapable of being ashamed of our country, we do not love it. It is a shame that can be valuably mobilized.' This is what the renowned scholar of nationalism Benedict Anderson said during an address at Wits last year. I have often locked horns with many of my fellow white South Africans over their lack of shame about apartheid. This lack of shame has often turned into outright denial of how apartheid gave them cruel and unfair advantage over black people. I suppose their logic is that any expression of shame would lead to pronouncement of guilt which would in turn to lead to punishment. But as Anderson puts it, there is something intrinsically redemptive about shame – without extending into guilt and punishment.

In the same way I have been astonished by this lack of shame in white society, I cannot see how black people cannot be ashamed by our complicity in the Zimbabwean tragedy. I will leave criticism of quiet diplomacy to foreign policy experts. I am talking about something much more basic and simple than such sophisticated concepts. I am simply asking whether we can feel proud about our South African identity and our values given our own collusion in what has happened in Zimbabwe. Collusion may seem like a strong word. After all, our country did not send troops to put down the people of Zimbabwe. But I would argue that we provided this monstrous dictator with psychological aid and comfort. Our leaders and intellectuals swallowed Robert Mugabe's lie that Zimbabwe's problems were a creation of the Western world. We gave him standing ovations and received him with thunderous applause whenever he came here. We put down his critics as agents of the West or sell-outs or coconuts of one type or the other. We argued for non-interference as articulately as our former oppressors did during those long dark decades of apartheid. We did and said all of these things even as we witnessed the destruction on our television screens. The idea of a country in which the government has to arrest shop-owners for increasing prices to stay in business is truly absurd.

Reasonable people have been asking how it is that a whole society can stand by while their ruler does as he wishes with the whole country. In many ways that is a question for the people of Zimbabwe to answer. The question for South Africans to answer is how could we have given psychological aid and comfort to this tragedy? Personally, I was sickened by the whole thing, and our participation in it. I always felt we had squandered our moral authority in defence of an irredeemable monster. I suppose part of the reason I write is to simply record my own reactions to history. And when it comes to Zimbabwe it is a history of which I am utterly ashamed. In the final analysis my expression of shame about our support for Mugabe also has something to do with our political future. I fear that in our support for Mugabe we demonstrated that we lost the basic value of ubuntu *that was supposed to underpin our political democracy. If we can show such callousness towards the people of Zimbabwe, what would stop us from such callousness to our neighbours here at home? After all, world history is littered with examples of neighbours turning on each other in the name of ethnic and racial nationalism, mainly at the instigation of thugs and gangsters lodged deep within the state. For example, there is still more we need to know more about the genocidal campaigns that Mugabe is said to have unleashed on the people of Matabeleland in the 1980s.*

In the final analysis Mugabe's terror raises questions about what happens when thugs take over the state, when citizens become accomplices to the terror, and when politicians and intellectuals become the chief theoreticians of the terror. But there again, the people of Zimbabwe must take the lead. Our responsibility to ourselves is to do some soul-searching about our own role in this sordid and tragic affair. Our first instinct may be to deny any such complicity, and say there is nothing we could have done. But did we really have to applaud this murderous dictator? What does that say about us, and our own cultural and political values? How did we become cheerleaders in an unseemly celebration of mass murder and gangsterism? We may have to begin with shame, but shame presupposes an articulation of pre-existing values. I still look forward to the day when all this racial nationalism is no longer with us, when we can speak openly about the values we hold in common.[2]

History and hypocrisy

There can be no gainsaying that Zimbabwe went through one of the most brutal forms of colonial rule on the African continent. This goes

69

back to land dispossession by Cecil John Rhodes's British South Africa company in the 1890s. The territory was given self-government in the 1920s but the new colonial government only intensified the processes of land dispossession. Black people were herded into barren parts of the country while whites kept the lush high rainfall areas to themselves. Things worsened when the white minority under the leadership of Ian Smith adopted the Unilateral Declaration of Independence in 1965, putting paid to any discussions of black majority rule.

This led ultimately to a bloody war of independence involving Zimbabwe's two liberation movements: Mugabe's ZANU and Joshua Nkomo's ZAPU (Zimbabwe African People's Union), each with its own military wing. The military struggle endured from the late 1960s right through the 1970s, waged mainly from Mozambique with the support of the late Mozambican leader Samora Machel. The war ended with the Lancaster House Agreement signed on 21 December 1979. This Agreement became a source of much unhappiness among Zimbabweans. This was mainly due to its provision that any land reform would have to be under the willing buyer, willing seller system. Moreover, Zimbabwe's white farmers were entitled to be paid in foreign currency if they wished. The guerrilla leaders baulked at this as yet another form of entrenchment of privilege. The impasse was broken when Britain and the United States agreed to co-ordinate efforts to fund the land acquisition programme.

However, this is where the narratives of the Zimbabwean government and Britain begin to diverge. The Zimbabwean government alleges that Britain reneged on this offer. They argue that this is why they have been able to resettle only 71 000 families instead of the 160 000 families targeted. The British government insists that the Zimbabweans never conformed with the conditions for support, particularly the specific requirement that the land be redistributed to landless Zimbabweans. However, there has been enough scholarship on the Zimbabwean land process to suggest that the Zimbabwean government could still have done many things, particularly on underutilised land. For example, the Land Acquisition Act of 1985 gave government the right to procure excess land. According to land reform expert Dan Wiener and his co-authors, the underutilisation of land was so acute that in a province such as

Mashonaland a farm with the average size of 1 640 hectares might only have on average 168 hectares under cultivation in 1981–82. As many as 468 farms or 17.8 per cent of the farms in that province were not growing any crops at all. Even under the most conservative estimates of available land there was still substantial underutilisation of land in Zimbabwe: between 50 and 75 per cent of land was neither being cropped nor fallowed.[3]

Land reformist Bill Kinsey also points out that the Lancaster House Agreement did not prohibit the government from

alternative methods of acquiring land, such as through a land tax, reparations, reclaiming historic subsidies, inviting nongovernmental organizations to take a more active role in resettlement, providing existing credit institutions with a window for 'small' land transactions, or swaps for long-term government obligations matched to a corresponding payment schedule for buyers.[4]

The limitations of the Lancaster Agreement notwithstanding, there were policy options available to the government. So why did it not move more vigorously? Several authors have argued that the Zimbabwean nationalists were never really interested in land reform in the first place. One of the more radical scholars Ibbo Mandaza argues that the nationalists were more than content with the one man, one vote victory. In liberation movement jargon, the social question was never really their priority.[5] Kinsey argues that ideologically the government no longer believed in land reform and small-scale agriculture as the means to national development. While this was the initial impulse in the early years of independence, the government moved towards a greater focus on the development of agribusiness and mechanised farming:

the rhetoric of reclaiming lost land that had animated the liberation war was ousted in favor of technical and economic interpretations of land reform. Emphasis was increasingly shifted to the ability of the resettlement program to produce marketed surpluses and, to meet this objective, the selection rules for beneficiaries, as well as the practices employed, were more and

71

more handed over to bureaucratic management. The language that animated conflicting claims to resources had no place, it seems, on the agenda of a centralized, modernizing state.[6]

The biggest beneficiaries of this were a small African capitalist class of farmers with close links to the government. For example, as part of its response to the Lancaster House Agreement the new government cancelled leases on government-owned land. But instead of redistributing that land to poor people, the government preferred to transfer it to high-ranking officials. Kinsey concludes that 'almost a quarter of a century following independence, agriculture in Zimbabwe is scarcely any less dualistic than was the system inherited in 1980, even if race is no longer the differentiating factor'.[7]

Horace Campbell, who was once very sympathetic to the Zimbabwe cause, makes similar observations in his book *Reclaiming Zimbabwe*. He argues that Mugabe believed that the protection of white large landowners was necessary for foreign exchange earnings. This was exacerbated by the government's embrace of structural reform programmes imposed in cahoots with the World Bank and the International Monetary Fund. Government support shifted from the promising resettlement programmes towards foreign-exchange earners among large-scale farmers. The government started providing support for horticulture, game ranching, wildlife farming and tourism. Meanwhile the resettlement programmes, which had seen improvements in productivity and asset ownership, were left to wither on the vine. The main reasons for the decline were that precisely because of their success, the resettlement programmes were attracting many people facing retrenchment and unemployment. And yet there was no backing from the government to help with the increased social pressures facing small-scale farmers. Thus improvements in agricultural productivity did not translate into improvements in social welfare. Add to this increases in input prices and cost recovery policies imposed by structural adjustment – many people simply abandoned farming. Campbell concludes that 'faced with two different kinds of political pressures, one from the poor and the other from capitalist farmers, the independence government made a conscious choice to support the white farmers on the grounds of stabilizing the economy'.[8] In the final analysis, Mugabe's government

72

was 'objectively an ally of the settlers under the guise of being hemmed in by the Lancaster House agreement'.[9] Campbell also argues that what undermined support for land redistribution was the decision to keep prime land out of the purview of resettlement, keeping it aside for large-scale farmers, and for the coterie of Mugabe's black supporters who wanted to go into farming. Campbell thus concludes that part of Mugabe's legacy was 'a class of African capitalists who treated the rural workers (in relation to wages, health care, housing and exploitation of children) in the same manner as the white settlers did'.[10]

There is another reason why the government was not that enthusiastic about taking over underutilised land. A great deal of that land was owned by Lonhro and Anglo American Corporation, both of which were supporters and benefactors of Mugabe's party. In fact, Mugabe would dare not make any land reform proposals without passing them through Anglo American Corporation, one of the biggest landowners in the country.

So when did Mugabe rediscover his 'commitment' to the people? These arguments are important if we are going to avoid the trap of mysticism and examine the actual record of Africa's leaders.

The violence of an insecure leader
Starting in the 1990s the people of Zimbabwe were become increasingly restive, and by 1995 were openly protesting against Mugabe's government. They particularly mobilised against his embrace of structural adjustment programmes. But Mugabe had an even bigger problem on his hands. The great beneficiary of the growing discontent was a newly formed opposition party called the Movement for Democratic Change (MDC). Formed in 1999 under the leadership of former trade union leader, Morgan Tsvangirai, this movement soon became a threat to Mugabe's rule and the hegemony of his party. This became increasingly apparent after the MDC defeated a ZANU-PF-initiated referendum on a new draft constitution. ZANU-PF wanted to change the constitution to expand Mugabe's powers, and in order to make this proposal attractive, cynically tied those changes to a proposal to acquire land without compensation. However, the people saw through it all and defeated the ruling party on the referendum.

With egg on its face, the government blamed racist whites for misleading the people. Zimbabwe's nativists branded the MDC sell-outs in the pay of the British government. Losing the referendum was a wake-up call for Mugabe's government, which then intensified its efforts to win the 2002 presidential elections. This started with Mugabe's support for the group of self-styled 'war veterans' who started invading white farms in February 2000 under the leadership of one Chenjerai 'Hitler' Hunzvi. This was rather ironic given that this was the very same group that had emerged initially as a protest movement against Mugabe's failure to redistribute land.[11] By this time Mugabe was openly calling white farmers enemies of the state. He cautioned them against resisting the land invasions if they knew what was good for them.

Mugabe's support for the veterans went beyond the matter of land invasions. In his view the white farmers were providing crucial support for the MDC, and a growing number of farm workers were joining the MDC. Some ZANU-PF leaders even declared that they would under no circumstances allow the MDC to run Zimbabwe because, in their leaders' view, 'the opposition is an extension of imperialism . . . they were put together as an opposing package by the British'.[12] Mugabe sees the country as his Zimbabwe, and thus regards himself as having exclusive monopoly to dispense violent punishment to those who threaten that self-image, which is exactly what the MDC sought to do.[13] The movement's leader and its sympathisers have been on the receiving end of Mugabe's violence. Tsvangirai was even accused of treason, a crime for which he could be sentenced to death. He sustained heavy injuries during the now infamous 11 March 2007 police beatings.

When the international community complains, Mugabe uses the very strategy that had enamoured him to so many people two decades previously. He tells everyone, particularly the West, to 'go hang'. And it still seems to be working. He still goes in and out of meetings with impunity, and nobody dares to tell him that he is out of line, and that he must step down. The land movement thus became part of a campaign for Mugabe's election in 2002. It was only a matter of time before the violence became part of an orchestrated campaign to eliminate the MDC. Mugabe's spindoctor at the time, Jonathan Moyo, continued to justify the attacks on the farm workers thus: 'Like in the old Rhodesian days, farm workers have been trained and armed to confront and disrupt the peaceful demonstrations of the War Veterans with the consequence of provoking violence.'[14] Almost a thousand farms were confiscated between February and May 2000. However, less than 2 per cent of the land that had been confiscated by the so-called war veterans was transferred to farm workers, most of whom are disenfranchised women and children.[15]

Despite his use of violence to deal with critics, the South African government continued to defend Mugabe. When asked to comment on the deteriorating situation in Zimbabwe, Foreign Minister Nkosazana Dlamini-Zuma defiantly declared: 'The economic crisis affecting Zimbabwe did not come from a reckless political leadership but out of a genuine concern to help the black poor. We will never condemn Zimbabwe.'[16] Mugabe gets protection from his other 'brothers' in the all-male club of the Southern African Development Community (SADC). He is regarded as a war hero, and therefore a racial insider who cannot be held to account by outsiders such as Britain and the West in general. In May 2007 *New African* magazine ran a series of interviews with Mugabe and other regional leaders where this racial solidarity was on display. It is worth citing a passage from the interview Mugabe gave to Baffor Ankomah. Ankomah asked: 'But I would like to situate the Zimbabwe case in the wider African context. Why should a Ghanaian or Nigerian or Kenyan or South African or an African American support Zimbabwe? Why should Africa stand with Zimbabwe?' Mugabe responded:

Well, obviously, our cause is their cause. The success of Zimbabwe is their success. And we don't live in isolation, we are not an extension of Europe, we are part of Africa, and so really our stand, as a fight, should be seen as an African cause, and wherever we have Africans, be they in the Diaspora or in Senegal or Ghana where we first got our revolutionary drink, they should be able to understand and appreciate the war we are fighting here, and when they are disillusioned, it is our duty to remove that disillusionment and get them back on the right track as our supporters.

Mugabe then went on to cite what Thabo Mbeki had said at the SADC Dar es Salaam meeting:

> And in Dar-es-Salaam, President Mbeki put it very clearly. He said, 'The fight against Zimbabwe is a fight against us all. Today it is Zimbabwe, tomorrow it will be South Africa, it will be Mozambique, it will be Angola, it will be any other African country. And any government that is perceived to be strong, and to be resistant to imperialists, would be made a target and would be undermined. So let us not allow any point of weakness in the solidarity of the SADC, because that weakness will also be transferred to the rest of Africa.'[17]

Mbeki's government has used the same language to protest against Zimbabwe's exclusion from the Europe-African summit of leaders. This is the tactic that Eric Hobsbawm described (and I first spoke about in Chapter 2), when he talked about how African leaders take on the role of gatekeepers protecting the African community from outsiders. Leaders such as Mugabe manipulate their followers' fears by keeping alive the idea that the non-Ruritarians might just return to oppress the Ruritarians again. And as I noted earlier, citing Isaiah Berlin, nationalism can even 'create a mood in which men prefer to be ordered about, even if this entails ill-treatment, by members of their own faith or nation or class, to tutelage, however benevolent, on the part of ultimately patronizing superiors from a foreign land or alien class or milieu'.[18] To their credit, the presidents of Botswana, Zambia, Ghana and Malawi have openly condemned Mugabe's reckless behaviour while South Africa helplessly looks on. But at its August 2007 meeting SADC leaders gave Mugabe a standing ovation, once again demonstrating what Cornel West calls the pitfall of racial reasoning.

The South African response and parallels

The Zimbabwe experience has been a shadow over South Africa – yet another test to our political morality. Other ANC people have weighed in on Mugabe's side. Leading ANC officials have argued that black people in their right minds could not really be against this 'nationalist hero'.

Deputy Minister of Home Affairs Malusi Gigaba suggested only whites and the West were against Mugabe.[19] In a spirited defence of Mugabe's actions Gigaba argued that those who were criticising Mugabe were doing so in order to protect white interests: 'They would elevate the rule of law and democracy, and not ask – for which class. Apparently in Zimbabwe the rule of law and democracy means the unfettered right of the propertied classes that are almost wholly white to property ownership and economic domination.' Gigaba thus contended that Mugabe's 'land reform programme had committed the cardinal sin to challenge white property rights or to reclaim the land historically expropriated by white settlers'.

One of those 'suspect' whites was none other than the seasoned deputy secretary general of the South African Communist Party and a member of the ANC's National Executive Committee (NEC), Jeremy Cronin. Cronin made the mistake of warning against the 'Zanufication' of the ANC, which was an allusion to the growing lack of tolerance within the ANC. In an interview with Irish academic Helena Sheehan in Cape Town, Cronin observed:

I think there are tendencies now of what some of us refer to as the Zanufication of the ANC. You can see features of that, of a bureaucratisation of the struggle: Thanks very much. It was important that you were mobilised then, but now we are in power, in power on your behalf. Relax and we'll deliver. The struggle now is counter-productive. Mass mobilisation gets in the way. Don't worry. We've got a plan. Yes, it'll be slow, but be patient and so on. That kind of message has come through.[20]

Cronin's colleague Blade Nzimande described the same phenomenon as the 'presidentialising' of the ANC.[21] Nzimande submitted a paper to the Central Committee of the South African Communist Party in which, among other things, he criticised the creation of a new presidential centre in the ANC. Mbeki did not take kindly to this and spoke of Nzimande's extraordinary arrogance. Nzimande in turn accused Mbeki of causing stress within the Tripartite Alliance: 'We expect the president to lead the ANC and the alliance rather than to personalize issues. He should engage with the alliance partners in a comradely and inclusive way that also respects the integrity of the other partners.'

It did not matter what Cronin's political experience was – it was enough that he had a white skin. This is part of the philosophical mysticism that if someone is black then they must by that very fact be reversing the legacy of colonialism. In this case the logic is that if someone is white, they must by that very fact be doing everything to preserve that colonial legacy. What their political consciousness might be is of secondary consideration. This is the racial essentialism of the Mbeki years.

I am always mortified to hear people invoke the history of struggle to find justification for the murder and mayhem in Zimbabwe. This is clearly not the Black Consciousness of my youth. I was brought up in a proud and exultant Black Consciousness whose critique of white racism was always accompanied by a process of self-definition informed by the concept of *ubuntu* – a fellow-feeling for justice towards others. Black Consciousness was never about hate and mayhem and corruption and uncritical following of despotic leaders.

Zimbabwe's experience under Robert Mugabe has affirmed something I had always suspected but never really wanted to believe, which is that, while necessary, a radical critique of white supremacy also risks depriving blacks of their own self-understanding. The Black Consciousness in which I was reared never required that I look the other way when those who look like me commit murderous acts against their own people. In fact, looking the other way would have constituted a betrayal of the very meaning of blackness as a 'political and ethical construct'. In the following column I reflected on the Black Consciousness of my youth, and what it taught me about black political morality:

'What Makes You Black?,' reads the title of the painting in my living room. The painting is a plain black canvas without any images on it. The artist then deliberately carved into the canvas to reveal the brown wood beneath it, so as to convey the deeper cultural content of blackness. If art is indeed a metaphorical representation of life, the painting is a representation of the orienting values that constitute my

identity. And as one of the leading figures in the Negritude movement Leopold Senghor once argued, 'far from seeing in one's blackness an inferiority, one accepts it, one lays claim to it with pride, one cultivates it lovingly.' And that's because blackness, in the words of Cornel West, is 'a political and ethical construct that embodies values of service and sacrifice, love and care, discipline and excellence.' No less than the revolutionary intellectual Aime Cesaire observed that 'blackness is historical, there is nothing biological about it.'

Yet another painting dominates my living room. It is a painting of Robert Sobukwe and Steve Biko in conversation with their supporters. This painting signifies black people's attempts to link their values to the creation of a new political democracy. In one of the earliest expositions of direct democracy in our country Biko suggested a mechanism for the institutionalisation of community values in the policy process: 'in a government where democracy is allowed to work, one of the principles that is normally entrenched is a feedback system, a discussion in other words between those who formulate policy and those who must perceive, accept or reject policy. People can hear, they may not be able to read and write but they can hear and understand the issues when they are put to them.'

It is this respect for the integrity of black people that I find lacking in our political discourse on Zimbabwe. I am mortified to hear people suggest that the political thuggery against helpless men and women in Zimbabwe is consistent with the values of Sobukwe and Biko. And of course the fact that those people might die from mass starvation is just another figment of the Western imagination. Ironically, this version of black nationalism depends for its critique of white racism on a process of black self-negation, literally and figuratively. It is indeed all the more ironic that we should hide our heads in the sand when it is those who look like us that are at the receiving end of tyranny.

No, my black brothers and sisters, this is not the black nationalism I was brought up in. I was brought up in a proud and exultant Black Consciousness whose critique of white racism was always accompanied by a process of self-definition informed by the concept of ubuntu. *That process of self-definition was absolutely essential if black people were to be truly free beings whose judgements were not to be always conditioned by white responses to the world. That is the moral autonomy I would like to pass on to my children, irrespective of how white people choose to define their own values. As Aggrey Klaaste once put it: 'It is increasingly becoming the responsibility of blacks to help this country from certain ruination. It is our responsibility because it is also our country, and we are, after all, in the majority.' Only then would the walls of our children's homes be filled with proud images of a post-liberation Black Consciousness that would have served as the moral anchor of this democracy.*[22]

The limits of economic nationalism in South Africa and Zimbabwe

However, above and beyond the naked nativism I suspect that something else is at play here. How could Mbeki criticise Mugabe if that would expose the U-turns of his own government? One area around which there has been intense contestation and disagreement is the management of the economy. As in Zimbabwe, South Africa started out on a social demo-cratic path under the Reconstruction and Development Programme. However, the 1996 Asian Economic Crisis provided the government with an opportunity to make a shift to a more neoliberal economic agenda under the Growth, Employment and Reconstruction (GEAR) policy programme. At the core of this strategy was that the government should introduce a series of structural reforms. Indeed the government has been successful in getting the prices right: interest rates, inflation rates and budget deficits are at historic lows, and tax collection has reached new levels of efficiency. South Africa is now in the odd position of having a budget surplus – which is attributed by many to the government's lack of capacity to implement many of its social spending programmes. Part of the logic behind GEAR was the assumption that getting the prices right would lead to higher levels of foreign direct investments and export growth, and that this in turn would lead to a 6 per cent economic growth rate and the creation of 600 000 jobs.

Suffice it to say that Trevor Manuel was the first to complain that the government had done all it had been asked to do, and yet there were no foreign direct investments coming in, and the record was even more disastrous when it came to job creation. Although official statistics put the unemployment rate at 25.5 per cent, overall unemployment – which includes both those who have been discouraged from seeking work and those who are actively seeking employment – stands at around 40 per cent. About one half of the population is said to be living in poverty, and we share the dubious honour of being one of the most unequal societies in the world. In apparent recognition of these facts, the government has shifted its policies to social welfare. The obvious question that all of this raises is whether, as in Zimbabwe, South Africa is ultimately headed towards what Campbell described as 'a clash between elite black males and elite white males'.[23]

A number of South African authors have argued that the increasingly radical nationalist rhetoric we see from Mbeki has been nothing more than convenient cover for the government's conservative economic policies – creating a false image of being progressive while the rest of the people wallow in increasing levels of unemployment and poverty under the government's austerity programmes. These writers argue that it is indeed ironic that Mbeki struts the world stage decrying world powers for Africa's poverty while presiding over neoliberal policies that have served only to deepen poverty, unemployment and inequality in his own country. Political economist Patrick Bond calls it a matter of talking left and walking right.[24]

As in Zimbabwe, the conservative turn in economic policy made it easier for black political leaders and business leaders to rationalise accumulation under the guise of black economic empowerment. The term black economic empowerment itself is misleading to the extent it gives the impression that black people are being empowered en masse. A turn of phrase thus makes possible the conflation of the elite and the masses. And yet members of this elite continue to invoke race even as they do nothing to contribute to the welfare of the people in whose names they benefit.

This dynamic is similar to what happened in the United States in the post-civil-rights era – a burgeoning underclass co-existing alongside a burgeoning middle class. In their book, *The Future of the Race*, Henry Louis Gates Jr and Cornel West describe how the so-called black leaders in the United States often resort to a politics of racial solidarity to mask the problems faced by African Americans:

Black cultural nationalism – make no mistake about it – is the figure in the carpet within African American society. Appeals to nationalism – and, at the extreme fringes, to anti-Semitism, homophobia and sexism – are drawn up to mask class differences within the black community. As economic differences increase, the need to maintain the appearance of cultural and ideological conformity also increases. But it is these fake masks of conformity that disguise how very vast black class differentials really are. And no amount of kinte cloth or kwanza celebrations will change this.

Gates then issues a call for 'something we don't yet have: a way of speaking about black poverty that doesn't falsify the reality of black advancement; a way of speaking about black advancement that doesn't distort the enduring realities of black poverty'.[25]

This would require a frank admission that the government's economic policies have left many people behind, and that black economic empowerment has had uneven impact in the creation of a black middle class. The main problem has been that political connections have become, by hook and by crook, the easiest way of accumulating wealth, and this has often meant that only a connected few are well positioned to siphon off public resources. *The Weekender*, a small but influential Johannesburg newspaper, described the relationship between politics and business thus: 'To every member, the state of play was now obvious. First, doing business and being a politician was okay because if the higher-ups were doing it, they could hardly complain if the lower ranks were doing it too. And, second, if you were found out, the ANC would contrive a way to defend you.'[26]

The Zimbabwe experience should at the very least caution us against a demagogue who will come along to blame white people or the West for the consequences of Mbeki's policy choices.

In the next chapter I discuss how corruption came to destabilise the ANC.

CHAPTER 5

The Chickens Come Home to Roost

Corruption Undermines Democracy

IN JANUARY 1997 I submitted my doctoral dissertation at Cornell University on Harold Washington's leadership as the first black mayor of the city of Chicago. For decades the city was under the rule of the notoriously corrupt Richard J. Daley. Daley was elected mayor in 1955 and ran the most corrupt city government in the United States for the next two decades. Legend has it that the mayor could greet by name half of the city's 40 000 employees – because he had had a hand in their hiring. Even matters as trivial as requests to cut down a tree or fill a pothole came directly to his office for approval. Daley was not only mayor but party chairman: 'Under Daley's leadership the Democratic party became a tightly integrated, highly centralized organization. It became a political institution through which the chairman-mayor ruled the city.'[1]

It was not unusual for senior managers to spend the morning preparing contracts, and in the afternoons to receive those contracts as private contractors.

Harold Washington rode on the strength of discontent among minority communities in Chicago to be elected mayor in 1983. The well-known American commentator Studs Terkel described Washington's victory as an American 'Soweto', while Jesse Jackson called it a political riot and an unprecedented act of disciplined rage. Distinguished academic Manning Marable argued that Washington's victory was 'the most recent and most politically advanced expression of a very deep tradition which is part of Black Chicago's history'. The newspaper columnist Vernon Jarrett spoke of the election as 'a zenith in black aspirations'.[2] Indeed, Washington's transformation of the city of Chicago remains one of the most celebrated examples of urban reform in the United States. Pierre Clavel and Wim Wiewel called it 'one of the high points in the history of American cities . . . his reforms marked the end of the notorious machine identified with Richard J. Daley'.[3]

All of these descriptions struck an emotional chord in me as a young Ph.D. student looking for best practices of urban governance for the emerging democracy in South Africa. It was even better that this model of urban governance was under a black leader. This is not to overlook that the tenure of black mayors in the United States is replete with contradictions. The most common criticism is that black mayors have done little to reverse the economic marginalisation of black people in American cities, many of which are regarded as poverty traps. Harold Washington experimented with different ways of bringing resources to Chicago's black neighbourhoods but it would have taken a national federal effort to deal with the deep-rooted poverty of south-side Chicago in particular. A number of dissertations have been written on the local economic development strategies pursued by Harold Washington's regime, and the turnaround that he brought about in the city's finances. My interest, however, was more on the meaning of this new experience for the city, and for African Americans in particular.

Part of my initial attraction to Mbeki's African Renaissance message was that it brought the cultural dimension to our conception of freedom. I had absolutely no idea that the cultural nationalism I was so excited about would soon be deployed as a shield against criticism of corruption among high-level government officials. And never did I imagine that corruption would threaten to rip apart the very liberation movement we had thought would clean up the political corruption of apartheid.

I often received and turned down invitations to anti-corruption conferences or to join one anti-corruption body or the other. But the subject of corruption just did not seem such a big problem to me. Even when the noted anti-apartheid cleric Allan Boesak was imprisoned for misusing donor funding I still thought of corruption as nothing more than the failings of individual leaders.

I did not think we had a systemic problem until the feisty Patricia de Lille, then leader of the PAC,[4] and the leader of the United Democratic Movement (UDM) Bantu Holomisa called for a judicial inquiry into the government's proposed purchase of arms worth tens of billions of rand, popularly known as the arms deal. They alleged the whole thing was riddled with corruption. De Lille was ready to reveal the names of senior government officials who were positioned to receive all kinds of favours and kickbacks from the arms deal.

My first public response came in the wake of allegations that the ANC's parliamentary chief whip and head of the oversight committee on intelligence, Tony Yengeni, had received a discount for a luxury vehicle from one of the companies bidding for the massive arms contracts: Daimler Chrysler. Yengeni strongly denied allegations that he had sold his influence for a discount on a vehicle. He even took out an expensive newspaper advertisement lashing out at his accusers as racist. But the courts thought differently. Yengeni was later found guilty of defrauding parliament and sentenced to four years in prison. However, he ended up serving only six months of his prison term because of changes in parole regulations. He flouted his parole regulations but pretty much got away with that too.

With the kind of social problems we had inherited from the apartheid era we did not need to spend that kind of money on arms. South Africa was not facing any external military threat. If anything, the security risk lay in the growing numbers of unemployed and the poor inside the country. But I was particularly incensed at the thought that we were not dealing only with a bad public policy decision but a bad policy decision deliberately designed to further the self-interest of various individuals in government, with race as the ready weapon of self-defence:

The truth is we have been deceived. We have been repeatedly served with a goulash of deceptions. We have been misled by Tony Yengeni and by our government. Yengeni has consistently refused to explain his acquisitions of luxury cars to parliament, choosing instead to make his case through a newspaper advertisement. Those who pointed to his lies have been vilified as either racist or reactionary or opportunistic. We have shot the messengers in the name of a perverted conception of black solidarity. I am black, alright, but mine is not a blackness of lies. The other night I waxed lyrical about how much of a redeeming moment Yengeni's arrest was for our young democracy. Indeed, Bulelani Ngcuka's unit must be commended for their leadership in this matter. In the midst of the controversy over Judge Heath's exclusion from the arms probe I had suggested that a black-led investigation could say to us, and a watching world, that this democracy is indeed safe in our hands. Ngcuka and his unit have done us proud, and I pray that they will do us even prouder.

But what about the macro-lies surrounding the arms deal? Why should we spend R66 billion on arms when our population is being devastated by unemployment, hunger and homelessness, when poor black children walk distances to dilapidated schools, when babies are being orphaned by the scourge of HIV/AIDS? The big macro-lie to which our gullibility has given credence is that 65 000 jobs will be created as a result of this arms deal. If you believe that, then I have a second-hand car to sell to you.

I truly wish those people who want to put an end to this arms deal all the success in the world. It's time to stop shooting the messengers, and listen to the message. The simple message is that this scandalous arms deal, and the president's appalling prevarications on HIV/AIDS, are a tragedy unfolding in front of our very own eyes. I am not a prophet or any such thing. But as with Yengeni, the chickens will come home to roost. The question is, at what social and human cost? And when that happens, shall we say we did not know?

I started this column by saying the truth is that we have been lied to. But even scarier is that the lies have become the truth in the halls of power, where people have come to believe in the lies they cover up. I hope, perhaps naively, that the Scorpions have broken that trend. But this should be a salutary lesson for parliament. It is disgraceful that it should take the judiciary to alert us to the gravity of what should have been clear to every member of parliament, irrespective of party affiliation. The law, after all, is supposed to be an approximation of the values of a people, and the judiciary the interpreters of those values. But if the very representatives of parliament consistently undermine those values by covering for each other, we shall end up living under the aristocratic rule of the judiciary, giving lie to any pretensions to democracy. And so the question must be asked of each man and woman in parliament. Given the spilt blood of our people, the sacrifices of our leaders, and the bright-eyed aspirations of our children at freedom's promise, how did we get into this mess? What tragedy will next awaken you to your responsibilities as custodians of our children's future? What price, solidarity?[5]

While I commended the prosecuting authorities for their stellar job of taking on even high-profile figures I still worried about the government's refusal to re-negotiate the arms deal. More recently Tokyo Sexwale criticised the arms deal, saying it was more about kickbacks than about defending South Africa. He questioned the choice of foreign fighter planes over local ones:

I told the comrades, let's get planes like the [South African manufactured] Cheetah.

Why choose the Gripen [Swedish- and British-made]?

Against who are we going to be fighting with it . . . where's the threat in the next fifteen years? This money is for schools, man!

Why on earth would you want five submarines [from Germany]? . . .

It's for kickbacks, man![6]

I was particularly outraged when Thabo Mbeki intervened to remove the head of the Special Investigations Unit, Judge Heath, from investigating allegations of corruption in the arms deal. The subtext was that Heath could not be trusted because he was an over-zealous white man bent on embarrassing a black government. This is notwithstanding that the unit Heath headed had been set up by the government as a supposed bulwark against corruption.

This was one of the first times it became clear that institutions of state were not above political and racial manipulation by the new government. It was also one of the first times that Mbeki would launch a racial tirade against the media as 'fishers of men' who had taken it upon themselves to spread stereotypes about black people:

> The same stereotypical conviction about our government being corrupt, unless it proves itself innocent has re-surfaced with regard to the defence procurement decided by our government in 2000. The fishermen (and women?) have recast their fishing nets, convinced that they will bring in a rich haul of corrupt government luminaries.[7]

Mbeki has been contradictory in his pronouncements on corruption. One moment he would be lambasting ANC members who were using their positions of influence to enrich themselves. The next moment he would react angrily whenever the same admonitions came from the media or individual commentators or members of the opposition. On certain occasions he would come to the defence of party leaders, and on other occasions he would argue for the processes of the law to take their own course. And even then he has been inconsistent. Some party leaders (for example, Jacob Zuma) have been prosecuted but others (for example, National Police Commissioner Jackie Selebi) have not. This gives the impression that for Mbeki corruption is part of a larger political game, depending on whether the perpetrators are his supporters or critics. This argument has been made explicitly by those who supported Deputy President Jacob Zuma during his corruption and rape trials.

Zuma's trials and tribulations

The bombshell came at the end of November 2004 when the *Mail & Guardian* published a story asserting that Zuma was being investigated for allegedly soliciting a bribe of R500 000 from the French arms manufacturer, Thomson-CSF (later renamed Thales), one of the companies bidding for the arms contracts. The specific allegation was that in return for an annual payment of R500 000 Zuma would protect the company from allegations of irregularity in the tender process. At the heart of the investigation was whether or not Zuma had met with Alain Thetard, chief executive of Thales International's South African subsidiary, Thint, to discuss the bribe. The person who is alleged to have arranged for the payment of the bribe was Zuma's friend Schabir Shaik. The problem is that Shaik owned a company, African Defence Systems, which had a stake in Thint. The allegation was that in essence Shaik and Thetard were going to benefit from the arms deal if they could only secure the protection of Shaik's highly placed friend. It was alleged that Zuma had put his name to a letter to the parliamentary standing committee on public accounts (SCOPA) to allay concerns that this particular company had been involved in any wrongdoing – although it was later suggested Mbeki had written the letter, giving rise to suspicion that the president himself might have been compromised by this company. Zuma suggested that the president was the person best positioned to provide answers since it was Mbeki who negotiated the arms deal.

The first victim of the investigation into Zuma's affairs was Schabir Shaik. It emerged that Shaik had provided a series of donations to Zuma. This was in return for Shaik's companies, including Thint, receiving government contracts and Zuma getting kickbacks. The politics of the matter came to a boil when the national director of public prosecutions and a man widely seen to be Mbeki's ally, Bulelani Ngcuka, issued a press statement saying that while there was prima facie evidence of corruption against Zuma he would not proceed against Zuma because he did not believe he had a winnable case. He said the state would, however, prosecute Shaik. Presumably a successful prosecution of Shaik would enhance the state's chances of getting a conviction against Zuma.

Zuma's supporters were outraged. They alleged that Ngcuka's actions were part of a broader political ploy to prevent Zuma from ascending to the presidency of the ANC. However, Zuma was a much weightier figure in the ANC. He had served many years on Robben Island, and later re-emerged in exile as the head of the organisation's intelligence.

There are fewer more important units in the ANC than that. Zuma was also the first person to be sent back, at great personal risk, to re-establish the ANC when it was unbanned in 1990. All of his long-standing networks were thus reactivated when the charges were made against him. Schabir Shaik's older brother and ANC intelligence activist Mo Shaik teamed up with ANC veteran Mac Maharaj to accuse Ngcuka of having worked as a spy for the apartheid government. The allegation was as desperate as it was audacious, a last-ditch political gambit to get Ngcuka to back off from prosecuting Shaik and Zuma. Maharaj himself was also being investigated by Ngcuka's office for irregularly awarding tenders while he was minister of transport. One of Schabir Shaik's companies obtained the contract for issuing the new drivers' licences. All that Mo Shaik and Mac Maharaj needed to do was to cultivate doubt in the public mind by insinuating that the charges were cooked up by older order bureaucrats lodged within Ngcuka's office.

I was one of the people who came to Ngcuka's defence, and called the allegations what they were – an act of evasion. Mbeki quickly established a Commission of Inquiry into the allegations. He asked a former apartheid-era judge Joost Hefer to lead the inquiry. The Commission was a big embarrassment for Mo Shaik and Mac Maharaj. The nation could see for itself as Shaik and Maharaj made complete fools of themselves – to the point of admitting in full public view that they had no basis for their allegations that Ngcuka was an apartheid-era spy. Zuma and his comrades had lost the first round in what was widely seen as a high-stakes political fight to succeed Mbeki as president of the ANC.

Ngcuka was exonerated, and wasted no time in going after Schabir Shaik. Shaik was charged with fraud and corruption and sentenced to fifteen years in prison. His lawyers have since argued before the Constitutional Court that the sentence is too long for the offence. Above and beyond the conviction, a whole lot of things turned on a mis-attribution. The judge in the case was reported to have said there was 'a generally corrupt' relationship between Shaik and Zuma. This statement (about which see more below) became the basis for a whole series of subsequent events, including various post-mortems on Zuma's political career. In quick succession Mbeki fired Zuma from his cabinet and convened a special meeting of parliament where he issued a terse statement on why the deputy president could no longer function effectively as a member of cabinet. In one of the most unbelievable sequences of events Mbeki then appointed Bulelani Ngcuka's wife, Phumzile Mlambo-Ngcuka, to Zuma's position as the country's deputy president. This seemed to give credence to the idea that Zuma's prosecution was politically motivated – to get rid of Zuma in order to make way for one of Mbeki's people:

I am shocked by President Thabo Mbeki's decisions over the past couple of weeks. Despite the appearance of decisiveness and closure, his actions will raise more questions than answers for the foreseeable future. In the short term his actions will gain him a lot of kudos with business and international elites. I am worried though by the long-term effects of his decisions on the ANC and our society more broadly. He has signalled in many ways that his prerogative is more important than any attempt to make peace with the alliance partners or Zuma supporters. He signalled this by the way in which he fired Zuma. In the midst of congratulations about the president's decisiveness, I have been asking myself whether the president should not have waited until Zuma had been charged before firing him? Mbeki could have then said to his deputy that his trial distracted him from his duties and asked him to temporarily recuse himself from office until the matter was settled in the courts.

I still maintain that a plea bargain is the best possible route in the Zuma matter, depending on what Zuma makes of his chances. If he knows he has no chance in hell, he must bargain for a political solution and abandon any aspirations to the presidency. But then again I don't know if the enmity in the ANC has gone so far down the road to even rule out any chance of a political solution. But if Zuma did not settle for the political solution and was found NOT guilty, he would become the most powerful man in this country, a seductive embodiment of injustice to the masses. Some say that even if he were to win the case, his reputation would have been so tarnished that he would not be fit for the presidency.

The trouble with democracy is that even if it were unwise to elect Jacob Zuma as president on those grounds, the way our system of democracy works is that the elites must live with electoral outcomes they don't like.

Bill Clinton remains one of the greatest presidents in the history of the United States, his improprieties notwithstanding. Nixon is still hailed for his China policy. And Ronald Reagan illegally channelled funds to the Contra rebels in Nicaragua, and remains a revered figure in the pantheon of US presidents. If the media and intellectual elites got their way, John Kerry would be the president of the United States. The masses ruled and we are stuck with George Bush.

While I accept the president's rather passive formulation that we must allow the law to take its course, I would also suggest that in the remote possibility that Zuma is found NOT GUILTY, the elites must be actively prepared to accept the decisions of the courts. No more Monday morning quarterbacking.[8]

Elsewhere I described the sequence of events as a perfect script for a B-movie:

The president of an African country wants the deputy president out. He appoints the attorney-general to investigate the deputy president on corruption charges. The deputy president is duly charged, and the president wastes no time in removing him from his cabinet. Within days the president appoints the attorney-general's wife to become the deputy president. The attorney-general and his wife move into the former deputy president's official residence and take over all of the cars and enjoy all of the privileges that go with the new office. Everyone in the country is convinced that the deputy president is as guilty as hell. However, the deputy president wins on a technicality. A judge rules that he could not possibly get a fair hearing because of the negative publicity around the case. The judge argues that the state has been particularly inept. The corruption case is dismissed, and the deputy president is instantly the most popular and powerful man in the country. He stands for the leadership of the ANC and cruises to victory. As the new head of state he eschews commissions of inquiry for inquisitions. All of those who persecuted him are now the targets of persecution – and a vicious spiral begins.[9]

Shaik's prosecution emboldened the prosecuting authorities to go after Zuma. The problem was that in their haste they made several mistakes, including a wide-ranging search and seizure at Zuma's home and offices. This was seen as a fishing expedition by a state institution desperate but clearly not fully prepared. In February 2006 the Durban High Court ruled that the raids were illegal, and in August 2006 Judge Herbert Msimang threw the case out of court. He found that the state had rushed to charge Zuma on the basis of the guilty verdict against Schabir Shaik, without preparing well enough for its case against Zuma. The gist of his ruling was that the continued postponements were prejudicial towards Zuma. With yet another round under his belt Zuma stood poised to take the fight to the Mbeki faction in the ANC.

Nevertheless, the state continued its efforts. The national director of public prosecutions appealed against the Durban High Court's decision on the warrants, and on 8 November 2007 the Supreme Court of Appeal upheld the appeal. The same Durban High Court had granted permission for the state to obtain Alain Thetard's diary from Mauritius. Zuma appealed but the Supreme Court of Appeal reserved the High Court decision.

These were major setbacks for Zuma but they were not enough to stop him from running for and winning the presidency of the ANC in December 2007. However, the state wasted no time in charging Zuma again. On 28 December he was served with an indictment to stand trial in the High Court on eighteen counts of corruption, money laundering, racketeering and fraud. Both Zuma's supporters and his ardent critics such as the *Sunday Times* questioned the timing of the announcement in the middle of the festive season, and so soon after Zuma's ANC presidency victory. As I shall argue in Chapter 9, this would provide another gist for the political mill in the period between Zuma's election as ANC president and the all-important ANC list conference that determines the party's candidate for the 2009 general elections.

Throughout these trials Zuma's supporters argued that there was an orchestrated campaign by Mbeki and in sections of the media. For example, shortly after the case was thrown out of court by Judge Msimang, Hilary Squires – the judge who had sentenced Shaik – disputed that he had ever said there was 'a generally corrupt relationship' between Shaik and Zuma. This phrase was widely used by almost all those who were concerned by Jacob Zuma's rise. Yet again Zuma's supporters pointed to the prejudice that had been cultivated through false reporting. The media was left with egg on its face as the judge challenged everyone to point to anywhere in the Shaik judgment – both oral and written – where he had made such an utterance. It was nowhere to be found. Journalists, editors and columnists were left groping for apologies and excuses for why they had not double checked their facts. There were also questions about why the judge had taken so long to come out with his clarification. So many decisions had been taken on the power of that statement. Even the Supreme Court of Appeal rejected Schabir Shaik's appeal against his sentence by invoking that statement. And for all intents and purposes the statement provided the backdrop to Zuma's firing, which is why some of Zuma's supporters called for his reinstatement as deputy president of the country. But in reality Zuma was better positioned to challenge Mbeki from the outside, even though this would be compounded by Zuma's rape trial.

The Zuma rape trial

It was during the course of the investigation into the case of corruption that yet another shocking revelation emerged. The *Sunday Times* published a story that all imagined would be a fatal blow to Zuma's political career. The newspaper revealed that a woman young enough to be Zuma's daughter had laid a charge of rape against the ANC deputy president. In fact, the young woman was the daughter of one of Zuma's comrades in exile who has since passed away. The identity of that comrade is still unknown, and the woman accuser is known only as Khwezi. Once again Zuma's supporters argued that their man had been set up by Mbeki. But even if that were true, the story was embarrassing in its own right, particularly the outrageous statements Zuma made during the course of the trial.

Zuma's court appearances revealed both his strengths and his weaknesses. His strength was the growing sympathy he was receiving from the public. He portrayed himself as a simple Zulu man who was the victim of a sophisticated conspiracy led by the educated elite within the ANC. However, the more troubling aspect of Zuma came through his invocation of Zulu culture. For example, he argued that it was against Zulu culture to ignore the advances of a half-naked woman. It also turned out that he had not used a condom during the sexual act, which was odd given that the woman did not hide that she was HIV positive. Asked if this was not risky and irresponsible behaviour by a senior political leader, Zuma said that he took a shower to minimise the chances of infection (although, unlike Mbeki, he subsequently has been quick to take ownership and apologise for his mistakes). Zuma was becoming more of an embarrassment by the day as he spoke about how delicious the sex act had been with the young woman.

Meanwhile his accuser came under bombardment and violent threats. Zuma maintained his innocence throughout the trial. In a day-long judgment the judge found Zuma not guilty. Zuma calmly accepted the judgment, congratulated his lawyers, and went outside to throngs of supporters at the Johannesburg Library Gardens. And there he issued a long tirade against the educated elites, the intellectuals and the media analysts for their prejudice against him. It was a scary moment in many ways. There were also the usual doses of ethnicity thrown into it: a Zulu man persecuted by the dominant Xhosas. Zuma did nothing to dissuade this and turned to dressing in traditional Zulu garb at public gatherings. He was by now a cult figure to many, the underdog who stands up to the bully and wins. Zuma had won the second round of the succession debate.

ANC stalwart Raymond Suttner captured the militarism of it all: 'As the court case and surrounding activities developed, Zuma came to present himself not only as a victim of conspiracy but as an embodiment of Zulu culture. This resort to a conservative version of Zulu culture was also a re-embodiment of Zulu warrior traditions, merging with its militaristic traditions.' Suttner argues that this militarism was consistent with the warrior traditions of the ANC and the machismo of the broader culture: 'The militaristic model of manhood continues to have resonance because many cadres felt a sense of betrayal, a sense of a mission not accomplished, when the ANC embarked on negotiations.'[10] The Argentinian political theorist Ernesto Laclau has described how people like

Jacob Zuma become powerful populist figures: 'Since any kind of institutional system is inevitably at least partially limiting and frustrating, there
is something appealing about any figure who challenges it, whatever the
reasons and forms of the challenge.'[11]

The criminal underworld and government

The impression that the National Prosecuting Authority was selective
in whom to go after became pronounced in the reluctance to do anything about allegations that the country's chief commissioner of police,
Jackie Selebi, is linked to the criminal underworld. The *Mail & Guardian*
laid out the charges in great detail. The newspaper specifically alleged
that Selebi was good friends with Glenn Agliotti, a leading figure of the
criminal underworld in South Africa. Selebi first denied knowledge of
the man. It was only when he was presented with evidence that the
two had held several breakfast meetings that Selebi owned up to knowing
Agliotti. With characteristic gusto he declared that Agliotti was his friend,
'finish and klaar'. He pleaded innocence of any knowledge of Agliotti's
criminal connections, leaving unanswered the question of how a police
chief could not be able to pick that up. Several more accusations have
dogged Selebi, including that he was at a drug bust where some of the
drugs confiscated disappeared and, most recently, that Agliotti allegedly
had routed through payments to Selebi. When Mbeki was approached
by senior religious leaders about the matter he simply told them to 'trust'
him. Mbeki's reluctance to go after Selebi may well have to do with the
latter's influence within the ANC. Mbeki would not want to alienate such
a powerful individual at this time of the leadership succession race.

Agliotti was later charged with the murder of another fraudster, Brett
Kebble, who turned out to be one of the ANC's major financiers. Mbeki's
right-hand man and minister of state in the presidency, Essop Pahad,
spoke of Kebble at his funeral as a great South African. Kebble's coffin
was draped with the South African flag. It was one of those surreal moments in our short history as a democracy: a known fraudster and tax
evader celebrated as a national hero by the ruling party. The influential
business magazine *Financial Mail* captured the gravity of the relationship
between Kebble and the ANC – a relationship that, by the way, would
make Daley's Chicago look like a Sunday school picnic:

Kebble's brutal death and the revelations of corruption that have followed it have shed light on unnerving degrees of corruption and malfeasance in SA. His death has laid bare sinister truths about the relationship between rogue capitalists, the underworld of criminal syndicates and politicians. This is a troubling development. Dirty money, corrupt cops, politicians and criminals make a potently dangerous cocktail.

The *Financial Mail* warns that 'once crime syndicates have the lawmen in their pockets, it is virtually impossible to wrest back control'.[12] In another editorial the *Financial Mail* concluded that 'in SA, almost the only route to patronage is the ANC. Many on the outside who want big government contracts or a prestigious government position, understandably perceive that such things are in the gift of the ANC, both as a party in government and as individuals.'[13]

In their book, *The Criminalization of the State in Africa*, Jean-François Bayart, Stephen Ellis and Béatrice Hibou argue that sub-Saharan Africa has become the staging-post of global importance for drugs that reach as far afield as North America, Latin America, Western Europe and the Persian Gulf.[14] Could it really be possible that our resources have been used to build up such staging posts with the collusion of our own police commissioner? Nobody yet knows, because there has been no investigation into the commissioner's activities.

A personal encounter with crime

I had my own taste of the criminal underworld when I was hijacked in Johannesburg in the early evening of 31 May 2005. I had just finished giving a radio interview when I heard loud banging on my windows. Initially I thought these were police but my instincts told me there was more to this than an ordinary police raid. I put my hands up in the air and pleaded for the guys to leave me alone. Before I knew it, I was in the back of my car with someone holding a gun to my head. I was lucky to come out of that incident alive – mainly because I did not resist.

I emerged from the ordeal with one distinct impression – these were professional criminals who were part of a larger network that extended beyond South Africa. They told me they were not in the business of killing people but simply wanted the car. As it turned out, they also had a bank card reader in the car with them, which they used to transfer money from my bank accounts. After driving around with me – extracting all kinds of information about my bank details and trying to get me to point to the tracker in my car – they took me to the bush on the outskirts of Johannesburg and told me to kneel with my head down to the ground. Here I was in the middle of nowhere in the middle of the night surrounded by three armed gunmen. I was convinced they were going to shoot me and leave me for dead. I consider myself lucky that they spared my life. I had to find my way out of the bush to the nearest township where I got help.

I sat on this story for years, afraid to feed into what I also feared were racist stereotypes about criminality. But how long would I be able to sustain such denial, even on a matter that had threatened my own life. I came out to share the story only after I saw the president denying and trivialising crime as the product of a fecund racist imagination:

I really blame white people for introducing race as a way of structuring the world. This time I blame them not so much for visiting untold human suffering on black people but for the manner in which they have made it impossible for us to think outside the racial framework they bequeathed us.

There was indeed a time when it would have been foolhardy to think outside of that racial framework, and to some extent the theme of non-racialism was one attempt at such an escape. The black nationalist movements used in rather creative ways the themes of race to construct identities of survival – which I have previously referred to as culture making.

And then the days of the struggle passed, and our freedom came. The non-racialists won, and the black nationalists lost, or so we thought. But this was a Pyrrhic victory for the non-racialists, something of a mere formality. The real substantive winners were the black nationalists, but even then only to a certain extent.

While the new rulers started out with themes of non-racialism under Nelson Mandela, this was soon replaced by black nationalism of a special type under Thabo Mbeki. I say black nationalism of a special type because for the first time in our history black nationalist themes were now tied to state power. And as often happened elsewhere in the world: race + nationalism + state power = tragedy. The tragedy is there for all to see – a country that had virtually no HIV/AIDS problem before 1990 has now one of the highest incidents in the world because its government denied the reality of the disease using race-based arguments.

I must say I am disappointed that someone I thought could be the president of this country – Mosiuoa 'Terror' Lekota – has also taken to this racial nationalism in his explanation of why certain people leave the country. I am sure there are many whites who leave because they cannot countenance black rule. But it is surely not prudent for a minister of state to make that his entire explanation. After all, what would the honourable minister call those black people who have left the country to settle overseas? Surely, they are not racists? Or are they mere coconuts – South African on the outside but deeply American or British on the inside?

I accept the minister's argument that crime is not government policy. I also accept the minister's argument that there are many valiant people who continue to endure the vicissitudes of crime. But endurance should not be the existential condition of a free people, black or white. I am not merely theorizing about crime. I was once hijacked. After driving around with me for two hours with a gun to my head, the hijackers finally took me to a veld in the middle of nowhere on the outskirts of Johannesburg. At that point I was sure they were going to shoot me and leave me for dead. And I can assure you, Mr Minister, there is nothing black or white about such an ordeal.

Different individuals will respond in different ways to such ordeals. I never left the country, but someone else might have been frightened enough to leave the next morning. Would I hold it against them? I am not so sure. Race may enter the equation but I am not sure if it would provide us with the range of human emotions that people go through during such ordeals. Sometimes people are just being people, with all the fears that go with that.

Whenever I think about crime I also think about what happened to one of my political mentors, the late Black Consciousness leader,

Muntu Myeza. Muntu died under very mysterious circumstances in the early nineties. His death was attributed to a car accident but many of us suspected political foul play. I predict that 'crime' will soon be a cover for political assassinations in this country. Someone will knock you off, and it will all be attributed to a random criminal incident. Case closed. So there is much more to the complexity of what we are going through than any racial explanation could ever provide.

And I often wonder whether we will ever be able to solve our political and policy problems within the current framework of race + nationalism + power. It is a defensive, denialist framework that has run its course. I was happy to read in the Sunday papers that the ANC has woken up to the idea that both Thabo Mbeki and Jacob Zuma must exit the political stage for a more unifying figure. This country desperately needs a new leader with a new political register, and new ways of talking about race. That's going to require some political ingenuity.[15]

I have heard similar stories from almost all of my friends: hijackings, robberies and house-breaking. Those who can afford it live in gated communities with all kinds of expensive security systems. And yet our president has the temerity to suggest that this is exaggerated. In which country do the president and his ministers live?

As with HIV/AIDS, Mbeki has demonstrated complete alienation with the experiences of his people. True to his style he probably does not know anyone who has been a victim of crime.

In the next chapter I make some suggestions about how to talk about race, and the kind of leadership required for us to steer in a different direction from where we are headed under Mbeki.

CHAPTER 6

Nationalism of a Different Kind
White Denial and Barriers to Non-Racialism

IN THE PRECEDING chapters I have explained how the politics of racial nativism (which are narrow and exclusionary) have shaped our political culture with grave public policy consequences. However, equally as important is why leaders such as Robert Mugabe and Thabo Mbeki are able to get away with this manipulation of race.

Part of the answer surely lies with the way white society has responded to the challenges of change. Judging by their largely dismissive reaction to processes such as the Truth and Reconciliation Commission (TRC) – see more below – it is fair to say that white South Africans still have to develop their politics of adaptation to the new society.

I am sure that just as black South Africans have had to change their identities to meet changing circumstances, white people have had to confront their moments of adaptation. For example, Dan O'Meara demonstrates

101

the transition from the politics of Afrikaner nationalism to the construction of a white identity that encompassed both Afrikaans- and English-speaking South Africans under H.F. Verwoerd in the 1960s.[1] This was seen as a form of selling out by the more radical nationalists who later formed right-wing Afrikaner nationalist parties such as the Herstigte Nasionale Party, which was an instantiation of the worst forms of authenticity and nativism in white politics. P.W. Botha took the National Party on the path of reform – daring this community to 'adapt or die'. However, Botha finally baulked at crossing the proverbial Rubicon, leaving the moment of adaptation to F.W. de Klerk.

As with many other societies that have gone through such transitions from dictatorial rule, South Africa is going through various forms of denial – mainly denials of white complicity to one of the worst crimes against humanity. There is a certain smugness and lack of contrition in the white community that is oftentimes quite breathtaking. It is as if there was no social catastrophe that literally consigned half the population to indigenes. I am not even talking the language of apologies and reparations but just an instinctive defensiveness and solidarity and ultimate denial.

This culture of denial and racial solidarity among whites provides the backdrop for understanding why black nativist leaders are able to entrench themselves further in power. They can always point to white people and say, 'See, look how they deny what they did to us. Look at how they refuse to share the resources. Look at how they continue to abuse and disrespect black people.' That kind of rhetoric can be quite seductive for a formerly oppressed community, especially when backed up by evidence of denial. It does not even require black radicals to point to the denial for what it is. I remember reading a *New York Times* headline describing as 'vitriolic' a speech Nelson Mandela gave at the ANC's national conference in Mafeking in 1997. Mbeki had just been elected to the presidency of the ANC at the conference, and many people suspected he might have had a hand in the making of that speech, a signal of things to come. In addition, Archbishop Desmond Tutu broke down, lamenting how white South Africans thumbed their noses at the TRC.

Author and prominent intellectual Njabulo Ndebele traces the denial in the white community to a callousness about black life that is deeply rooted in white society:

There is a continuum of indescribable insensitivity and callous-ness that begins with justice minister Kruger saying Biko's death leaves him cold . . . in all this there is a chilling suggestion of gloating which borders on moral depravity. This culture of callousness can be seen in continued white silence about the desecration of black bodies in present-day South Africa.

Ndebele calls for 'a shift in white identity in which whiteness can undergo an experiential transformation by absorbing new cultural experiences . . . an historic opportunity has arisen now for white South Africa to participate in a humanistic revival of our country'.[2] That is the adaptive challenge that has confronted white South Africans over the past thirteen years.

To be sure, I would not want to minimise the changes in attitudes that have happened among whites since 1994. And I would not want to paint white people with one broad brush. The white community is as complex and differentiated as the black community. But on the whole the politics of solidarity are just as strong in the white community as they are in the black community. The political vehicle or manifestation of the indifference is what the renowned African American political scientist Ron Walters describes as a conservative nationalism.[3]

In the public discourse this plays itself out through what I have on occasion described as a racialised mobilisation of sympathy. The way this bias works is that when black people are caught out in violation of the law, there is an instinctive call, often by white people, to hang them high. This punitive culture is perhaps consistent with long held prejudices and stereotypes about the black as the child who needs to be punished. How-ever, when whites do similar things there is amongst the same community an instinctive call to understand, and forgive.

This is what happened when the former South African cricket captain Hansie Cronje was caught for match fixing. Before we knew it, Cronje was being rehabilitated as a hero of South African cricket. The racialised mobilisation of sympathy has been invoked even in instances where whites have committed gross crimes against black people. The stories of desecration of black bodies abound: a black man pulled by a rope by a truck; a black youth painted all white because he is suspected of theft; a black child shot dead on her mother's back; a group of whites beat a black man to death and walked away with a slap on the wrist. That is the daily reality of poor black people at the total mercy of white racists on the rural farmlands.

I remember being woken up by a friend one evening in late 2000 telling me to turn on the television to see six white police officers setting their vicious dogs on three defenceless young black men. What angered many in the black community were the all-too-familiar defensive metaphors: 'these are isolated incidents'; 'pockets of racism'; 'a few bad apples'; etc. And I thought: how mockingly hollow these responses must be in the ears of the victims.

It is this inability to empathise with the experience of others that remains the adaptive challenge for many white South Africans. I argued this point in one of my columns about good apples covering for bad apples in the white community:

Too often the executioners are able to mobilize public sympathy by hogging media conferences, and calling on an amazing array of sophisticated diversions and metaphors developed in less than six years. And before we know it, a reversal of roles has taken place. As in Ariel Dorfmann's play, Death and the Maiden, *the original perpetrator has become the victim, and the victim's sanity is questioned. The victim is subsequently advised to be an agent, forgetting that agency is called into being by pre-existing victimization. As Harvard University's Cornel West puts it: 'to call on black people to be agents makes sense only if we examine the dynamics of the victimization against which their agency will be exercised.' By denying these victims' experience of racism, even in the face of incontrovertible evidence, we risk driving them into the margins of wanton violence. We make the very legal and civil agency we demand impossible to realize.*

104

Frankly, I find white resistance to the idea of apologizing to black people astounding. I had always thought that the ability to apologize to those we have wronged, our families, friends and even strangers, was a hallowed moral value. To reconcile with others was to reconcile with oneself. So why not apply this most redeeming human quality to racial reconciliation?[4]

The racial mobilisation of sympathy was evident more recently around the prosecution of former minister of police in the apartheid government, Adriaan Vlok. Earlier Vlok came out to apologise for his actions towards Reverend Frank Chikane, who is now the cabinet secretary in the Mbeki government. As a sign of contrition Vlok offered to wash Chikane's feet, a gesture that was met with a mix of ridicule and appreciation by different sectors of the community. Not long after that the National Prosecuting Authority announced that it would prosecute Vlok for attempted murder. There was also the question of why Vlok had not confessed during the TRC. The announcement of Vlok's possible prosecution was met with loud protestation in the white community. The arguments were that similar prosecutions needed to be taken with respect to ANC leaders who had committed comparable acts but were never prosecuted.

I suggested a simple exercise for white South Africans in a column I wrote about their responses to the Vlok issue:

In this exercise you are required to examine your instinctive response to the prosecution of Adriaan Vlok – a man who thumbed his nose at the Truth and Reconciliation Commission and then years later publicly confessed to attempted murder. You are allowed to draw some kind of legal equivalence between Vlok and members of the ANC who did not apply for amnesty. However, it is not your legal genius I am interested in. I am interested in something more personal – your instinctive, gut response. Is your response a genuine response to a double standard in the application of the law or is it a reflection of the all-too-common instinct to defend one's own? And if you think that despite flouting all the rules of the TRC it is enough that Vlok has shown contrition – would you extend a similar sense of sympathy towards Jacob Zuma, who has also expressed contrition for his wrongs.

You may of course say their circumstances are different – except that the difference won't carry very far in the townships. I am asking you therefore to suspend your legal and technical analysis and focus a little more on your gut response. If the exercise reveals that you are more concerned about protecting your own then I have a story to share with you. The story is that when he was the head of the South African Students Organization the more radical students used to send Steve Biko for negotiations with the white administration. If the administration baulked, Steve would simply say, 'Okay then I suppose you will have to deal with other guys.' The administration would end up conceding to the demand and averting radical action. Failure to own up to the legacy of apartheid may leave white people with no option but to deal with the bigots amongst us. Like will deal with like, and we will not be able to make out the difference. And we'll be on our way to Zimbabwe in a hand basket.[5]

I am personally of the view that we should bring an end to all prosecutions now. This is not because I think there is some kind of moral equivalence between those who fought on the side of liberation and those who fought on the side of oppression. The only argument I would make against prosecutions is that it is like opening a Pandora's Box. This is about the only area of our public life where I am willing to say let bygones be bygones. I would urge whites to see this as yet another window for reconciliation. That would mean among other things confronting head on the potential consequences of their racialised double-standards when it comes to the prosecution of black and white people respectively.

This will not be easy, given that this racialisation is not only a part of white public discourse but has found institutional form in the politics of opposition – in what is in many ways a parallel development to Mbeki's own racial nationalism.

White conservative nationalism as a barrier to adaptation

Ron Walters has described white political culture in the United States as a form of white conservative nationalism. It is a form of reaction against what is perceived as a black attack on white entitlements.[6] In South

Africa conservative nationalism found institutional form in the politics of the opposition party under the leadership of Tony Leon.

Leon catapulted the liberal Democratic Party into the official opposition by playing up white fears. He offered a muscular brand of liberalism that promised to 'fight back' on behalf of the endangered white minority. This strategy worked brilliantly in undercutting the support for the old National Party. The National Party had lost its credibility among the more conservative sections of white society. Not only had it brought their world tumbling down but it had also joined Nelson Mandela's government of national unity. Even when its leader, F.W. de Klerk, took the party out of that government to become the official opposition in 1996, it was not taken seriously by the white conservatives. Many of them looked to the emergent muscular opposition presented by Tony Leon and the Democratic Party, which later merged with certain sections of the nationalists to form the Democratic Alliance (DA).

Through his actions Leon revealed the limitations of white 'liberal' politics in South Africa. The DA's fight back campaign was in bad taste, and led ultimately to the deepening of the crisis of legitimacy for liberalism in South Africa. American political theorist Benjamin Barber might as well have had Tony Leon in mind in his description of contemporary liberalism:

> Liberals, ever wary, still preach: 'Defend yourselves! The enemy is everywhere!' And, to be sure, wherever there are policies, policemen, and power, there lurk potential enemies of liberty. Yet the price we pay for this vigilance is also to see enemies where there are only neighbors, antagonism where there may be cooperation. In safeguarding our separate bodies, we neglect the body politic; in expressing our dignity as individuals, we fail to dignify our sociability and give it a safe form of expression.[7]

That is Tony Leon's legacy for South Africa: a politics of fear, rooted in liberal racialism. I described this legacy in an op-ed article:

> *Some years ago the political analyst and academic Dan O'Meara published his seminal book* Forty Lost Years. *This is an account of how successive generations of Afrikaner governments dug South Africa*

deeper and deeper into crisis. He argues that 'throughout these "forty lost years" the subjective aspects of NP [National Party] *politics – including the contrasting personalities of its various leaders – played a central role – in fashioning the overall evolution of the apartheid state.' O'Meara also makes the rather prescient observation that subjective politics are as likely to play a crucial role in the evolution of the democratic state as they did in the past. However the problem is that 'the collective minds of different groups of South Africans are living the nightmares of different histories. They are thus also haunted by very different fears over what these unresolved pasts mean for their individual and collective futures.'*

What emerges from all of this is that the relationship between identity and leadership matters a great deal in politics. The question I would like to pose then is whether Tony Leon's leadership of the Democratic Alliance can equally be characterized as 'thirteen lost years.' Did Tony Leon help white South Africans go beyond the fears of an unresolved past? This immediately brings to the fore an interesting contradiction – his objective success in building an opposition and his subjective failure to help his constituency transcend the fears of their unresolved past. Does his use of the latter to achieve the former give credence to the saying that the ends justify the means? Before answering that question let me explain this contradiction further.

In an objective procedural sense Tony Leon has done a great job in building a formidable opposition party, thereby strengthening our democracy. No matter how much the ANC leadership may detest Leon and the Democratic Alliance, there is no discounting their importance as a political force. One of the great challenges of a democratic society is not just the existence of opposition parties but also the understanding that there is nothing we can do to eliminate such opposition. The democratic temperament teaches us always to accept our enemies as opponents. In a sense Leon has taught us to begin to accept the value of living with the contradictions that come with plurality. I am increasingly of the view that those of us who come from the liberation movements must disabuse ourselves of the notion that we can get everyone to think exactly as we do, or look at South African society in the same way that we do. That would be an ideological, intellectual and political pipedream, achievable only under fascist conditions. Our challenge is not to coerce but always to persuade through democratic politics that section of the population Leon represented to embrace the values of the new society, or what Rousseau would have called the new civil religion . . .

It is at the level of political socialization of his constituency into the new society that Leon failed spectacularly. Instead of helping his mainly white constituency transcend the fears of their unresolved past, Leon capitalized on those fears. What this means of course is that the DA does not have as much of a leadership succession problem as it has an identity problem . . .

In his magisterial work, Leadership, *James Macgregor argues that the modal values that leaders use must be consistent with the end-values that leaders want to achieve. For example, it is oxymoronic to use tyrannical modal values to establish democracy. In the final analysis Tony Leon failed to use his pivotal position to transform the identity of white South Africans. And so as Dan O'Meara predicted white South Africans are still haunted by 'fears over what these unresolved pasts means for their individual and collective future.' Fear, which comes out as anger, is at the heart of white political discourse thirteen years after Leon's ascendancy into the leadership of the DA.*

How will history then judge Leon as a leader? Almost everything I have read on leadership emphasizes the importance of leadership as a normative concept premised primarily on the transition from authoritarian values to democratic values. The Harvard academic Ronald Heifetz argues that the leadership challenge is the ability to get one's followers to adapt to a new environment and its values. Great leaders are those who are able to mediate the conflict between the unresolved fears of their past and the challenge of charting new values. Leaders are risk takers but more importantly they should be able to help their followers to become risk takers in embracing sometimes different values. It thus still remains to be seen whether the DA will transform its conservative-liberal identity – which itself is a source of confusion within the party – and thus build on the remarkable role it has played in the opposition.[8]

However, Tony Leon is no longer the leader of the opposition. In an exemplary move for other political leaders, Leon voluntarily stepped down as leader of the opposition in May 2007. He was replaced by Helen Zille.

In many ways Zille comes from a more activist background than Leon. She worked as a journalist for the *Rand Daily Mail*, helping to expose the truth behind Steve Biko's death. She has also had experience with a number of civil society organisations in the white community, such as the Black Sash movement and the End Conscription Campaign. Leon, by contrast, comes from a more conservative political tradition, having himself gone into the army as a conscript. The question on many people's minds was whether or not Zille would bring a new transformative liberalism into opposition politics?

Mbeki, who has never met Leon, started off by meeting Zille. A photograph of Mbeki straightening her shirt collar was on the front page of the major South African newspapers. Some interpreted this as a power-laced patronising image, while others saw it as a sign that Mbeki was beginning to loosen up and be kinder to opposition leaders. He probably sees in Zille the opportunity to let his guard down. Much of his response to Tony Leon was characterised by a hostility that I suspect came from a sense of being disrespected by Leon. There was always a sense of one-upmanship between the two men, each trying to outsmart the other.

The ANC's Carl Niehaus articulated where white South Africans could begin their transformative process in an article that appeared in *City Press*:

> The underlying implications of the lack of preparedness to accept, and confront oneself with, the full evil of and depravity of apartheid has become a stumbling block for continued transformation in South Africa. As long as the deep and unmitigated racism that was the heart and essence of apartheid is denied by a substantial part of the white community, it will become impossible for them to become part of the new South Africa.[9]

Niehaus could have easily adopted the tack taken by many white liberals. He could have said: 'I am not part of a morally depraved past. I languished in apartheid's jails for fifteen years.' From a liberal individual perspective he would have been more than justified. Instead he says: 'I am a white man and I want to address all the whites in this audience. You are white in this country with its particular history, and it is an undeniable fact that each one of us, myself included, benefited from apartheid. No one of us can escape the guilt of that reality.' Not only does Niehaus refuse to point to his own sacrifices (which itself is a remarkable act of sacrifice and selflessness), but he acknowledges that simply by virtue of his whiteness terrible things were done in his 'name'.

Where is the leadership to take white South Africans forward into this humanistic revival? I raised this question in an op-ed piece for *Rapport* newspaper, which is the largest Afrikaans weekly, read by both white Afrikaners and a significant section of the coloured population. But it was really to a white audience that I directed the article:

Aphi Amadoda! – *that is the rallying cry that black people have used to call for leadership in times of crisis. Despite the age-old patriarchal assumptions of men as leaders, this is a call that both men and women have heeded in different times of our history. This is a call that has rarely been heard in the white community. Who and where are the moral leaders of white South Africa? Who are the white equivalents of Mandela and Tutu? These, of course, are questions that can only be answered by first understanding leaders as products of their environments and, secondly by resolving the question of whether we need race-based leaders or not.*

Let us begin with the first proposition – which is essentially that communities and nations get the leaders they deserve. People like Nelson Mandela rose to leadership positions as part of broader political movements espousing values of freedom, justice and inclusion. While these values defined the kind of leaders that the black community would have, the values of separation, exclusion and oppression defined white leaders like Verwoerd and Vorster. But ultimately, and at great human cost, freedom and justice triumphed over tyranny. Nelson Mandela became the most exalted embodiment of these values throughout the world. Admittedly, this is too stark an opposition for there were many whites who upheld progressive positions and many blacks who collaborated with apartheid. But the general picture remains – blacks fought apartheid and whites supported it. And as sociologist Dan O'Meara has observed, as time went on the National Party increased its share of the white vote beyond the Afrikaner community into the English speaking white community.

The vindication of democratic values also necessarily entailed the repudiation of the value systems that underpinned white society. All of a sudden the old value system disappeared and many white people had to adjust to the new world. What this meant is that in all sectors of our society white leaders started feeling that they had no moral standing to provide leadership to blacks without seeming either arrogant or hypocritical. Three options presented themselves: to 'fight back' or to withdraw or to define a totally new conception of white leadership. For the most part white leaders chose the first option of fighting back and as that option becomes more unviable, they may take the second one of total resignation and withdrawal.

Instead of crafting a new vision for their people in the new South Africa, the current crop of leaders advanced sectarian conceptions of freedom and justice. Constand Viljoen spoke of a sophisticated cultural pluralism but one that could not break free from narrow conceptions of race and Afrikaner self-determination; Louis Luyt's self-image is that of a white male who can stand up to Nelson Mandela; Tony Leon conducted an unmistakably racial 'fight back' campaign; and Marthinus van Schalkwyk did not inspire even the confidence of the white community he was trying to protect against the spectre of a dominant black government.

But the lack of a larger than life moral leadership is not only limited to the conservative whites. Even liberal and progressive whites have not taken up the cudgels. Helen Suzman, who could easily have become a stateswoman like Mandela, could not elevate herself beyond her association with the Democratic Party with all the racial baggage it now carries. And Frederick Van Zyl Slabbert could not be bothered with attempts to have him lead an Afrikaner cultural movement.

And so we must still ask our white brothers and sisters: Aphi Amadoda – *who could be role models for all our children, but particularly white children growing up in a new era? In hundreds of*

112

classrooms throughout the country black and white children are learning to live with each other without all the racial fuss of their parents. Maybe the project of injecting new value systems in the white community and therefore a different breed of white leaders in the broader society will be the task of the children. But can this be done without white role models?

This then leads me to the second assumption in the preceding discussion – do we need race-based leadership if we profess to live in a non-racial society? There are at least two ways of looking at the world – and your reaction to this article will depend on which view you subscribe to. There is the old non-racial view that we should all be colour blind – it should make no difference if white kids have Nelson Mandela or Nadine Gordimer as their role models. People are all the same. I do not subscribe to this view. I believe that race, culture, tradition matters. The challenge is to acknowledge, respect and celebrate difference . . .

Roelf Meyer's decision to lead the United Democratic Movement is historic and significant for one important reason – the willingness to risk leading in equal partnership with Bantu Holomisa a people whose cultural idioms, values, traditions are in many ways new to him. Risk-taking is the finest quality of leadership, and it may well be that leap of faith that is needed in building a new value system and therefore a new corps of white leaders. The Roelf Meyer model may well be 'the third way' for white leaders – away from either fighting back or withdrawing. And, perhaps, we can let the children lead.[10]

For as long as both blacks and whites are locked in their respective domains of denial – the black denial of the experience of HIV/AIDS, crime, corruption and Zimbabwe, and the white denial of racism in their midst – then for that long the goal of building a truly non-racial society will remain elusive.

Building a joint culture

The late Aggrey Klaaste, former editor of the *Sowetan*, once argued that in the end it will be the responsibility of black people to save South Africa from certain ruination. Klaaste argued that this was so because blacks were after all in the majority and for all intents and purposes were likely to provide the political leadership to the country. It is therefore absolutely important that even as we call for white leaders to play their role we should not forget this responsibility. In a column titled 'Denial can be Experienced as a Form of Attack',[11] I alluded to Njabulo Ndebele's argument that

> the black majority carries the historic responsibility to provide in this situation decisive and visionary leadership. Either it embraces this responsibility with conviction or it gives up its leadership through a throwback psychological dependence on racism, which has the potential to compromise severely the authority conferred on it by history.[12]

I then posed the questions: 'But what about us blacks? Are we up to the challenge of taking this country out of its moral morass?' I answered them by commenting:

> *I submit that black people will not be able to offer an alternative moral ideal for as long as they mimic the dominant culture's pathology of denial. The black community will fail to assert its moral authority for as long as it denies the legacy of Biko and his call for a new consciousness predicated on psychological liberation, self-definition, self-reliance, creativity and initiative. As Harold Cruse put it with respect to the American experience: 'As long as the Negro's cultural identity is in question, or open to self-doubts, then there can be no positive identification with the real demands of political and economic existence.'[13]*

The worst thing we could do, I argued, would be to succumb to play out the very attitudes of racial nativism or exclusivity that have been so much a part of white society. As Steve Biko put it:

> Blacks have had enough experience as objects of racism not to wish to turn the tables. While it may be relevant now to talk about black in relation to white, we must not make this our

preoccupation, for it can be a negative exercise. As we proceed further towards the achievement of our goals let us talk more about ourselves and our struggle and less about whites.[14]

Our duty as black people is to recuperate ideas such as liberalism from the limitations of their white moorings and locate these ideas within the black political experience. Given our historical experience with oppression, and the tolerance and forgiveness we have demonstrated in the past ten years, black people may turn out to be the true guardians of a properly contextualised and progressive, transformative liberalism, joining the collective solidarity of *ubuntu* to respect for the individual. This is what Biko once described as a 'joint culture' that would draw on both black and white experiences in building a new South African identity.

The austere policies of his administration notwithstanding, Thabo Mbeki has been able to utilise the language of black victimhood and has been able to mobilise some black intellectuals to varying degrees on that basis. And given that members of the middle class are often positioned to articulate the black experience through the media, they are able to articulate the language of blacks as victims in ways that resonate with the reality of black people. However, when this happens it is very easy for nationalism to come together with socialism in murderous ways as has happened in so many countries throughout the twentieth century – from Germany to Yugoslavia to Zimbabwe. The question is, how do we bend the twig of nationalism to be less ferocious? How do we avoid the manipulation of race and ethnicity by leaders bent on holding on to power at whatever cost, as has so tragically happened in Zimbabwe? In short, as I explore in the next chapter, what does South Africa need to get back to the language and vision of a non-racial nationalism that animated the struggles for freedom?

CHAPTER 7

In Search of Goodness
Rebuilding State–Society Relations

AS PART OF any re-examination of where South Africa has been and where it needs to go, it is only appropriate that we revisit our approach to nationalism. My experience with Thabo Mbeki – whom I initially embraced as a nationalist hero – has taught me that, left on its own, nationalism can lead to deadly consequences. In talking about nations we therefore need to look out for what is bad and what is good about them. The preceding chapters certainly encapsulate what is bad about nationalism, but what is it that we can do to accentuate the goodness of nations?

In August 2006 I hosted Benedict Anderson at a public forum at Wits University. Anderson is widely regarded as one of the world's leading scholars of nationalism, best known for his path-breaking study, *Imagined Communities*. I asked Anderson to speak about the subject of his latest work, *The Goodness of Nations*, and he focused on the paradox of nations.

On the one hand, all nations are characterised by various kinds of fault-lines: race, class, religion, ethnicity, gender, generation, ideology, etc. He also observed that 'nations only too frequently behave badly, choose leaders who are cruel, corrupt, or incompetent, and have plenty of black pages in their histories'. On the other hand, those very same nations cling to the idea of nationhood, and to this day demand to be recognised as nations in bodies such as the United Nations.

Anderson identifies three elements that make up the goodness of nations. Firstly, nationalists believe the nation will exist well into the future. The language is always suffused with the idea of posterity. We call on each other to 'do the right thing' in the present in the interests of future generations. In the words of the German economist and sociologist Max Weber, we need to be 'worthy ancestors' to the innocent unborn. Anderson notes that it does not matter that some of the unborn will turn out to be criminals or murderous dictators or hooligans of various types. In the present imagining they are all wonderfully innocent.

The second quality is that all nationalists think we have a past worth preserving. The Czech-born writer Milan Kundera is appealing to the same goodness when he says 'the struggle of man against power is the struggle of memory against forgetting'.[1] Desmond Tutu is doing the same thing when he calls on us to look to the rock from which we have been hewn.[2] Nation building is thus an act of active remembering and forgetting, construction and reconstruction.

The third element of the goodness of the nation is in the invocation of national inalienable rights, inalienable precisely because we are national citizens. We are not South Africans by blood or by the past, but because we are citizens. Great social movements are able to make their claims for freedom and for socio-economic rights on the basis of their national belonging. Thus African Americans could make their claim on freedom in the United States by arguing that they were citizens like everyone else, and that by treating them as non-citizens the United States government was violating a principle sacred to its very foundation. In his book, *The Story of American Freedom*, the historian Eric Foner has documented how the success of the civil rights movement was in large part predicated on appeals to America's own values. And as I argued in Chapter 3, the success of the TAC was predicated on appeals to South

Africa's constitutional values, particularly the constitution's guarantee of socio-economic rights.

The nineteenth-century French intellectual Ernest Renan encapsulated all of these time dimensions of the nation in a seminal lecture he presented at the Sorbonne on 11 March 1882. In that speech Renan argued that 'the nation is a soul, a spiritual principle . . . a large-scale solidarity, constituted by the feeling of the sacrifices one has made in the past and of those one is prepared to make in the future; [and] the clearly expressed desire to continue a common life'.[3]

Achille Mbembe, a research professor in history and politics at Wits University, argues elliptically about the present: 'More philosophically, it may be supposed that the present as experience of a time is precisely that moment when different forms of absence become mixed together: absence of those presences that are no longer so and that one remembers (the past), and absence of those others that are yet to come and are anticipated (the future).'[4]

It may be argued that what makes nation building difficult in South Africa is that we do not share a common past. This is quite similar to Dan O'Meara's assertion that 'the collective minds of different groups of South Africans are living the nightmares of different histories. They are thus also haunted by very different fears over what these unresolved pasts mean for their individual and collective futures.'[5] But surely a society must construct ways of getting out of this trap of the past if it is to address the challenges of the present? The past is of great importance in nation building but it should never be used as a crutch, preventing us from forming new identities. The promise of liberation was the creation of these new identities. It was an exultant moment for many South Africans with Nelson Mandela as the embodiment of what can be good about nations. However, under Mbeki's leadership we have moved into what can be bad about nations.

The history of the idea of the nation would therefore suggest that any discussion of its 'state' should speak to this collective, albeit ambivalent, identity. This must begin with an acknowledgement of the irreducible plurality – the differences that cannot be overcome – of society. Ideological uniformity or blind racial solidarity can hardly be instruments for nation building in a pluralistic society such as South Africa. An important element in such an effort must be civil society.

In his book of essays, leading political philosopher Michael Walzer describes the important role that civil society should play in the making of national identities in plural societies. Plurality will no doubt introduce an element of instability. But as I shall argue in Chapter 9 this is more of a leadership challenge than an essential challenge. One of the interesting things in this regard is the nation building that Julius Nyerere undertook in Tanzania. With all of its 126 ethnic groups Tanzania has been one of the most peaceful countries on the African continent. It is therefore better to experiment with managing plurality if we are to avoid a drift into authoritarianism. Or as Walzer puts it: 'No state can survive if it is alienated from civil society. . . The production and reproduction of loyalty, civility, political competence and trust in authority are never the work of the state alone, and the effort to go it alone – one meaning of totalitarianism – is doomed to failure.'[6]

However, Walzer warns against ignoring that civil society is itself an unequal terrain characterised by its own inequalities. Some groups, because they are well financed and better organised, can be more effective in getting their voices heard and their issues put on the agenda of government. This may be bad or good depending on what civil society groups we are talking about. But then again we must accept the fact of their existence.

The civil society groups I have in mind in the process of nation building are those seeking to deepen South Africa's democratic project. The more prominent ones have been COSATU and the TAC. The TAC is effective in part because it has mobilised our constitutional values and general values of caring that come from our past, but it is also effective because individuals with the same challenges in the present have come together to act in concert about their survival into the future.

Paying attention to plurality in civil society will also involve accepting that even those who committed the worst atrocities against us are in fact part of us – even if we are all ashamed of the past they bequeathed to our national identity and our national memory. As I first discussed in Chapter 4, Anderson argues that a sense of shame is an essential element of national pride and national identity. There may come a time when future generations will look back with embarrassment and shame at the absurdity of apartheid. But such a break can only come with the present generation – which is why my writings give special attention to the leadership challenges facing the ruling ANC. As I shall argue in Chapter 9, the ANC's dominance at this juncture of our national life gives the organisation a special responsibility to build that bridge into the future that will free future generations from the past.

In short, we need to be 'worthy ancestors' – in the manner and example set by leaders such as Nelson Mandela – to those who come after us. This applies with equal force to both black and white South Africans. It requires that whites resist the instinctive denial of the past, and that blacks resist the racial insider/outsider discourse that has taken root in our political culture. Moving forward as a nation will require the abandonment of the idea that some of us have more authentic voices than others – on account of the colour of our skin or participation in the revolutionary struggle. This is the kind of racial nativism that has brought Zimbabwe to its knees.

I have been arguing that our political, intellectual and civic history has for the most part been that of syncretism. Through this syncretism black communities were able to build new identities to face up to the challenges of the day. For example, at various points in our history black people have constantly named and renamed their collective identities – all the while challenging and rejecting derogatory names given to them by the white power structures. I experienced syncretism in my own home with my parents and grandparents taking the best that the West had to offer and mixing it with the best that African traditional life had to offer to create new identities – what Steve Biko would have called a 'joint culture'. The strength of political consciousness and activism in South Africa was in many ways a reflection of the underlying strength and quality of these processes of adaptation. The genius of the Black Consciousness movement of the 1970s was its recognition of the importance of this identity as an essential element of what the American civic activist and academic Harry Boyte calls 'culture making' and political mobilisation.[7] The concept of culture making describes how communities generate creative responses to life's varied problems. Culture making is not just about civic and political actors mobilising millions into the streets but also about how individuals, families and communities reproduce their lives on a daily basis. Key to all of this was developing in people a sense of their own agency in everyday life as part of the process of building national pride, and in the process impelling them to be political agents. A new nationalism with a light touch would have to develop what Mbembe describes as 'languages of life':

> For each time and age, there exists something distinctive and particular – or, to use the term, a 'spirit' (Zeitgeist). These distinctive and particular things are constituted by a set of material practices, signs, figures, superstitions, images, and fictions that, because they are available to individuals' imagination and intelligence and actually experienced, form what might be called 'the languages of life'.[8]

I have argued in many of my writings that the ANC needs to rediscover non-racialism as its language of life. Even though I have not always been a great supporter of non-racialism as a strategy for struggle, I never had any doubt that the ultimate aim of our struggle was the creation of a non-racial democracy. The ANC and its internal organisations, particularly the United Democratic Front (UDF), used the concept of non-racialism as a powerful generative metaphor for what kind of society we could attain. The ANC thus needs to retrace the steps of its own history. Even if it can be claimed that a great deal of that history contains Africanist strains of various types, and that Mbeki represents a re-emergence of those strains, by the 1980s the dominant language of the ANC was non-racialism.

The impact of exile

I suspect that the departure from non-racialism as the language of life of the ANC also has something to do with the experience of exile for Thabo Mbeki and his cohort. Exile can induce in people a heightened sense of longing as well as resentment against those who drove them away from home. The South African writer Es'kia Mphahlele captured the rage that informs the experience of exile thus:

> There is something about the act of and fact of communal survival inside a situation of racism that either tones down, or

lends another complexion to, the hate that is mixed with anger. Outside the situation you are on your own, you have little communal support: at best, it is intellectual. So you hate the whites you left behind with a scalding intensity. Could it be that distance creates a void and that the burning lava of hate must fill it?[9]

Ngũgĩ wa Thiong'o offers a slightly different account of why the distance of exile turns into a more radical orientation. He argues that it is the memories of home that are passed through the generations that turn the experience of exile into a radical longing,[10] and I suspect it is that experience that informs so much of the anger in Thabo Mbeki and many of his exile comrades. But a radical nationalism that is driven by anger and ignores the plurality of society can only lead to the kind of death and destruction that nationalism has wrought on the African continent and elsewhere in the world. That nationalism in turn is likely to generate the kind of denialism and social outcomes on HIV/AIDS, Zimbabwe, corruption and crime that we have seen under Mbeki's leadership.

People in power need a new and smarter kind of radicalism, a radicalism that recognises and accepts the fact of social plurality and seeks to build new alliances, even with former oppressors. There was a time when I did not understand Mandela's constant urgings that we should not think with our hearts but with our brains. Now I cannot imagine a more important strategic leadership challenge for our country as we enter the second decade of our freedom. We cannot continue to assume the position of victims even as we are in power. However, thinking with our brains does not mean the kind of intellectual and emotional distance that Mbeki has developed with South Africans.

Building bridges with civil society
The relationship between civil society and the state must also extend to the development agenda. One of the unfortunate consequences of the transition to democracy was the decline in the quantity and quality of civic leadership as former civic leaders took up new roles in government and others pursued opportunities in business and elsewhere. An oft-asked question by those in power was: what do we need civil society for now

123

that we have a government of the people? Civil society began to lose its special place in the language of development. Civil society organisations were seen as at best a nuisance and at worst a threat to the democratic government. The argument was that they would delay service delivery. But it is in the nature of societies to find ways of regenerating leaders. And it is indeed the re-emergence of organisations such as COSATU that has provided a mirror for the ANC to examine itself in.

The ANC has embraced the idea of the developmental state as the strategy for development, an idea that owes its origins to scholars such as Chalmers Johnson but has been more recently resuscitated by University of California sociologist Peter Evans's 1995 work, *Embedded Autonomy*. Evans offers the concept of embedded autonomy as a way in which the state can effectively manage relationships with the rest of society.[11] He argues that inasmuch as states need internal bureaucratic coherence and autonomy, they also need to be connected to and embedded within civil society. This is a departure from the Weberian idea that the most important task of bureaucracy is to provide a certain level of predictability and efficiency of action by decision makers. For Weber this clarity of state actions could be achieved only by an autonomous state unencumbered by the clamour and clatter of community participation in the processes of governance. Evans argues that while bureaucratic coherence is necessary for effective action, social connectedness is necessary to bring forth the creative energies of the population into the decision processes of government.

Under Mbeki the South African state has erred on the side of autonomy. The little social connection that exists is mainly to business organisations represented by groupings such as the Big Business Working Group or the International Marketing Council. Organisations representing labour are weak, ineffectual and hardly have any weight. The National Economic Development and Labour Council (NEDLAC), a body set up for joint consultation on economic matters, was bypassed when the Mbeki government adopted its controversial economic policy, GEAR, in 1996.[12]

It is still unclear, though, how the labour movements and civil society groups that seek to replace Mbeki would go beyond collective action to create a coherent bureaucracy. However, there is a crucial element of the concept of embedded autonomy that hardly finds any expression in ANC discussions. This is what Evans calls 'encompassing embedded autonomy'.

One of the ironies of embedded autonomy is that it sometimes leads to unintended consequences. The very social and civic actors that the state empowers discover in themselves a greater sense of agency, and they may sometimes build coalitions with other social groups to confront the state with their demands.

Former allies become sworn enemies, and state actors feel betrayed. I have frequently suggested that Mbeki's behaviour gives a sense of someone who feels betrayed – betrayed by the white liberal and business community who fêted him with lavish reception when he came back from exile and by the black intellectuals who failed to come to his defence during his troubled relations with the media and white society more broadly.

The developmental state thus extends beyond just state–society relations to the appreciation and acceptance of the irreducible plurality of society, and the inevitability of criticism and disagreement and 'betrayal'. This requires a state that is able to relate to disparate groups that are pulling it in different directions. Evans describes the experience of encompassing embedded autonomy thus:

If labour cannot be marginalized or ignored, a dependable arena for centralized bargaining between capital and labor is essential. A competent coherent state apparatus provides that arena. Far from making the state irrelevant, the comprehensive organization of class interests makes it essential. As actors in civil society become more organized, a solid and sophisticated state apparatus becomes more rather than less necessary.[13]

However, much as its attempts to embrace the developmental state are a laudable correction to the prevailing orthodoxy, the ANC still sees itself as the custodian of society. To solve the conundrum of managing the plurality of social voices and forces the ANC rather cleverly places itself on both sides of embedded autonomy. Members of the ANC deployed in government will represent the state and engage with members of the party in civil society. The ANC reworks Evans's concept thus: 'While we seek to engage private capital strategically, in SA the developmental state must be buttressed and guided by a mass-based democratic liberation movement in a context in which the economy is still dominated by a developed but largely white capitalist class.'[14]

In July 2007 the ANC held a policy conference in anticipation of the all-important December leadership conference. No doubt the most contentious policy issue was the rightward shift in the ANC's economic policy. The economic policy document reads like an exercise in economic revisionism. Because this is an ANC policy conference – and because government is supposed to get direction from the party – the document suggests that the adoption of these economic policies was not a departure from the party's reconstruction and development programme. Instead, the adoption of these policies is presented as a tactical move forced on otherwise loyal ANC leaders in government by the exigencies of governance. In other words, this is not a philosophical and ideological U-turn but a practical, technical matter. ANC leaders in government cannot hold a policy conference every time they have to fashion policies: 'Whilst the ANC had elaborated a clear strategic perspective on macro-economic policy, the details of our tactical positions were – correctly – left to those deployed in government who had to respond to an evolving and complex environment.'[15]

The document provides an interesting mix of quaint Marxist jargon to prove to the masses that the organisation has not abandoned its radical origins. Drawing on Marx's *Eighteenth Brumaire*, the document waxes lyrically: 'We have not approached our goals in conditions of our own making and the outcomes we seek are partly the consequence of objective factors beyond our control.' I asked one of the authors of the document why the ANC continues to present itself as a revolutionary organisation – the document is indeed littered with references to the National Democratic Revolution. He was quite unapologetic about the need to keep the base. The ANC is a brand and like any brand it has to keep its base, while also trying to attract new customers. And of course the way to keep brand loyalty is through the language used. To wit, a revolutionary party must speak to people in the language they understand, even if it does exactly the opposite. The ANC successfully kept its deliberations from public view.

The most publicised aspect of the policy conference was under the general topic of organisational review, which for all intents and purposes was about the leadership succession debate. Mbeki had tried to keep any discussion of leadership succession outside of the conference, urging conference delegates to limit themselves to matters of policy and warning against all those who sought to use the conference to divide the ANC.

Perhaps he was sensing he might be defeated and embarrassed if the ANC decided to discuss the possibility of him serving a third term as ANC president. Maybe this was not an opportune time to launch his campaign. Mbeki is prohibited by the constitution from serving another term as the country's president. However, there are no such limitations on the presidency of the ANC. The first person publicly to suggest a third term for Mbeki was KwaZulu-Natal premier Sbu Ndebele. This was taken up by the Eastern Cape ANC in its provincial executive conference in 2007. Whether this was a decision of the conference is hotly disputed by some members of the ANC in the Eastern Cape. This is probably because in this province the ANC has always been divided between Mbeki and anti-Mbeki camps. The influential ANC Youth League declared its unequivocal opposition to a third term for Mbeki. They said that given that Mbeki was barred from being president of the country again, his election to become president of the ANC would lead to division and confusion. It could easily lead to what we have seen in the rest of the continent – a former president who still calls the shots from behind the scenes while installing his puppet to do his bidding.

The ANC Youth League was now putting its weight behind the beleaguered Jacob Zuma. One of the first signs of the rebellion against Mbeki came not long after he had fired Zuma from his cabinet, and Zuma was relieved of some of his responsibilities as ANC deputy president. The ANC general council in 2005 was the first in what would be a series of humiliating moments for Mbeki by the Zuma camp. As Mbeki and Zuma shared the stage, Zuma supporters openly sang songs saying Zuma was their president. They restored Zuma's responsibilities as the party's deputy president.

The ANC policy conference in 2007 was taking place within the context of a longer history of contestation – and Mbeki could not have been sure what would happen if the delegates used the policy conference to discuss leadership matters, which were properly meant for the December 2007 congress. But it was also widely suspected that anyone who wanted to make a bid for the leadership had to use the conference to consolidate networks and mobilise within the party. It is no surprise that ANC heavyweights and would-be kings were seen at the conference.

The ANC basically ignored Mbeki's injunction and deliberated the leadership issue under a general discussion of organisational review. The outcome of that discussion could not have been any more irritating for Mbeki. The star of the show was ANC Secretary-General Kgalema Motlanthe. To be more accurate, this was a kind of comeback moment for Motlanthe. When Mbeki became president he created a completely new unit called the presidency with Smuts Ngonyama as its head. This created tension between the office of the presidency and office of the secretary-general – a position traditionally seen as the engine of the ANC. Suddenly Ngonyama was more prominent than Motlanthe – at least in the public domain, which partly explains why Motlanthe is still a stranger to members of the public outside the ANC.

The policy conference re-asserted the centrality of the secretary-general's office. In what would be seen as a clipping of Mbeki's wings, the conference resolved that its president would no longer unilaterally make appointments without consulting the office of the secretary-general. The organisation sought to protect itself from Mbeki by removing from him the carte blanche powers of appointment it had given him at its policy conference in 1997. Mbeki had the power to appoint everyone from cabinet ministers to directors-general to premiers of provinces and mayors of cities. It was an incredible concentration of decision making in one individual in the hope that he would be fair and prudent in the exercise of such responsibility. However, it was a matter of time before Mbeki consolidated power to hire and fire without so much as informing the party. Increasingly ordinary ANC members felt they had to be on the president's good side if they were to make it. As the saying goes: 'You gotta go along to get along.' Over the years Mbeki has built a formidable oligarchy, and as the Austrian political scientist Robert Michel has argued, once elected those oligarchies tend to rise above their electors.

In addition, the ANC went a step further to repudiate the two centres of power argument. Mbeki is barred from serving a third term as president of the country but was keen on being re-elected president of the ANC at its leadership conference in December 2007. Such an arrangement would have resulted in what has been described as two centres of power. The ANC has rejected this scenario, thereby indicating support for an alternative candidate. The conference resolved that members of the ANC preferred that the president of the ANC should be the same person as the president of the country when the country elects a new president in 2009. Pallo Jordan later confirmed the conference position thus: 'The ANC would not prefer Mbeki to continue as president of the ANC. That is the view of the majority.' In the same interview Jordan argued: 'It is not desirable for one president to lead, especially in a young democracy like ours, for such a long time.'[16]

The conference outcome was a slap in the face for Mbeki but he tried – with the help of the SABC – to put a positive spin on it. At the close of the conference he appeared on SABC news saying it would be fine if members of the ANC thought they wanted someone else to lead them but it was also fine if they wanted him to lead.

The irony of it all is that Mbeki had urged members of the ANC to abide by the conference's policy decisions, and here he was violating its most important decision because it was not in line with his own interests. The next chapter is an in-depth discussion of this leadership style, and what it has meant for the country.

CHAPTER 8

The Lone Warrior
Limits to Mbeki's Leadership Model

THE AREA OF leadership studies is vast and well-traversed, going back to Thomas Carlyle's great man leadership theories. Carlyle's Victorian concept of leaders was based on the idea that great men have innate traits – they are born to lead.

Cornel West also traces leadership to influences of nineteenth-century scholars such as Carlyle, and Matthew Arnold, and ultimately to freedom fighters such as W.E.B. du Bois, the African American scholar and political leader. Du Bois coined the idea of the 'Talented Tenth' precisely to indicate that there was a specific group of exceptional men whose duty it was to bring salvation to the masses.

There were essentially three pillars to the idea of the Talented Tenth. First, a cultural elite works in service of the 'impulsive and irrational masses'. Second, this elite manages educational and bureaucratic institutions for the benefit of these masses. Third, by moulding the values and opinions of the masses through these institutions this elite becomes the driver of spiritual and material progress. As Du Bois put it in his essay on the Talented Tenth, 'the Negro race like all races, is going to be saved by its exceptional men'.[1]

This tradition would come to influence the ANC's approach to leadership. One of the ANC's leading thinkers Saki Macozoma gave a paper at the Platform for Public Deliberation at Wits University in which he traced the history of leadership in the ANC. In the early days the shortest route to the leadership of the ANC was societal prominence. If you were a lawyer, doctor, journalist, prosperous farmer and/or chief you stood a better chance of being a leader. These early leaders provided a link between the ANC and what was going on in the world. And, of course, matters of the world could only be dealt with by those equipped with the relevant education.[2]

The leadership literature continues to be marked by this assumption. Even James MacGregor Burns's influential work is informed by the idea that it is the task of leaders to elevate their followers to a higher moral, spiritual and material plane.

This is the framework of leadership I will use to attempt to understand Thabo Mbeki. Mark Gevisser's biography of Mbeki captures what informs both the substance and the style of Mbeki's leadership: 'The person who does good, and does it honestly, must expect to be overpowered by the forces of evil. But it would be incorrect not to do good just because you know death is coming.' Gevisser concludes that 'whatever anyone else thought of him [Mbeki], he remained, in his own mind, a person doing good and doing it honestly'.[3]

Mbeki himself enunciates this idea of self-determination in a commemorative collection of essays on Oliver Tambo. Mbeki's essay is a recall of a process of divination by the ANC's revered leader Oliver Tambo, who entrusted Mbeki with the ANC thus: 'He then communicated another mission, the most challenging since I first met him in Dar es Salaam 27 years earlier: look after the ANC and make sure we succeed. You will know what needs to be done.' Tambo authorised Mbeki to make contact with people like Mandela because he knew that 'I would not make mistakes that would compromise the advance of our struggle and revolution'. Most important, Mbeki would not allow himself to be swayed by the passions of the masses:

Similarly, I came to understand why OR [as Tambo was called by many comrades] insisted on maximum precision in the preparation of his public statements. He taught me the obligation to understand the tasks of leadership, including the necessity never to tell lies, never to make false and unrealisable promises, never to say anything you do not mean or believe, and never to say anything that might evoke an enthusiastic populist response, but which would ultimately serve to undermine the credibility of our movement and struggle.[4]

In his book *Certain Trumpets* Garry Wills describes how the suspicion of the masses can be a problem for the electoral leader operating in a democratic context: 'That may be a proper credential for the lonely genius, the martyr to a truth, the austere intellect – people who forge their own souls in fierce independence. But what have such heroes to do with leading other people?'[5]

The essence of this chapter is that this is the dilemma at the heart of Mbeki's leadership – by all indications he is a fiercely independent individual but in the end has proved to be tragically ineffective in providing leadership at a crucial moment of our encounter with democracy. On the contrary, while Nelson Mandela was himself moulded by the Victorian understandings of leadership – after all, the man is a chief – he was, unlike Mbeki, able to transcend the limits of self-conviction.

Harvard University leadership guru Ronald Heifetz provides a theory that could take us a long way towards addressing our leadership challenges. Heifetz describes leadership as adaptive work: adaptive work consists of the learning required to address conflicts in the values that members of society hold, and to use those conflicts both within individuals, and in relations between individuals or groups, to foster new ways of learning. Adaptive leadership requires introspection, self-criticism and being open to criticism by others. It requires accepting the bona fides and integrity of those who criticise you, and at times questioning the comfortable assumptions and dogmas of your own history and of your own constituencies. It requires entering as much as you can into the world of your protagonists, and trying to understand the world from their point of view.[6]

One of the most remarkable demonstrations of adaptive leadership was when Nelson Mandela described F.W. de Klerk as a man of integrity. As a militant activist I could not understand how Mandela could readily ascribe integrity to someone who had presided over the apartheid government. Besides, what did Mandela know about De Klerk's motives and end-game that the rest of us did not know? But in time Mandela has challenged us to accept that you cannot negotiate with someone whose bona fides and integrity you do not accept. I think by that act alone he sent a message to black people to accept the integrity of the white people who had oppressed and exploited them for so long. That was the only way black people would be able to co-exist with white South Africans as their fellow citizens. Failure to do that would result in endless bitterness and recrimination.

It did not matter much that white South Africans did not reciprocate that gesture, and instead chose their own kinds of denial. It mattered for black people's own healing, and it mattered for the stability of the country.

Mandela criss-crossed South Africa saying the same thing over and over again. At every turn he emphasised in word and deed the importance of the ANC's ideal of non-racialism. He had tea with Betsy Verwoerd, the wife of the apartheid architect, Hendrik Verwoerd, and reached out to Percy Yutar, the prosecutor who led to his long-term imprisonment. He even appointed his former prison guards as part of his security brief. In one of the most public gestures of reconciliation he donned the Springbok rugby jersey in support of the nearly all-white national rugby team when South Africa hosted the Rugby World Cup in 1995. When the popular ANC leader Chris Hani was shot dead by a Polish immigrant associated with the Afrikaner right wing, Mandela went on national television to appeal for calm thus: 'A white man full of prejudice and hate, came to our country and committed a deed so foul that our whole nation teeters on the brink of disaster. A white woman, of Afrikaner origin, risked her life so that we may know, and bring justice to this assassin.'[7]

Again, Mandela's leitmotif was that of a black and white community united against evil. He turned to the theme of racial reconciliation during the 1994 elections:

But we are also concerned about the minorities in the country – especially the white minority. We are concerned about giving confidence and security to those who are worried that by these changes they are now going to be in a disadvantaged position. I again repeat that I have throughout my life as I pointed out in the Rivonia Trial: 'I have fought very firmly against white domination. I have fought very firmly against black domination. I cherish the idea of a new South Africa where all South Africans are equal and work together to bring about security, peace and democracy in our country.'[8]

Dan O'Meara describes Mandela's inaugural address as 'a moment of absolution and unity the likes of which the country had not known since the first white settlement at the Cape 342 years ago'.[9] Mandela, of course, gave all of his support to the TRC. As discussed in Chapter 6, the TRC gave amnesty to the perpetrators of apartheid crimes on condition they came clean about their activities. This was not always the case. Some of them rejected participation in the commission and chose to see it for what it was not – an instrument of retribution. Over time this led to growing resentment within the black community. I was among those who felt the otherwise laudable project of reconciliation was being abused to distract from the challenge of confronting white privilege.

Mbeki's tryst with destiny

When Mandela left office it would indeed be left to his younger successor Thabo Mbeki to tackle the issues that were uncomfortable to raise in the early period of the transition – and in a sense to bring the honey-moon to a close. Racial transformation, not racial reconciliation, became the watchword of Mbeki's agenda. The imbalances our society had inherited could not be merely wished away by romantic appeals to a harmonious 'rainbow nation'.

On America's *Newshour* programme on 24 July 1996 Mbeki was asked about the drop in the number of whites (from 70 per cent to about 34 per cent) who believed that race relations were good. Mbeki attributed this decline in white attitudes to the imperatives of change. He argued that you cannot leave the process of transformation at the political level without addressing economic imbalances, and he continued: 'I would imagine that you would find whites who would be fearful of that kind of change.'[10]

I would not for one moment fault Mbeki for taking on the difficult task of confronting the challenge of racism head on. He was absolutely right in his argument that there would be whites fearful of change. The problem is that for Mbeki the fight against racism became conflated with his defensiveness over his government's policy failures. By so doing he allowed white people to trivialise racism, thereby giving credibility to the overused concept of the 'race card'. Instead of preparing whites for the changes he wanted, Mbeki succeeded only in alienating them. In the process he has proven unable to rise above the divisions of the very society he is supposed to lead. Instead of playing the role of national leader he has become a factionalist, both inside and outside his own political party.

Where did it all go wrong?
Soon after Mbeki was sworn in as our new president I suggested that his challenge was to foster unity and forge a sense of national identity in a country riven by the fault-lines of racial and economic inequality. If India's leaders could forge a pluralistic democracy for India, the world's largest and most diverse society, then there was no reason Mbeki could not do the same for South Africa. I urged him to avoid the mistakes that big political parties often make, which is to abandon civil society (see previously in Chapter 7). Again drawing on the Indian experience, in, June 1999 I suggested that Mbeki should do what Gandhi called 'building bridges' with the people:

'Long years ago we made a tryst with destiny, and now the time comes when we shall redeem our pledge.' Jawaharlal Nehru, Prime Minister of India, 1947

'The people have spoken' – that was Thabo Mbeki's humble, dignified and assertive refrain at the ANC's victory rally at Gallagher Estate. While not exultant as Jawaharlal Nehru's 'tryst with destiny' speech or John F. Kennedy's 'ask not what your country can do for you,' Mbeki's words will be remembered nonetheless for their self-assured

and declarative message. Mbeki will no doubt interpret what the people have spoken to mean an overwhelming mandate for the ANC. But I hope he will take a broader approach, as he hinted he might do when he described his inauguration as 'a festival and celebration of democracy'. . .

The policy question though is now that Mbeki has obtained the overwhelming mandate of the people, how will he sustain their interest in democracy until the next elections and beyond? Will he use his party's dominant position to deepen the roots of democracy? Whether Mbeki can link the party interest to the national interest of building a democratic society will depend in turn on whether he can do what Mahatma Gandhi called 'building bridges' with the people. His biggest challenge will be that of building unity and forging a national identity in a country riven by the fault lines of racial and economic inequality. But if Nehru could forge a pluralistic modern Indian identity for India, the world's largest and most diverse society, Mbeki can learn from India's imperfect experience and Nehru's personal experiences, which are remarkably similar to his, and brilliantly portrayed in his auto-biography, The Discovery of India. *Like Nehru, whose father was one of the founding fathers of the Indian National Congress, Mbeki also comes from 'struggle royalty'. . .*

Both Nehru and Mbeki can be described as detribalized intel-lectuals who were educated away from their traditional communities and yet were given the historical responsibility of building democracy in their societies. Nehru was educated at two of England's most prestigious institutions: Harrow and Cambridge. Once at a public rally with the great Mahatma Gandhi he asked: 'What do I have in common with these people?' Mbeki was educated at Britain's University of Sussex and hobnobbed with high society. The ceremony at his Transkei home last December was perhaps an attempt to start building bridges with his roots. Hopefully, he will take Gandhi and even Mandela's connection with traditional communities more seriously than Nehru was ever able to, without pretending to be what he is not.

Much has been said about Mbeki's 'formality' as an impediment to his ability to connect with the people. But Mbeki should be just himself, and he may be surprised to learn that people like him just the way he is. Dressing down will go only a certain distance. What is more important is whether he comes across as an authoritative leader who is respectful of the people . . . What people will most appreciate is his respect for their ideas and their ways of doing things. One practical suggestion is for him to go back to the townships and villages he visited during his campaign to engage people directly in the policy process. If he could do it over the short space of an election period, he can surely do it during the term of his administration. Finally, if Mbeki is going to translate the overwhelming vote for the ANC into a victory for our society, he should also build bridges with civil society institutions . . .

Mwalimu Julius Nyerere's words on the matter could be instructive for Mbeki: 'We committed two basic mistakes in Tanzania. First, we abolished local government. We thought local officials did not have the vision that we had at the national level. They seemed not to realize how urgent the business of transformation was. I had been writing all these things about freedom and participation and yet taking away power from down there and centralizing it in national government because I thought things would move quicker. That was one basic mistake. Second, we abolished the cooperative movement. During the process of the liberation struggle we had built up a strong cooperative movement as an economic power base for the people, and now we were abolishing it. However it soon became clear that we could not sustain the path of a centralized bureaucracy. We had to make government responsive and accountable to the people. That's when I started calling for a multiparty democracy. I had thought I could reform the party from within but the ineration of corruption was too heavy. The pressure had to come from outside. In addition to political parties we had to build self-governing communities and people's organizations.' Mbeki's historical responsibility is thus to make sure that we do not find ourselves repeating the same mistakes.

There's one final international parallel I would like to draw. Just as Thomas Jefferson in the United States followed George Washington in the founding of the United States, and just as 'crown prince' Nehru followed in Gandhi's footsteps, Mbeki follows in the steps of the

towering Nelson Mandela. Like those other crown princes Mbeki has
an historic opportunity to help us develop a positive national
consciousness and identity. That is his tryst with destiny. Whether he
fulfils it is for future generations to tell. It is that long-term perspective
that differentiates nation builders from party builders.[11]

We have had close to two terms of Mbeki as the leader of the country.
The question to ask now is whether or not he has fulfilled his 'tryst
with destiny'? On the basis of what I have been describing in the
previous chapters it is hard to escape the conclusion that Mbeki has been
a great disappointment for those of us who looked to him to herald the
African Renaissance. On the one hand, he clearly had the potential to
be one of Africa's great leaders and a true visionary for South Africa.
On the other hand, he seemed guarded, turgid and removed from the
experiences of South Africans.

With the passage of time my concerns about Mbeki's leadership style
have turned into firm hunches about the man. The African Renaissance
was better articulated in foreign capitals than in the rural villages and
urban communities of South Africa. He spent more time on the
international stage than he did interacting with the communities. The
Financial Mail's Barney Mthombothi put it this way: 'One always gets
the impression that the president finds SA – and its problems – too small,
too constraining for his prodigious talents. He likes to play in a bigger
pond . . . He's unlikely to know, let alone care, about the trivia troubling
his fellow countrymen and women.' Mthombothi offers the exile
experience as a possible reason for Mbeki's alienation from ordinary
South Africans: 'I don't think Mbeki has made an effort to understand
this society in all its complexity; to press and feel its pulse. He leads the
country with an exile mind-set. Attending the odd *imbizo* won't do the
trick.'[12] The *Mail & Guardian* described Mbeki's leadership style as follows:
'In his sonorous intellectual voice Mbeki has denied that crime is out
of control. He is using and misusing statistics again, as he did at the height
of AIDS denial. Now, as then, he is not feeling the (weakening) pulse of
his people. And, again, he is revealing his propensity to believe in conspiracy theories.'[13] *The Weekender* put it this way: 'At his best, Mbeki has
been able to find the words to exhilarate and unite South Africans. But

at his worst, he comes across as distant, overly technical, and lacking in real appreciation for the plight and joys of ordinary South Africans.'[14]

Another leadership guru from Harvard, Abe Zaleznik, wrote a classic piece in the *Harvard Business Review* in which he drew a distinction between leaders and managers, which I use to analyse the tragic paradox of Mbeki's style.[15] Zaleznik argued that managers tend to value stability and control and are infatuated with strategy. Leaders, by contrast, are driven by a restless search for change and innovation. There is a widely held perception, for instance, that the president is a stickler for detail and facts. Cabinet ministers are like managers directly accountable to the chief executive. As happens in many organisations, daily transactional leadership has substituted for long-term visionary and inspirational leadership around issues of values. The privileging of strategic details gains a momentum of its own and detracts from the development of an over-arching leitmotif for the country. Loyalty, survival, formalism and 'not rocking the boat' – the hallmarks of managerialism – take precedence over risk-taking, experimentation, and innovation and openness – the hall-marks of leadership.

In February 2004 I elicited a vicious response from Mbeki's spokes-men when I dared to suggest that his formalism alienated him from the people. What follows is my column and extracts from the responses from Mbeki's spokesmen:

I have never met President Thabo Mbeki. I am told, though, that he possesses a formidable intellect, holding his own among world leaders. He is suave, articulate and generally genteel, save for the moments he pushed Winnie Madikizela-Mandela in her face or when he seemed visibly flustered by a question about HIV/AIDS on television last Sunday night. When SABC journalist Redi Direko asked if he gets irritated by questions about HIV/AIDS the president responded: 'No it does not irritate me. What irritates me is why people do not want to think.' This particular response betrays an all-too-common flaw among a certain category of intellectuals.

In his book Certain Trumpets *the American public intellectual Garry Wills identifies two types of intellectuals. There are those who engage in a severe and lonely quest for the absolute truth, and end up frustrated with those who 'do not want to think.' Wills cites the case of the great philosopher Wittgenstein as an example: 'Unlike Socrates, who engaged citizens in philosophical self-examination at public meeting places, Wittgenstein could not bring himself, very often, to meet with a small circle of students. He feared that not even those select Cambridge philosophers would understand him.' However, an intellectual president does not have the luxury of a Wittgenstein, whether on HIV/AIDS or any other matter. He also has to attend to the business of the nation. How then to be an intellectual and president at the same time? For that you must pursue what Wills describes as the second type of intellectual excellence, and that is to work towards 'a less exacting but more accessible truth.'*

The father of administrative science, Herbert Simon, called this satisficing – making decisions on the basis of imperfect information. In many ways one could say that the government's strategy on HIV/ AIDS follows the latter kind of intellectual inquiry until of course the president or the minister of health lapses into solipsistic arguments that leave us all agape, perhaps because we 'do not want to think.' The model of the intellectual president as Wittgenstein hampers the ability of the president to communicate on other dimensions as well. As Wills puts it 'calls are always going down the vasty deep; but what spirits will respond?' He feels frustrated because no one understands him. Instead of calling forth the energies of the people, he then becomes self-absorbed. His speeches take on a particular predictable and uninspiring pattern. First, there is the usual acknowledgement of the struggle family in the gallery, then the characteristic quote from a poet or writer, preferably white, either William Butler Yeats or John Donne or Ingrid Jonker or Willie Esterhuyse or Rian Malan or a white couple now living in America that is all of a sudden crazy about the spirit of Vuk'Uzenzele. I must say though the least attractive of the president's rhetorical devices is the by now familiar refrain: 'there are some among us.' In Xhosa it's called 'uku-kwekwa,' and it's just not a very nice way of talking. The reality is that when the president says there are some among us who are not as mature as Rian Malan we know he is referring to Tony Leon. Why does he not just say so? And then there's the reference to 'we are on course' or some other similar constant refrain such as 'as president Mandela said ten years ago.' Frankly, I do not know if comparing the present government's current achievements to a dysfunctional apartheid government is the proper benchmark for measuring social progress. Of course we could only do better.

I suspect, though, that the predictable structure of the president's speeches is a case of form following function. His rhetorical predictability is linked to a need for a broader predictability in the eyes of international markets. When he says there shall be no policy changes he is not so much talking to us as he is talking to international markets. That is the path the ANC chose, and that is the path we are stuck with for the next five years. It is path dependence of the worst kind. There will be none of that exhilarating stuff about 'bold, persistent, experimentation' that Franklin Roosevelt spoke about as he confronted America's poverty and unemployment in the 1930s. And yet that's exactly the kind of social experimentation this country needs if we are to confront our social challenges. But I also know I am howling in the wind. That kind of social experimentation would require a different kind of intellectual leadership from the president, away from the Wittgenstein model to the Socratic model of public engagement. A new social function could perhaps yield a new form of speech, one that, for example, speaks to the young people of this country. I'm sure the markets can wait, they might even appreciate that.[16]

I had no idea what was coming. In a letter headed 'Mangcu's Song' presidential spokesman Bheki Khumalo wrote:

Sir – What to Make of Xolela Mangcu? His column, 'Cryptic Mbeki Runs Risk of Losing Touch with Common People' (12 February) has an undertone of hell having no fury like a columnist spurned. From Mangcu's whimsical opening ('I have never met President Thabo Mbeki') one can see trouble ahead. Wittgenstein could never bring himself to meet with students, wails Mangcu. And you do not have to be a student of psychology to understand the particular axe that Mangcu is grinding. Mangcu decorates his column with big names; it seems that the president's sin is not to play along. How dare the president quote Rian Malan and the tragic heroine Ingrid Jonker, but not the great Mangcu, a legend in his own mind? Mangcu's columns tend to be overburdened, undigested polymathism and the present column is an example . . . Mangcu is singing for his supper. Not long ago the *Business Day* editor urged South African conglomerates to shower Mangcu's institute with money. But then comes the irony: Mangcu is not only a trader and entrepreneur in ideas, he is a sectarian advocate of Black Consciousness. That is why, methinks, he resents the president's citing of Malan and Jonker. Whites must get little or no credit in Mangcu's world – except, of course, when white-run corporates bring gifts to fund-raising dinners. In our president's world, non-racialism is the governing principle of true Africanism.[17]

The ANC's head of presidency Smuts Ngonyama followed the same line of argument and concurred:

Xolela Mangcu's broadside against president Thabo Mbeki and the African National Congress (ANC) in his article, 'Cryptic Mbeki Runs Risk of Losing Touch with Common People' (12 February), betrays a deeply insecure intellectual who chooses conjecture over fact. While he claims never to have met the president, he nevertheless ventures out and casts deep aspersions on his person and integrity. The average reader would assume that his admission that he has never met the president would suggest that he is less than qualified to make the kind of judgement he makes. The fact that he has never met Mbeki is indeed telling, as we are certain numerous opportunities had presented themselves to him, but he failed to oblige. Selective amnesia has never made a man honourable, and it certainly does not make the writer seem any more intelligent . . .

Mangcu makes an issue out of the president's quotation of Ingrid Jonker and Rian Malan. It is mind boggling why it should be wrong for the president to acknowledge South Africans like Jonker and Malan. Is he perhaps suggesting they are less South

African because they are white? Mbeki is the president of SA, a multi-racial nation that has acknowledged every one of its citizens across the racial spectrum as an equal citizen. Mangcu continues his tirade and ridicules the president when he remarks that there are people who refuse to think in our society, and misses the context entirely. It is indeed true that there are many in this country who are fixated to a particular point of view and do not want to look at issues from others' point of view. Those are the people who refuse to think and see the bigger picture. Those are the kind of people who do not make any meaningful contribution to our national discourse . . . We believe a person of Mangcu's calibre has an incredible role to play in shaping our future discourse. It is rather unfortunate that he chose not to take up the challenge to play a meaningful role in building our nation. The ANC believes that African scholars like Mangcu can and should become beacons of hope and inspiration to the rest of the nation.[18]

Troubled by the tone and language of these letters Njabulo Ndebele chimed in with this response:

Sir – I have always found Dr Xolela Mangcu's column thoughtful and insightful. He has consistently come across as a genuinely concerned and candid commentator on a range of public issues, persuading most people who read him that his views deserve serious consideration. In this, he is often provocative and succeeds in eliciting sometimes very robust public reaction. I do not believe that he, nor anyone else who dares to express considered opinions, deserves the *ad hominem* attack that presidential spokesman Bheki Khumalo made in his letter (19 February). It is not too much to expect of the presidential spokesman to enhance rather than diminish public discourse. In my view Mangcu's 'offending' article could have been better viewed as feedback for the president's speech writers who have to understand a complex national environment and then grapple, I suspect, with the search for appropriate and most effective rhetorical strategies to achieve desired effects in the president's speeches. A response in this regard could have helped the public better understand the challenges of preparing the president's speeches. Instead, righteous indignation has left us in the dark. An opportunity to clarify has been lost.[19]

But it is really Heifetz who describes what I think is at the root of Mbeki's leadership failure: 'the lone warrior model of leadership'.[20] The irony is that Mbeki fits snugly within South Africa's long history of strong warrior models of leadership – from early Afrikaner leaders such as Smuts, Hertzog, Verwoerd, Botha and De Klerk. The political party was central to the implementation of their segregationist vision, and without fail they unquestioningly followed their leaders. Unfortunately, Mbeki's self-image as a philosopher-king reinforced this historical leadership mould, and he ended up fighting all kinds of battles, with all the mishaps that entails. But as Heifetz argues: '. . . leadership cannot be exercised alone. The lone warrior model of leadership is heroic suicide. Each of us has blind spots that require the vision of others.'[21]

In a rebuke of the philosopher-king model of leadership, Wills argues that the paradox of great intellectual leaders – which is Mbeki's greatest aspiration – is that their leadership comes from a perception of the absence of knowledge: 'the great teacher is the strategically igno-Intellectual'.[22] Thus the late Mwalimu Julius Nyerere defined leadership as the ability to say 'I don't know'. Or as Benjamin Barber puts it: 'Public officials displaying an omnicompetent mastery of their public responsibilities unburden private men and women of their public responsibilities.'[23] This results in what psychoanalysts call work avoidance, with citizens constantly passing the buck to The Great Leader. And then before we know it we cannot imagine ourselves without his leadership. The future is inconceivable without him. As Barber comments: 'The people are apt to cry "What will we do without him?" and doubt whether they can go on. What is really only a departure is experienced as a loss and an incapacitation.'[24] This sense of incapacitation partly explains calls for Mbeki to make himself available for a third term as president of the ANC. I have raised my own objections to such a possibility:

Here are ten reasons why President Thabo Mbeki should reject calls for a third term as party president coming from certain sections of the African National Congress in the Eastern Cape. First, such a development would take the ANC down the slippery slope of one-man rule. A party that stays in the thrall of one individual is veering dangerously close to changing the constitution to extend his stay as leader of the country. I may have been brought up differently but there is something quite unseemly and downright pathetic about a whole group of adults being so fixated on another adult that they would mortgage their fate to him. Where I come from bright people never got the kind of adulation Mbeki gets from certain sections of the ANC, and that's because there were always other equally bright and assertive people around them. Second, we know the horrors of one-man rule from the experience of other African countries, with Zimbabwe being the latest example . . . Third, the call for a third term for Mbeki could lead us to a tribal conflagration like we have not seen in our democracy. The call could be interpreted by all sorts of ethnic entrepreneurs as yet another attempt by the Xhosas to hold on to power. Mbeki and Zuma should forestall such tribal Armageddon by gracefully exiting from the political stage. It is outrageous for people to suggest that the ANC lacks leaders. What about Cyril Ramaphosa, Tokyo Sexwale, Mosiuoa Lekota, Kgalema Motlanthe and many others? Fourth, a Mbeki third term would be more of the same in terms of public policy. For years Mbeki has refused calls to become a champion in the battle against HIV/AIDS – the most devastating public policy problem of our times. We would likely see more of the same also in terms of government's economic policy, leading to endless battles with other members of the Tripartite Alliance. Fifth, perhaps such battles would bring forward the prospects of a split in the ANC. An emboldened Mbeki might be tempted to ostracize the ANC's alliance partners even further. At the moment the alliance partners do not have a political champion. Such a champion could emerge from within the ANC were Mbeki to be elected for another term. The development of such a left-wing opposition could augur well for our democracy but I doubt Mbeki would want to go down in history as the person under whose leadership the ANC split. Sixth, the call for a third term is a

146

political gambit that could backfire with increasing vocal opposition from within the ANC in other provinces, and could ultimately leave the president with egg on his face. Already delegates at the Eastern Cape conference give different accounts of what actually transpired putting into doubt the authenticity of the call. Seventh, even if Mbeki were to adopt a reconciliatory approach to his opponents within the movement he would be hobbled to act against powerful individuals by the desire to hold the party together, and to get backing for his preferred successor. In my view Mbeki's inaction against Jackie Selebi has more to do with internal balance of power issues than anything else. After all, Jacob Zuma was dismissed for something far less sinister than what is being alleged against Selebi. Eighth, governance could be reduced to the fending off of rivals, a classic case of power for power's sake. As political analyst Thabo Rapoo argues, as former head of state Mbeki might be tempted to intervene in the processes of government from behind the scenes. Ninth, growing perceptions of tribal, political and criminal instability would put South Africa's prospects of hosting the World Cup in further jeopardy. Tenth, this country needs a changing of the guard – a fresh face, a fresh soul and a fresh voice. That would send such a powerful, evocative message to the world – a leadership change without a gunshot being fired. Nelson Mandela left us a wonderful legacy when he stepped down from just one term in office. Surely two terms must be enough for Mr Mbeki?[25]

The NEC of the ANC and most of the provinces seem acutely alive to the danger posed by Mbeki's quest for a third term. At an NEC meeting Mbeki's supporters suggested that the NEC should compile a list of consensus candidates that would then be presented to the branches for endorsement. Apparently Minister of Public Enterprises Alec Erwin was one of the most fervent supporters but came up against the opposition of people such as Matthews Phosa, who described the whole proposal as unethical. Most provinces also presented lists of people they would like to see as president and Mbeki found himself on the back foot, trying to fend off the challenge from ANC Deputy President Jacob Zuma's supporters. Influential organisations such as the ANC Youth League and the MK Veterans Association came out in support of Zuma.

Mbeki was increasingly isolated within his own party, adding to his sense of paranoia. One of the more bizarre demonstrations of this paranoia was when, early in his administration, Mbeki and his safety and security minister, Steve Tshwete, appeared on television to suggest that Cyril Ramaphosa, Tokyo Sexwale and Matthews Phosa – all of them respected ANC leaders – were plotting to overthrow his government. It was one of those moments that have unfortunately become characteristic of the Mbeki regime. A similar kind of paranoid intolerance was Mbeki's response to Archbishop Desmond Tutu's Nelson Mandela Lecture in 2004. Tutu pointed to a truism that is as old as the history of democratic thought itself – that a people unwilling to countenance dissent is a people blind to their collective possibilities. Tutu criticised the lack of debate in the ANC. Mbeki argued that Tutu was not a member of the ANC and thus could not presume to know what went on in the organisation. It was an unbelievable moment, this dressing down of one of our greatest icons on account of ANC membership. How convenient, I thought. After all there was a time when Mbeki would have been happy with Tutu's association with the ANC.

This shutting down of dissenting voices is unfortunately Mbeki's legacy. Those who dared to disagree have either been dressed down or fired from his cabinet. These include Jacob Zuma, Nozizwe Madlala-Routledge, Vusi Pikoli and Billy Masetlha. In one column I argued that we were saddled with an individual who having been elected by the people had simply risen above the people:

There is something sick at the core of our constitutional government. With time it is likely to consume us all.

At the heart of any constitutional democracy is the principle of accountability. Literally this means accounting to those who have put you in a position of authority. Sometimes this is called reason-giving. I do not know how we got to a point where one individual does as he wishes without so much as seeing a need to explain himself to the public. It goes against every leadership tradition we have ever had in the liberation movement.

Our president goes about as if we are in a monarchy and he is the king. Perhaps even more troubling is that he could not care less how his decisions are received by the public or the political party he leads. The pattern is there for all to see. First, it was Jacob Zuma. The ink had hardly dried on Judge Hilary Squires's judgment on Schabir Shaik than Mbeki fired Jacob Zuma as the deputy president of the country. For someone in such a senior position in the party and in the government a little more reason-giving both to the party and the public would have been the right thing to do.

When Zuma was fired I suggested that Mbeki was signalling for all who dared to listen that his prerogative is more important than any attempt to make peace with the alliance partners or Zuma supporters. He signalled this by the way in which he fired Zuma. In the midst of congratulations about the president's decisiveness, I asked myself whether the president should not have waited until Zuma had been charged before firing him.

There have been several casualties since then, and it's the same story over and over again: a breakdown in relationships. The best way to avoid explaining yourself is simply to say there has been a breakdown in communications. What the breakdown consists of, why and how it happened are details the president need not bother himself with.

What country would we be living in if bosses willy-nilly fired their subordinates with such ease? There is something of a contempt for the citizenry in all of this. I did not know that public servants are paid to be servants or friends with their bosses. But even being friendly with the boss is no guarantee. Look at Billy Masetlha reduced to crying in public because of what he calls Mbeki's betrayal. Again we were simply informed that there was a breakdown in the relationship with Mbeki, and Masetlha had to see his way to the door. And now Masetlha is going around saying embarrassing things about the president, including that Govan Mbeki did not approve of his son's elevation to the leadership: 'akakavuthwa lo mfana nje'. Oh, and then there is the case of Nozizwe Madlala-Routledge who was fired because she took an unauthorised trip to an HIV/AIDS conference in Spain. The whole thing smacked of vengeance when she was made to pay all kinds of money to the government.

149

And now it is Vusi Pikoli, supposedly one of Mbeki's trusted lieutenants. Again we are left groping for answers with opposition leaders demeaning themselves by going to the Union Buildings for answers.[26]

It was COSATU, one of the ANC's partners in the Tripartite Alliance, which summed up Mbeki's legacy. COSATU raised questions about conflicts of interest around one of the 2010 projects, the construction of Gautrain, a high-speed railway between Johannesburg and Tshwane. Mbeki responded by questioning the organisation's integrity, to which it replied:

We find it particularly offensive that President Mbeki has seen fit to play the race card in a manner that suggests that the people with business interests – whom he is defending – are somehow blacker than the working class components of the Alliance.

Moreover the President's style of engagement leaves much to be desired. He never debates on the strength of his arguments or correctness of the points he is raising. He always seeks to misrepresent people's genuine concerns in order to ridicule those he disagrees with and question their integrity. He throws the race card even against organisations whose membership is constituted mainly by the very ANC members he is leading. In the process of doing so he has antagonised countless organisations and left the ANC and the Alliance fractious and deeply divided.[27]

I went further with my own commentary on Mbeki's profound failure of leadership by describing him as representing 'the end of black political morality':

Thabo Mbeki has come to represent a completely new phenomenon in black politics: he represents the end of black political morality. I want to be careful here by what I mean by morality; I use the term in its deep and strictly philosophical sense.

Morality is not, as is often assumed, a matter of self-righteousness. Morality is simply what we owe to each other.

In his wonderful book The Ethics of Identity, *Kwame Anthony Appiah makes a distinction between ethics and morality. The ethical ideal is what it would take for any individual to lead a successful and meaningful life. The moral ideal is what individuals owe each other. The saying* umntu ngumntu ngabantu *is an expression of both ideals at work. To be* umntu *in an ethical sense depends on what we individually need to do to make ourselves successful and meaningful, but that depends on* abantu *and what they make possible for us to succeed. Of all our ethical needs we have as individual human beings, there is none as dependent on the morality of others as our survival. Our survival depends on what society makes possible . . .*

Since 1789, no political movement has played a greater role in the evolution of democracy than the black political movements, particularly the decolonization movements in Africa. Our greatest achievement was pushing humanity to embrace in so many ways the values of human solidarity. That is our claim to civilization – being at the centre of human morality despite all the vicissitudes of slavery, colonialism and apartheid and neoliberalism. As Steve Biko put it, despite all of the technological and military achievements of the West, the contribution of Africa would be to give to the world a more human face. Biko was very clear about what this human face meant: it was what we owe to each other, black political morality.

What does this have to do with Thabo Mbeki in present day South Africa? If it is indeed true that survival is at the heart of our ethical desires, then there is no greater moral responsibility societies have than safeguarding the survival of their citizens. There will always be contending values and interests – from protection of private interests to education to public transport to economic growth. But I can think of no more important moral responsibility for society than the health of its individual citizens – when they are at their loneliest and most vulnerable. As I put it in one of my columns, in the Eastern Cape you send your relatives to public hospitals for them only to die.

This is not mere theoretical postulation on my part. I have watched hopelessly and helplessly as my mother, my aunt and several other relatives died in Eastern Cape hospitals because they needed medical operations that people like Manto Tshabalala-Msimang take for

151

granted. The distinguished writer Phyllis Ntantala wrote an article not long ago in which she lamented the disgraceful state of Eastern Cape hospitals. There is no reason that Manto Tshabalala-Msimang should have more privileged status than my mother or Phyllis Ntantala or any other person. And yet we have a president who sees fit to protect her privileged treatment over other citizens.

We have a president who sees fit to question the experience of people who have actually experienced the horrors of our hospitals by saying what is happening there is statistically average.

In other words, we have a president who at every opportunity is always more interested in how clever he is than in empathizing with the rest of the population. Thabo Mbeki is an aberration in the long history of black political morality. Our history tells us that we deserve better than his leadership.

As the ANC goes to elect a new leader in December they should find someone in whom we can proudly see our glorious history of moral leadership. We need to do this if we are to salvage our history, before we forget that we were once a good and caring people. It is therefore time for Mbeki to go.[28]

Chapter 9 discusses the election of Jacob Zuma as the ANC's new party president and what the implications of this are for the future of democracy in our country.

Will he Pull us back or Push us over the Brink?
Jacob Zuma and the Prospects for Democracy

HOW TIME FLIES. It seems like only yesterday that Nelson Mandela stood at attention ready to be sworn in as the first president of a democratic South Africa. Almost every leading statesman and -woman was here to witness the event for themselves and for their people. All over the world people stayed glued to their television sets in virtual communion with South Africa as we celebrated one of the greatest political moments of the twentieth century – the birth of a new country under the leadership of the most loved political leader in the world.

I have never felt more proud of my country. At academic conferences and seminars, at dinner parties, at musical and cultural events, the mere mention of South Africa captured people's interest. The conversations would turn on the miracle unfolding in South Africa. Even though I knew that our achievement was not a miracle, I enjoyed the voyeurism of it all.

Amilcar Cabral, a great African revolutionary, once warned his people to 'claim no easy victories'.[1] This applied with even greater force to me. I had never been part of the ANC. I came from the other side of the liberation movement, the Black Consciousness movement. We had rejected the ANC's non-racialist approach to the liberation struggle even though we always insisted on building a democratic, non-racial society. Our political strategy, based on an exclusivist radicalism inspired by Steve Biko, succeeded in giving ownership of the struggle back to black people in the 1970s and in restoring pride and dignity to a people under the barrage of white supremacist doctrine. But our movement became a victim of its own success. The youths we had conscientised had swelled the ranks of the ANC military wing, Umkhonto we Sizwe, in exile. The liberals we had criticised became radicals. They did exactly as we had asked them, which was to organise in their communities. They became part of a militant groundswell against apartheid that ultimately became part of the UDF in the 1980s. Our movement, the Azanian People's Organisation, simply failed to adapt to the changing times, and to build new allies.

One of the worst mistakes – and perhaps an indication of how irrelevant we had become – came in 1985 when we staged a boycott against American politician Senator Edward Kennedy, one of the most well-respected and influential allies of our struggle. Kennedy was in South Africa as a guest of Desmond Tutu, and all we could do was to go to the airports with our placards: 'Yankee go home!' The mere thought of it makes me feel so embarrassed.

The UDF and the civic organisations took the initiative and mobilised the entire country into action – following to the letter Oliver Tambo's call to make the country 'ungovernable'. By the late 1980s the civic movements were part of new local government forums all over the country, prefiguring the emergence of new local government authorities in the 1990s. This went hand in hand with national-level negotiations and ultimately led to the announcement of democratic elections – an event brought forward by the murder of Chris Hani in 1993. That was the only way to avert further bloodshed.

Mandela governed with the assistance of F.W. de Klerk and the younger, princely Thabo Mbeki. Mandela had wanted Cyril Ramaphosa to succeed him as president but Mbeki had been groomed from exile for this moment. Mbeki was to be to Mandela what Nehru had been to Gandhi or what Jefferson had been to Washington, a worthy successor – or so we thought. Then with remarkable rapidity things began to change for the worse.

Mbeki put in place a celebrated programme of economic restructuring and stability. It was, however, not celebrated by those who saw their economic fortunes decline as unemployment and poverty took a toll on the quality of life in most black communities. The political temperature began to rise with Mbeki taking to calling his critics racists or foot lickers of the white system. The language and tone of the discourse became more coarse. And then there was Mbeki's denial of the greatest public health problem facing the country: HIV/AIDS. What has transpired since then has been surreal.

Fourteen years ago I never would have predicted that a country that was the toast of the free world would become the butt of jokes over its leadership's refusal to acknowledge that HIV was killing its population at unprecedented levels. Back in 1994 I never would have imagined that we would provide cover for a brutal dictator, Robert Mugabe, under the guise of black nationalism. I would have laughed anyone out of the room if they had dared to suggest that some of our political leaders would be carried shoulder high by their supporters to prison to serve time for corruption. The most surreal incident would be the president's suspension of the national director of public prosecutions for issuing a warrant of arrest for the national police commissioner who is suspected of ties to the South African criminal underworld. The last thing I would have believed was that just over a decade after our freedom the ANC would be split down the middle because of what *Sunday Times* editor Mondli Makhanya calls 'that darn arms deal': 'the deal that poisoned our souls and turned our heroes into grubby mortals. It was the arms deal that made corruption okay, and made good liberation fighters realise just how easy it is to cheat their people.'[2]

Who would have thought that an arms deal would implicate the deputy president of the country in the solicitation of a kickback, and that there would be calls to investigate the country's president for possible corruption in that same arms deal? And barely a decade after Nelson Mandela had gracefully exited the political stage, his successor was manoeuvring to cling to power for a third term as president of the ANC. Thankfully, members of his party would have none of it. This all happened so quickly that the African writer Ayi Kwei Armah could have been describing Mbeki's South Africa in this passage: 'How horribly rapid everything has been, from the days when men were not ashamed to talk of souls and of suffering and of hope, to these low days of smiles that will never again be sly enough to hide the knowledge of betrayal and deceit. There is something of an irresistible horror in such quick decay.'[3]

The irony of ironies is that the person most publicly identified with the arms deal has been the one to gain the most politically because of a strong anti-Mbeki sentiment in the ANC – the prevailing view being that Mbeki uses state power to persecute his political enemies. That at least has been part of Jacob Zuma's political mobilisation for the presidency of the ANC. In one of the most remarkable political comebacks in history, Zuma unseated Mbeki from the presidency at the much anticipated ANC leadership conference in Polokwane in December 2007. Zuma obtained 2 329 votes and Mbeki 1 505, a wide margin that reflects Mbeki's unpopularity within the party. Now that Zuma has been successful, the question is: what kind of leader will he make, both in his capacity as president of the party and as the person in pole position to be the president of the country in 2009?

Naturally and understandably the South African public has been asking how it is that a man implicated in bribery allegations and in a damaging rape trial could still even be considered for the exalted position of the president of the country. Where will Zuma get the authority and legitimacy to speak about HIV/AIDS after sleeping with an HIV positive woman and then claiming that he had a shower to protect himself from the disease? How will he speak with any authority and legitimacy when he is still under a cloud of suspicion for corruption? How will the public trust a man who has surrounded himself with characters such as convicted fraudster Schabir Shaik? These are all important questions and it will take some doing for Zuma to be seen with an untainted eye.

A different set of questions for Zuma

The reality of the situation is that Jacob Zuma has been elected by the majority of the members of his party. Whatever our feelings about his social behaviour, Zuma is the president of the ANC. I wrote a column in the *Sunday Times* in early December 2007 in which I urged South Africans to accept the outcomes of the courts and of legally constituted electoral processes. Failure to do so would lead to the same kind of mob rule that critics of Jacob Zuma claim to fear:

> *I have never understood the idea of President Thabo Mbeki as an enigma. Mbeki is just like any other African leader who cannot resist the lure of power. I always thought I was alone in that observation but by the look of things the majority of ANC branches seem to be feeling the same way.*
>
> *The president must have been shocked by the drubbing he received at the hands of his comrades during the nominations for the ANC presidency. I suspect he will get an even bigger thrashing if he should proceed to contest Jacob Zuma in three weeks' time; the ANC leadership conference would go down as the biggest repudiation of any sitting president in ANC history.*
>
> *It is indeed ironic that this should be the repudiation of a man who saw himself as the only rightful heir of the ANC's leadership mantle. In that self-perception Mbeki committed one fatal political error: he acted like an oligarch in a country with strong democratic traditions. He took members of his own party for granted, and some might even say abused them. His stay in power is littered with all manner of political corpses – with only one that refuses to die. With each and every stab, Zuma seems to rise from the dead.*
>
> *My purpose here is to make a few observations about how important the nomination process has been for South Africa, and how better to analyze the prospects for democracy under a Zuma presidency. First, in a society where one party is as dominant as the ANC it is vitally important that democracy be cultivated within the party. Political plurality is now the ANC leadership challenge, as never before. Second, the nomination process demonstrated the power of ordinary people when they are well mobilized – even against a strong*

state-backed candidate. Mbeki has been the beneficiary of all kinds of propaganda – SABC nightly news, pro-third-term newspapers, and all manner of biographies on the eve of the leadership elections.

The ANC in government has to find a way of keeping this base energized if it is to keep communities engaged with policy processes. An energized base will also provide a ready bulwark should Zuma start behaving like Mbeki.

Third, in the long-term interests of our democracy, Mbeki's campaigners should respect the decisions of legitimately constituted electoral and judicial processes.

Zuma was acquitted on rape charges by a court of law, and has yet to be found guilty of corruption by a court of law. Democracy requires that our passions should never substitute for respect for the law.

It would be ironic if it were to be Mbeki who undermined the decisions of our courts by constantly speaking of 'rapists and criminals' in his political rhetoric. Even though Mbeki has denied this is a reference to Zuma, the rhetorical style is classic Mbeki. He has long relied on a form of political argumentation that I can only describe in isiXhosa as 'ukukwekwa' – a form of argumentation by indirect allusion and never through direct engagement. Hence his constant reference to those he disapproves of as 'some among us,' without referring to them directly.

Another example comes from the HIV/AIDS controversy. The president could pose a rhetorical question about whether it is really possible for a virus (HIV) to ever cause a syndrome (AIDS). This enables his defenders to deny he ever denied the HIV/AIDS link thus: 'Where is the exact sentence where the president ever said HIV does not cause AIDS?' Yet the denial is there in the rhetorical question itself.

Similarly, it is hard to believe that the references to 'rapists and criminals' are not directed at Zuma. These rather self-indulgent language and rhetorical games may make a philosophy seminar a little more interesting, or be interesting kindergarten riddles, but they can never fool an adult citizenry all of the time. At least that is what the nomination outcomes seem to be suggesting. The consequences of this fake intellectual formalism are deadly, whether we are talking about HIV/AIDS or the integrity of our justice system.

The Zuma affair raises an interesting question about the relationship between the private morality and the public morality of elected officials. My own view is that while a leader's private morality may compromise his or her ability to lead, a leader's public morality may not always be reduced to his or her private morality.

An example of a leader whose private morality affected his public duties was the nineteenth century American president, Martin van Buren. Van Buren was known to disappear from work for weeks on end on account of his drinking.

But equally there are those leaders – Franklin Roosevelt, John F. Kennedy, François Mitterand, Bill Clinton – whose questionable relationships never detracted from their public achievements or what Hannah Arendt would call their 'public virtuosity.'

The question to ask is whether Zuma is so incapacitated by the scandals of his personal life. But even if we think that to be the case, we must still respect the outcome of the democratic processes. Failure to do so would be the real precedent for mob rule.

Finally, in evaluating the prospects for democracy under a Zuma presidency, we should also bear in mind the institutional and cultural matrix within which any leader would have to operate: parliament, the courts, the media, the ANC and civil society.

If the rejection of Mbeki by the ANC is anything to go by, there is no reason why Zuma should be so powerful as to be beyond the recall of this institutional and cultural matrix.

If I had my way I would have neither of these folks as my leader. This country is way ahead of both of them.

But if you put a gun to my head, then I would have to go with Zuma. Better to confront the Zuma challenge now than go down the path of the leader-for-life model that Mbeki represents.[4]

What type of questions might a worried public ask about Zuma? Well, I posed some of these questions in one of my *Business Day* columns. Put together, the questions are about whether Zuma's private morality is so egregious as to hobble his ability to run a government and become the leader of a nation:

If Zuma should not be charged, and enter the ring as a candidate for the presidency his supporters would have to answer at least four questions. The first question is whether Zuma's corruption is congenital – in which case we definitely don't want him as our president – or whether we are dealing with a lapse in judgement? . . .

If Zuma can in the interim show remorse for his lapse in judgement we may give him another chance. But then such forgiveness would have to be taken in conjunction with consideration of a second question: Would Zuma come out of this gruelling experience a bitter man, ready to take revenge on those who 'persecuted' him? This would lead to even greater degrees of polarization than we currently have, both within the ANC and the country at large. Consideration would have to be given to whether Zuma can separate his personal feelings about perceived or real 'enemies' from the intellectual, political and social contributions they could make to his overall agenda.

Zuma's ability to compartmentalize would in turn depend on the answer to a third question: Is he a democrat by disposition? Oftentimes we complain about today's centralized authoritarian political culture. However, just as bad, if not worse, would be a form of decentralized civic authoritarianism – the kind we experienced with the intolerance of some of the civic movements of the 1980s.

Would Zuma be the kind of president who could retain autonomy from his grassroots backers or would he be so beholden as to be stymied by their demands? The Schabir Shaik trial shows a picture of someone beholden to his financiers, but can he change and overcome that weakness, if it is indeed proven to be a weakness. This is important given the multiple interest groups that one way or another seek access to the highest office in the land.

The fourth question is whether Zuma's lack of formal schooling would lead to insecurity about his ability to lead the nation? Given his record I see no reason for suspecting such insecurities. He could well use his story of overcoming adversity as a leitmotif for inspiring the young and marginalized. In recent weeks I have been arguing against the idea of a president who is also an intellectual. Such leaders tend to do the thinking for the nation . . . What we need is a leader who can call on us to think and act together – that's the true meaning of democracy.[5]

Zuma has done very little to bring the nation into his confidence on these questions. The reluctance to open up is partly a function of the politics of the ANC. Zuma may feel that he has explained himself to the ANC, and that is all that matters. He is too much of a party man to engage seriously with the public on these questions.

This is not to say that Zuma is not a people's person, or that he would not be good at building bridges and relationships with communities. In that respect he would be a welcome break from Thabo Mbeki's distance and aloofness.

Zuma and Mbeki: The 'benevolent chief' and the 'stuffed shirt'
I once asked an ANC and Communist Party veteran to describe Zuma's leadership style for me. 'He is Mandela-esque in a feudalistic kind of way,' he explained. Like a chief in a village Zuma likes to have many people and many different voices around him. The ANC and the Tripartite Alliance are constituent parts of his village. He reached out to the other members of the Tripartite Alliance, even as they came under heavy attack from the ANC leadership. In short, he is not the kind of person to banish from the room those with whom he disagrees. He does not see it as beneath him to reach out to political opponents, which probably explains his success in bringing about peace between the warring ANC and Inkatha Freedom Party factions in KwaZulu-Natal. Zuma's supporters even claim that the only sustainable peace process in Africa is the one he presided over in Burundi. There might be some spin in that, but the point is well made: Zuma has earned a reputation as a peace builder.

However, the idea that he is 'Mandela-esque in a feudalistic kind of way' also means he is a conservative traditionalist in his social views about women and homosexuals. He once castigated same-sex marriages as 'a disgrace to the nation and to God'. He used the derogatory Zulu word for homosexuals: 'When I was growing up, *ungqingili* [homosexuals] could not stand in front of me.'6 For Zuma there is no greater earthly authority than the ANC, which he joined when he was only seventeen years old. The organisation is such an important part of his outlook that he often proclaims that the party will rule until the Second Coming of Jesus. He has an unquestioning reverence for the ANC that one usually sees only in religious groups. While he is accommodating of different views, his dismissal of those who are not part of the ANC 'religion' can be quite condescending and patronising. By his reckoning, those who criticise do so because they do not understand the ANC, and in fact can never understand the ANC unless they join it.

This is a radically different reaction to criticism from what we have come to expect from Mbeki. For Mbeki those who criticise the ANC do so because they want to undermine the organisation. Critics are enemies. Zuma sees critics as wayward individuals who can be won over by persuasion about the rightness of the ANC. While Mbeki's instinct would be to isolate and ultimately banish, Zuma's instinct would be to proselytise and win over. Zuma's reputation as a peace builder may stem from this sense that others can be persuaded to come around to his position.

These radically variant political temperaments will lead to different leadership styles. The question is whether Jacob Zuma can be persuaded to see things differently from his ideological certitudes. This is important if he is going to avoid the gargantuan mistakes of his predecessor.

What characterised Mbeki's presidency was a strong resistance to the idea that he might be taking his cue from other people, let alone that he might be wrong. Frederick van Zyl Slabbert, a South African political analyst, captures Mbeki's leadership style as follows: 'One of the dilemmas of our very important, intellectual President is that he has what I call Andy Capp's disease: he has many [faults] but being wrong is not one of them.'[7]

Mbeki and Zuma are also different kinds of nationalists. All nationalists are driven by a search of identity of one sort or the other. However, they do not always do so in similar ways. Mbeki's search is intellectual and abstract, and Zuma's is through a mix of militarism and tradition. While the former is pursued as a lone project, the latter finds expression through symbolic appeals to community. Both can manifest in perverted ways.

According to Mark Gevisser's empathetic biography, *A Dream Deferred*, Mbeki is an intellectual nationalist in search of an identity. Gevisser effectively argues that Mbeki was disconnected from his roots and from his community from a very early age. Gevisser lays much of the blame for this on Mbeki's father, Govan, who abandoned his family in the

Transkei while he joined the broader family of the struggle. The young Mbeki so much wanted to be like his father that he too soon joined the revolution and began to look at the world in the same unsentimental fashion as his atheist, communist father.

In an interview for Gevisser's book Mbeki's mother says the children were not allowed to play in the streets with other boys after school. She recalls: 'There was to be no lolling about in the village with other boys. No aimless roaming about.'[8] Gevisser quotes Mbeki attesting to the disconnection thus: 'We were sort of disconnected from many things in the surroundings. Growing up among these *amaqaba*, we lived with them and all that, but we were not *amaqaba*. So in that sense we were disconnected: you can see it, you live in it, but it is not you.'[9] An even more revealing passage comes from his mother's recollection of Mbeki's response to an invitation to his birthplace: 'I've told Thabo the villagers want to see him. But he told me that this is the very last village in the whole of South Africa he will ever come to.' According to Gevisser, Mbeki's 'modernism does not seem to sit easily with the conventions of being a member of a clan, of having a "home-town" or roots. There is no apparent nostalgia for the tobacco-and-cowdung-scented hills of the Transkei. One senses it is little more than a place, like many other places, that must be improved.'[10]

This explains many things about Thabo Mbeki's political and policy leadership. To him human beings are an abstraction whose fortune can be improved by application of scientific methods and economic progress – no room or time for sentimentality there. Gevisser argues that Mbeki's disconnectedness is not an entirely bad thing because it allows him to have some remove and thus gives him a certain degree of objectivity about the world, or what he describes as 'relative freedom from the feudal constraints of traditional hierarchies'.[11]

Gevisser has come under intense criticism – including from me – for a psycho-biographical explanation of Mbeki that seems to excuse him from the political choices he has made and the shifts and alliances he has brought about over the years as a scheming adult politician. I have also argued that there are many leaders who have had far worse personal experiences than Mbeki, who was the child of two university graduates who owned a shop in a rural village. It did not get more privileged than that in the black community under apartheid. This is perhaps why Govan Mbeki rejected the hardship of his children with a dismissive and perhaps even defensive flourish: 'I don't think they lost out on anything. They grew up well.'[12] Gevisser is not to be easily discouraged. He writes about the pain of a young Mbeki who had to read the letters of migrant labourers to their families. This led to a loss of Mbeki's childhood innocence. But, as Gevisser himself points out, Chris Hani was doing the same thing in his village in another part of the Transkei: 'But Mbeki seems to have responded to it in a particularly profound way.'[13] It is not immediately clear why Mbeki's response would have been any more profound than Hani's. This profundity extends from Mbeki's youth and later translates directly into the theme of his government, the African Renaissance: 'It is no coincidence that Thabo Mbeki first started talking about an "African Renaissance" publicly at around the time he was "called back home by the elders of his clan".'[14] Gevisser might as well trace Mbeki's position on HIV/AIDS, on GEAR, on Zimbabwe, on the arms deal to his childhood experience. Gevisser further insists that Mbeki's independence of mind also comes from this childhood experience. He would be willing to go against the world before kowtowing to popular opinion.

Garry Wills mocks this independence in leaders: 'That may be a proper credential for the lonely genius, the martyr to a truth, the austere intellect-people who forge their own souls in fierce independence. But what have such heroes to do with leading other people?'[15] Unfortunately that's the kind of nationalist intellectual Mbeki became.

When Gevisser launched his book at Wits University, I asked him why we should all be implicated in Mbeki's search for identity; why was it our business? I never really got an answer back. But what I should have said in addition is that the mark of a great leader is not someone who collapses under the weight of his or her own history, but one who uses that personal history to inspire others to greatness. It is not the leader's psychological baggage that matters, but the psychological freedom the leader gives to the people – indeed, drawing on his or her own troubled past. For example, Franklin Delano Roosevelt understood what was ailing the American people during the Great Depression. He understood that the best psychological response was to tell them that their salvation lay in their own hands. If he, a man suffering from polio, could have confidence in recovery, so could the able-bodied men and women of the United States about their country. He became through his own difficult life-situation the nation's metaphor for recovery. He did not make his individual burden their collective burden.

Jacob Zuma had a much harder upbringing in the rural village of Inkandla in northern KwaZulu-Natal than Mbeki would ever have had. Perhaps no one would have had a greater claim on history to explain his wayward behaviour than Zuma. But he has not come out to say 'blame me on history' – at least not yet. He has embarrassed us a great deal with some of his shenanigans but, unlike Mbeki, he has not been shy to apologise for his gaffes, including his remarks about having a shower after sex to prevent the contraction of HIV.

Journalist Jeremy Gordin is reportedly writing an empathetic biography of Zuma. It will most likely portray Zuma as the opposite of Mbeki. Instead of disconnection we will find connection and rootedness in an extended rural family. It will most likely paint a picture of a rural boy who grew up 'lolling about' with other kids, while retaining a sense of connectedness to family.

If Mbeki is a detribalised African, Zuma's tribal and ethnic identities are an important part of his identity. Ethnic identity is not in and of itself a bad thing for as long as identities are not essentialised as possessing innate qualities. But Zuma has been guilty of essentialism. An example is his comment during his rape trial that when a woman is dressed in a particular way, a Zulu man is duty-bound to respond to that as an invitation to sex. But his tribal essentialism comes across more as conservative traditionalism and machismo than as an expression of tribalism as a set of political beliefs.

Zuma is also acting out a typical nationalist script when he says the ANC will rule until the Second Coming. In more intellectual terms this is the idea that the nation never dies. Benedict Anderson described this phenomenon in his public lecture at Wits, with a reference to a famous passage about the nation's transcendental quality from German sociologist Max Weber:

If we could rise from the grave thousands of years from now, we would seek the traces of our own being in the physiognomy of the race of the future . . . we can wish that the future recognizes in our nature the nature of its own ancestors. We wish, by our labour and our being, to become the forefathers of the race of the future.[16]

Zuma promises the disenchanted that as the leader of the ANC he will hold the fort here on this earth until the Second Coming. To that extent he is what Achille Mbembe called '*umprofethi*' (a false prophet) leading an undifferentiated millenarian, eschatological movement. Like the nineteenth-century prophetess Nongqause who urged the Xhosa people to kill their cattle and burn their grain in anticipation of a new season of prosperity, Zuma will lead his people to self-annihilation.

However, Zuma's election as president of the ANC demonstrated something much more sophisticated at work here. In his book *Certain Trumpets*, Garry Wills gives a contrasting picture of two American politicians, Franklin Delano Roosevelt and Adlai Stevenson. In many ways Stevenson has all the makings of Thabo Mbeki. The child of a prominent political family in Illinois – his grandfather was vice-president to President Grover Cleveland – Stevenson fancied himself an intellectual. According to Wills:

Stevenson had noble ideas – as did the young Franklin for that matter. But Stevenson felt that the way to implement them was to present himself as a thoughtful idealist and wait for the world to flock to him. He considered it below him, or wrong, to scramble out among the people and ask what they wanted. Roosevelt grappled voters to him. Stevenson shied off from them.

Wills continues:

Liberal intellectuals stayed true to Stevenson in the 1950s despite misgivings, because they were horrified at what they took to be the anti-intellectual alternative of Dwight D. Eisenhower. It was literally inconceivable to these people that a rational electorate would prefer Ike to Adlai – which shows how far out of touch they were with the American people.[17]

This rings a bell, does it not? In the words of a letter writer to the *Business Day*, Pauline Morris: 'Thabo Mbeki represents a stuffed shirt from Sussex University, Zuma a benevolent chief from childhood.'[18] There has indeed been a great deal of incredulity among Mbeki's liberal-middle-class-intellectual support base at the fact that he was upstaged by his very antitype – the anti-intellectual Jacob Zuma.

Mbeki, the urbane, suave, whisky-drinking, pipe-smoking Renaissance man gave it all away when he said he did not understand what must have been going through the heads of the ANC Women's League when they rejected him in favour of Zuma for the presidency. The *Financial Mail* vividly captured elite angst in its headline: 'Be Afraid'.[19] But the person who most accurately reflected the sense of alienation of the media with what is going in South African society is Wits University academic Anton Harber:

> The blind spot, however, was to believe that Zuma's colourful record would make him unelectable. The real error was the assumption journalists often make: that their values are those of the wider society. Mbeki was cocooned in the presidency; and journalists are often cocooned in their own world, listening and talking to each other and their experts much more than to anyone else.[20]

But what was it about Roosevelt and Eisenhower that made them such effective and well-loved leaders? Despite differences in class background, the one thing that Jacob Zuma seems to share with Roosevelt is an instinctive connection to people. Roosevelt was physically impaired at a time when that was a stigma. He could have easily wallowed in his condition, and hit back at those who stigmatised 'cripples'. Instead, he used his condition to inspire the nation. Beyond his own personal biography Roosevelt was simply an excellent political leader. He understood the power of public opinion: 'If Roosevelt had power, it came precisely from his responsiveness to public opinion.'[21] At the centre of that responsiveness was his attitude to the media – using his fireside radio chats to reach far-flung places in what his listeners experienced as intimate conversation.

Central to any strategy of governance must be a smarter approach to the media from that which has prevailed under the Mbeki administration. *Business Day* journalist Renée Bonorchis captured the strategic role of the media for any administration: 'Rightly or wrongly, the way the press perceives the president is what makes it into the papers and goes on to shape public opinion.'[22] She uses the George Bush and Al Gore presidential campaigns as an example of how much of a difference the press can make: 'While George Bush was goofing around with reporters and playing on his down-home image, Gore kept himself aloof and his communications people went as far as to keep the press at arms length.' Bonorchis draws an analogy with the Mbeki and Zuma campaigns. Like Al Gore, Mbeki competed against a candidate 'who is good at relating to most people, if not all of the people'. That may well be Zuma's greatest strength – in his Mandela-esque but feudalistic kind of way.

Now that Zuma is indeed ANC president, he should put into practice this piece of advice from Bonorchis: 'If Zuma were to be the next president we would already know he has a low regard for the media. But that's not the point. As long as his communications people are able to engage the press and keep them close, then his previously tainted image will continue to be reworked.' Zuma's rantings against the media and analysts after his acquittal on rape charges may have been understandable, but he would be better advised to change his tack on this one.

This is related to an argument that Ronald Heifetz makes, and which I referred to in Chapter 8, which is how important it is for leaders not to take the work of public leadership personally. Leadership is an activity to be shared among a range of people with different skills and the prospects for democracy will depend as much on the leader as they will on the group who surrounds that person. If a leader is surrounded by a bunch of mediocre yes-men and -women, then the leader will find himself or herself speaking for almost all of them, and mangling up in the way Mbeki has done over the past decade or so. However, if well-qualified, competent and well-respected individuals are appointed, then the battle for a 'reworked image' will be half-won at the outset.

A man of the people or a wolf in sheep's skin?

One of Jacob Zuma's great challenges is that he will soon be confronted with a fractious alliance – and that will call for some tough decision making on his part. Contrary to the idea of an irrational, millenarian movement, what we have with Zuma is a well-organised political movement arranged around what the sociologist Ernesto Laclau describes as a 'populist frontier'. According to Laclau, populist movements are by definition political. They are all about the construction of a popular 'we'. Although I find Laclau's three-stage theory of populism a little formulaic, it is useful in understanding the Zuma phenomenon.

First, a whole series of disparate movements emerge to challenge the centralisation of power – but they all act in silos. The HIV/AIDS group fights its battles on its own, paying little attention to the anti-privatisation forum, or the freedom of expression group or environmental protection organisations. The populist movement does not really emerge until all groups move to the second stage, that is, until they have established what Laclau calls a populist frontier. The frontier attracts people and groups from across the political and ideological spectrum, inside and outside the production relationship. Hence Laclau describes populism more as a 'dimension of political culture' than an ideological movement.[23] A leading expert on populist movements, Harry Boyte, similarly argues that 'populism is not a text or dogma. It has no written codes, no finished works, no canons of orthodoxy.'[24] And this is when someone like Jacob Zuma emerges to hold a non-ideological frontier together. As Laclau puts it: 'Since any kind of institutional system is inevitably at least partially limiting and frustrating, there is something appealing about any figure who challenges it, whatever the reasons and forms of the challenge.'[25] In a sense our calls on Jacob Zuma to say what he really thinks are misplaced. No populist leader in his or her right mind would risk dividing their frontier by proclaiming on ideology.

The third stage is the most precarious. Once the populist movement attains power, the frontier begins to dissemble, partly because positions must now be taken: on the economy, on wages, on HIV/AIDS, etc. The once united populist front – from Black Economic Empowerment wannabes to ethnic entrepreneurs to fugitives from the law and the ever-dodgy lumpen proletariat – is not an ideologically coherent movement.

There is no reason why Zuma should escape this stage. In a sign of developments to come, COSATU has already complained about its representation on Zuma's national executive committee, insisting that there be a reduction in the number of delegates of one of the organisations in the frontier – the ANC Youth League. This tussle is unavoidable, and will be a great test of Zuma's Mandela-esque, feudalist leadership style.

However, it would be a mistake to say populism does not have any content. It may not have an ideology but it certainly has an orientation towards the small man and woman. In the following column I complained about the denigration of populism in the commentary about what kind of leader Jacob Zuma might become:

> *Would our writers, commentators, activists, politicians please stop misusing the term populism? I am amazed by how much of the political analysis of Jacob Zuma hangs on a mischaracterization of populism as irrational, delusional mob rule.*
>
> *Populism is one of the finest traditions in democratic history, based on the struggle of small men and women in farmers cooperatives against big business and political oligarchs in the nineteenth century. One of the world's leading authorities on populism, Lawrence Goodwyn, author of the classic book,* The Populist Moment, *argues that the very experience of existing as members of farmers' co-operatives required a deliberative culture among populists: 'Populists would not fear that people, once encouraged to be really candid with one another, would promptly want the moon and ask for too much.'*
>
> *The eminent sociologist Ernesto Laclau recently wrote a book titled* On Populist Reason, *so named deliberately to make the point that reasoning is at the heart of the populist political experience. The point is that all politics is populist to the extent that it is about the imagination of a new community. For example, there is no sentiment more populist than the first sentence of the preamble to our constitution: 'We the people of South Africa,' or the Freedom Charter's 'The people shall govern,' or the American Declaration of Independence's 'All people are created equal.'*
>
> *So how did such a noble concept come to be so misrepresented? We can trace it to a number of developments in the nineteenth century. First, the denigration of populism was nothing less than the rearguard*

response of business and political oligarchs fearing the rise of democratic movements. Second, populism was denigrated because it came up against the prophets of Enlightenment rationalism – for whom political rule was the preserve of only a few scientifically educated elite. Third, the misrepresentation of populism coincided with an important sociological shift in Europe – the break of the elites from their communities.

Gianna Pomata describes this break as follows: 'In 1500 educated people could despise the common people but still, to a certain extent, understood and shared their culture. By 1800, however, in most European countries, the clergy, the nobility, the merchants, the professional men had withdrawn from popular culture, abandoning it to the lower classes, from which they were now separated, as never before, by profound differences in worldview. By then, from the viewpoint of the learned, popular culture had become a thoroughly alien world.'

Each and every one of these reasons for the denigration of populism applies with equal force in present-day South Africa. The political elites are in a panic because suddenly 'the natives are restless.' The policy elites cry wolf because the assumptions of their development model are under attack. And this is not an unreasonable attack, given the poverty, unemployment and inequality and the concomitant culture of intolerance all over the place. And the social elites are frightened because they have been so alienated from their communities they can barely recognize their own people. So they choose to describe them as nothing more than an undifferentiated, irrational, deluded mob fit for voyeuristic conversation at the suburban dinner tables ...

Unfortunately, it is precisely because of this mischaracterization of populism that we have failed to ask the real political question of whether Zuma is a real populist. Does Zuma believe in the interests of the small man and woman or is he beholden to his financiers and behind-the-scenes lobbyists? What is it about his political programme and the political programme of the ANC that says they would restore power to the people in the finest populist traditions of the farmers' movements, trade union movements, civic movements and movements for community revitalization and entrepreneurship that gave rise to civic populism all over the world?

South Africa's problem is not populism, which is to be properly understood as the creation of a popular democracy. What Zuma's critics are perhaps searching for is a phrase that comes from Hannah Arendt's essay 'Law and Power', in which she identifies the usual three types of government – monarchy, aristocracy and democracy. Monarchy can easily slide into tyranny; aristocracy can easily slide into oligarchy; and democracy into ochlocracy – another word for mob rule.

So I am going to shriek the next time I hear anyone mischaracterize populism and I will smile wryly when I hear people asking whether with Zuma our democracy will slide not into populism but into ochlocracy.[26]

The question then is what manner of populist leader would Zuma become? Earlier I suggested that Mbeki adopted an overly intellectualised leadership style, alienating many people in the process. Zuma presents a different kind of problem: how exactly might the citizenry engage a leader who is convinced that his organisation has History, Tradition and God on its side? I have in my writings about the ANC presidential race often made a distinction between what the sociologists Richard Sennett and William Whyte respectively called 'public man' and 'organization man'.[27] Zuma is a true ANC cadre, but he is a master at using what Njabulo Ndebele calls 'spectacle'. When Zuma leads thousands in singing the popular revolutionary song 'Awuleth' Umshini Wam' (Bring me my Machine Gun), he is sending a clear message to party members and potential rivals: I have the support of the people.[28] As I argue in the above column, there is really nothing about Zuma's record in government that suggests he would return power to the people in the classic populist sense. Political analyst Steven Friedman describes Zuma as 'a mainstream figure who was a bosom buddy of Thabo Mbeki. He's not some wild man coming from the hills to destroy the palace.'[29] In addition, Zuma's primary loyalty is to the party before the public. One of Zuma's backers and an influential leader in Gauteng, Angie Motshekga, had this to say about a Zuma administration:

Some will ask whether anything will be different from the present administration. In this all ANC leaders are guided by its policies. Hopefully Zuma is the archetypal party man and will seek the genuine involvement of the party membership in this process, as well as its allies. The party, too, will be closer to the ordinary citizen so that it more accurately reflects their needs and concerns.

Motshekga argues that this connectedness will most likely be interpreted as populism: 'Much is being said about populism, careerism and about people who want to be elected so that they can steal from the public. The ordinary people and members of the ANC are not stupid. They know what is in their best interest.'[30] While Motshekga is right about the misrepresentation of people's movements by members of the economic and social elite, her populism is based in an unshakeable faith in the party. While Zuma may stabilise and unify the ANC at the present time, he is unlikely to be the kind of leader to take the country to the open society of our dreams (I will return later to a discussion of who the leaders of the future might be in the ANC).

Zuma as a transitional figure
Given both his age and his travails, Jacob Zuma is most likely to be a transitional figure hemmed in by his own self-consciousness about his misdemeanours, and by the institutional and cultural matrix within which he has to operate if he were to be the president of the country.

There are three possible scenarios in which Zuma can play this transitional figure. First, by setting the trial date for August 2008 the state has put Zuma at a clear political disadvantage with respect to the presidency of the country. The ANC has to meet six months before a general election to select a group of people it would put on its list of parliamentary representatives. The party would be reluctant to put at the head of its list someone who runs the risk of a conviction. Given that the election must take place before April 2009, the list process must take place in October 2008. If Zuma won in his application for a mistrial then he would have a better chance of gaining his party's nomination for the state presidency. Barring an early election Zuma would take over as the president of the country at the age of 67, and would be 71 at the end of his first term. He would finish his second term at the age of 76. This is not unheard of – Mandela was in his seventies when he was president.

The difference is that Zuma and his cohorts – the so-called Class of 1942 – come from a culture of exile, secrecy, solidarity and vertical hierarchy. And yet the world we live in demands openness, accountability and horizontal networks. It's a new world with new policy challenges – ranging from energy security to climate change to shifting geopolitical realities characterised by the emergence of China and India.

Even if Zuma were to serve for two terms, there can be no questioning that the ANC has come to the end of the leadership of the Class of 1942.

The second scenario would be one in which Zuma voluntarily stops short of making himself available for the presidency of the country. This could happen either before or after the mistrial application. His supporters would then most likely put their support behind one of two candidates: Kgalema Motlanthe or Tokyo Sexwale.

The third scenario is not much of a scenario were it not for the social consequences that would flow from it. In this scenario he would be found guilty and automatically barred from holding public office. However, a jail term for Zuma could lead to violence and instability. A political solution may have to be found as has been done in many other cases including, most recently, that of Adriaan Vlok, who was found guilty of atrocities but given a long suspended sentence. A presidential pardon as a quid pro quo for staying out of politics could be another option.

It is the first two scenarios that I am more interested in. Let us first examine what would happen if Zuma obtained a mistrial and became a 'transitional president' of the country.

A state president hemmed in by our institutional and cultural matrix

South Africa has a panoply of institutions that no single individual can ignore: parliament, the courts, the ANC NEC, as well as our resurgent and sophisticated constitution. And as I observed in the *Sunday Times* article above, Mbeki's mistake was to act like an oligarch in a community with strong democratic sentiments. Zuma's most feudalistic instincts will soon run into public challenges and demonstrations by women's groups; into court challenges by gay and lesbian groups; into a parliament that consists of people who never wanted him in the first place; and a media that were afraid of him to begin with. Each and every utterance he makes will come under instant national and international scrutiny with the currency as a proxy indicator of what the world thinks about us.

His biggest mistake would be arrogance and haste that comes out of what political scientist Richard Neustadt calls 'newsness', particularly in the closely watched and highly contested areas of economic policy and foreign affairs. Neustadt describes the dangers of a badly managed transition thus: 'Everywhere there is a sense of a page turning, a new chapter in the country's history, a new chance too. And with it irresistibly, there comes the sense, "they" couldn't, wouldn't, didn't but "we" will. We won so we can.'[31]

To guard against such triumphalism and its consequences we need to do more to strengthen our countervailing institutions – and that would apply even under the most loved president. Parliament is in desperate need of revitalisation. We inherited a parliament that has historically rubber-stamped executive decisions. In the apartheid years what the prime minister wanted, the prime minister got. Parliament was seen as one of the principal means by which Afrikaner nationalists sought to impose their Christian national vision on the rest of the population. Public policy was always a tussle between the powerful and ubiquitous secret think tank – the Broederbond – the party, the cabinet and the prime minister. Early nationalist leaders such as J.G. Strijdom tried to keep the Broederbond out of policy making, but Hendrik Verwoerd relied on the Broederbond before its influence declined again under John Vorster. At the height of its influence the Broederbond set up expert task groups to decide on various aspects of public policy.[32] Their recommendations would be presented to the prime minister and cabinet, and would get the sanction of the parliamentary caucus, which was in turn filled with Broederbond members. However, whether it was the Broederbond or the prime minister and his cabinet that prevailed at any given time, parliament played the least influential role. According to Dan O'Meara: 'It was not unusual for one or more MPs [Members of Parliament] to find themselves in conflict with this or that aspect of government policy. However, given the vast pressures to conform – not the least of which was each member's hopes of political advancement –

it was very rare for individuals or groups within the caucus to oppose cabinet policy openly.'[33]

So diminished was the role of the ordinary MP that one Dr Albert Hertzog complained bitterly:

> It strikes me more and more that the ordinary Member of Parliament actually has no say at all. If he wants to achieve anything, then he must go and speak with the Cabinet Ministers and quietly try to influence them, otherwise he will get nothing done. The Prime Minister chose his Ministers before even knowing us ordinary MPs, without first asking our own opinion. They make their appointments without taking the slightest notice of us. Without us the National Party could never have won. But the moment that he had won, together with a few of his old friends, this man whom they call the Prime Minister simply decides what they want. They take the whole machinery into their own hands, they accept our loyalty and they make and break us as they see fit.[34]

A great challenge facing South Africa is to revisit the role of parliamentarians in holding the executive accountable. One way of building such accountability would be to have some kind of direct constituency representation in the electoral system. Constituency representation is no guarantee that parliamentarians would not be victimised by party leaders, but at least the constituency would have an opportunity to weigh in and express its opinion, whether that is in support of its MPs or to recall them. The power of the executive in South Africa is palpable. For example, even though the constitution provides for parliament to change money bills, the ANC has not passed legislation authorising parliament to do so. Parliamentarians would rather look to the executive for authority than exercise their constitutional responsibilities. Another example of parliament's weakness and powerlessness is the manner in which the senior members of the cabinet intervened in the inquiry into the arms deal. According to former ANC MP Andrew Feinstein, Minister in the Presidency Essop Pahad literally instructed the parliamentary committee investigating the arms deal to lay off the investigation, saying:

'Who the fuck do you think you are, questioning the integrity of the government, the Ministers and the President?'[35]

Parliament needs to be revitalised so it can be the space where a new layer of leaders might find their way into the political system. As pointed out in Chapter 7, senior ANC leader Pallo Jordan has argued for a generational shift in the leadership of the ANC. One of the better ways to identify such leaders is to see them as they rise through parliament, having been directly elected by their constituencies.

Reimagining the relationship between the NEC, government and the public

Zuma also cannot run roughshod over the NEC of the ANC. True, many of the members of the NEC have been elected onto that list on his ticket, but it is hard to imagine an NEC that is as docile as the one under Mbeki. In many ways the ANC contributed to the creation of Mbeki's 'imperial presidency'.[36] At its 1997 leadership conference the NEC gave the president the power and prerogative to appoint premiers and mayors. The NEC became emasculated under Mbeki's presidency, and was packed with Mbeki's yes-men and -women, a sizeable number of whom served in his cabinet. Those were the people least likely to question the president's decisions and controversial public policy positions.

However, the ANC came to its senses at its July 2007 conference and stripped Mbeki of those powers of appointment. Mbeki had used this power to appoint his own people as premiers, and in the process alienated the provincial executive. From now the provincial executive committee will recommend the person to be the premier of a province.

This is not a bad thing. For as long as our electoral system says we should vote for the party then it is appropriate that the party should send its people into government. This must be done without the party micromanaging government and usurping the work of government employees. The practice of deploying party members to strategic institutions needs to be tempered by attention to professional competence and a sensitivity to the line between party and government. This is a tricky balance; it needs a party leadership that knows its limits, and a government leadership that knows the source of its legitimacy and authority.

While Mbeki tried faithfully to enforce the line when it suited his desire to come up with his own policies, he failed to appreciate that ultimately his authority came from the party. By keeping the ANC and its alliance partners outside the policy process, he undermined his own legitimacy and authority within the party. His supporters tried to justify his unilateralism in drafting the ANC's economic policy document. For example, as shown in Chapter 7, they argued that the departure from the RDP to GEAR was simply a function of the exigencies of everyday decision making – of what was required of another day in the office, if you like.

It is almost inconceivable that Mbeki could initiate such a major policy shift without paying attention to the party he represented in government. And yet he did. To have consulted with the ANC would not have amounted to micromanagement by the party. He probably feared that the party would not approve his economic programme – a programme whose outcomes were unsatisfactory, to say the least.

Jacob Zuma is therefore not very far off the mark when he says he will represent the interests of the party in government. It may well be that he does not have his own original ideas, but the more important question is whether the ANC, through its NEC, has any credible, original ideas of its own. If the party develops such a programme it can trust Jacob Zuma to implement it more than it could ever trust Thabo Mbeki.

However, the democratic challenge goes beyond the relationship between the ANC and the government – which Zuma could manage quite ably – and extends to the relationship of both to the broader population. The government is elected into power by a broader population than members of the ANC. In that sense it has to approximate as much as possible the classic populist maxim contained in the Freedom Charter: 'The people shall govern.' This immediately raises the question of how best to bring that into effect. One of the great ironies of democracy is that while leaders are often elected by the majority of the poor, they soon find themselves dancing to the tune of a rich few. It is this disjuncture that has given rise to the emergence of Jacob Zuma.

There are numerous models for participatory governance that a Zuma administration could study: from the Harold Washington administration in Chicago, which inspired American presidential hopeful Barack Obama's approach to politics and governance, to the experiences of progressive movements in places such as Kerala in India. Spain is an interesting example of how to deal with issues of diversity without compromising the national integrity of the country. Gordon Brown is experimenting with citizen participation in government policy making, and the November 5th coalition in the United States has put together citizen transition teams to influence public policy making in the new administration.

What many of these examples have demonstrated is that there is no necessary trade-off between issues of equity and participation on the one hand, and efficiency and rational administration on the other. New technologies should enable new forms of public participation in governance, and new public platforms need to be established to maintain constant communication with the general public, particularly at the local government level.

In other words, the ANC as a party and the ANC in government would need to reinvent itself as a public organisation. The centralised, technocratic approach of the Mbeki years has been disastrous for South Africa, and there is much to be gained by experimenting with new forms of participation – starting at the local government level.

Paving the way for a new leadership

There is another way in which Zuma could exercise his influence and in the process secure a place for himself in history. He could do this by voluntarily stepping aside for someone else to take over as state president while he retains the role of party president. He could even step down from the party presidency and become an elder statesman. That would require a special congress to elect a new president and that might have the added benefit of aligning the election of the ANC presidency and the state presidency.

Depending on how long the corruption trial takes, Zuma could use his role as party president to prepare for a smooth transition to a new kind of leadership in the ANC. It has been reported that Zuma's Plan B, or at least the Plan B that has been announced by his supporters, is that ANC Deputy President Kgalema Motlanthe should then be elected to take Zuma's position.

Motlanthe is not well known outside the ANC, but nothing has stopped lesser known figures in other parts of the continent from acceding to power. For example, how many people readily know who Sam Nujoma's successor is in Namibia?

Like Zuma, Motlanthe is a true 'organisation man', a comrade's comrade. Motlanthe is well liked by the rank and file of the ANC, and as a former secretary-general of the National Union of Mineworkers he is also favourably viewed by the trade union wing of the Tripartite Alliance. He is affectionately referred to as *mkhuluwa* (older brother). As secretary-general of the ANC, Motlanthe has been a father figure to ordinary party members, and has often been called upon to mediate disputes among warring factions.

Motlanthe's reputation came under question when he became associated with the so-called 'hoax email saga'. The allegation was that Jacob Zuma's supporters had created emails that were disparaging of their candidate in an effort to demonstrate that there was a political conspiracy against him, and thereby elicit sympathy for the Zuma campaign. At least, that was the finding of the government's report into the matter. But clearly the ANC, and particularly Motlanthe, would not let government have the last word on a matter so politically sensitive. The party initiated its own investigation, which exonerated Motlanthe, providing in the process yet further evidence of the divergence between a party leadership mostly sympathetic to Zuma and a government leadership under Mbeki.

An added boost to Zuma's party presidency is the support he has received from business tycoon and ANC leader Tokyo Sexwale. Sexwale caused waves in the ANC when he announced that he would be available for party presidency if he were to be nominated. This was viewed as an unconventional path to leadership in the ANC. The injunction is often that leaders must wait until they are called upon by the membership – even though everyone knows there is behind-the-scenes campaigning. After it became clear he did not have the votes, and given his own criticism of Mbeki, Sexwale withdrew from the race to lend his support to Zuma. The businessman is likely to play a significant role as a voice for openness and tolerance of debate in a Zuma-led national executive committee of the ANC. He could still be the person that the ANC looks to as an alternative or partner to Motlanthe. In such a situation Motlanthe would take charge of the government–party nexus, while Sexwale would focus more on the more public role, building alliances with groups outside the party both in the country and beyond. But even if Sexwale does not end up being the president of the ANC, and Zuma might be the popular choice rather than the intellectual elite's ideal candidate, both leaders have openly criticised the accumulation and abuse of power we have seen under the Mbeki presidency.[37] The question is: will they walk the talk as we proceed to yet another phase of our democracy?

I raised some of these issues in a piece on the role that Tokyo Sexwale and Jacob Zuma have played in opening up the ANC, but nonetheless suggesting it is perhaps time for Zuma to step aside for people such as Motlanthe and Sexwale:

That ultimate social quality called leadership has become a matter of inheritance. Thabo Mbeki writes about how a dying Oliver Tambo divined him with leadership of the ANC, and Jacob Zuma claims it is now his turn.

No one will spare a thought for us – the people who actually elect these dudes into power. No one but Tokyo Sexwale dared play that role in the lead-up to the ANC leadership conference. In the end they all came around to appealing to the public for support. That is how it was supposed to be in the first place. The best countries are those in which individuals and parties compete for leadership in the public domain. The worst countries have historically been those in which leadership is a fix among a set of unaccountable comrades. It took the Soviet Union decades to recognize that and make a turn, and one hopes that the genie of open leadership contestation is out of the bottle for the ANC.

One of my friends complained that I attribute this cultural shift to Sexwale instead of Zuma. In response, I said Zuma and Sexwale opened up ANC culture in radically different ways. Zuma was forced to defend himself against political persecution. It is quite likely that had there been no such persecution he would have kept quiet as a matter of old-fashioned party solidarity. This is not to say Zuma lacks courage. After all he was Sexwale's commander in the ANC's military wing Umkhonto we Sizwe. And those who know Sexwale will readily attest to his courage as a soldier. It is simply to say that there is a difference between military courage and democratic courage.

The great political philosopher Hannah Arendt described democratic courage this way: 'It requires courage to even leave the protective security of our four walls and enter the public realm.' This is the cultural shift in our conception of courage that we need to spread throughout our land if we are to make this a truly successful democracy.

The ANC showed us glimpses of it in the way Zuma got so many people to be active in his campaign. But Zuma's appeal is limited mostly to the ANC and disaffected members of society.

I have in previous writings suggested that Tokyo Sexwale has that transcendent appeal required of a national leader – to assure business while working in the interests of the poor. Some have said Sexwale has shown courage because of his wealth. Frankly, that is not always such a bad thing. Wealth enabled Moshood Abiola to challenge the worst dictator in Nigerian history, Sani Abacha. And wealth enabled John F. Kennedy to free the Democratic Party from party bosses and patronage politics . . .

It is, of course, possible that Kgalema Motlanthe would be the person the ANC could look to if Zuma should either falter or voluntarily step aside. Motlanthe would be entitled to that because he was voted into the position of deputy president. He would not be my ideal candidate, but would be a big improvement on both Mbeki and Zuma. And even if Sexwale did not become president, it would still behove leaders of his generation to follow his example and show some democratic courage.[38]

Over the past few years South Africa's leaders have rubbished Nelson Mandela's legacy by their racialisation of every little policy disagreement, and ethnic mobilisation became a big part of the ANC presidential campaign. Now is the time to reinvigorate the sense of common belonging and creativity that Mandela epitomised. The question is whether or not the ANC has the common sense to recognise how far we have veered from the original promise that our newly created democracy held, and whether the organisation will have in it the wisdom and capacity to bring us back from the brink. But then again, getting back from the brink is a task for all of us.

An Open Letter to Former President Nelson Mandela from Xolela Mangcu

Business Day, 16 October 2007

Dear Tata

I hope this letter finds you well. I am not well. Tears came to my eyes as I read news of the imminent arrest of *Sunday Times* editor Mondli Makhanya and Jocelyn Maker. I am not exactly sure whether I was crying for Mondli or for myself or for our country or for you in particular.

I was probably crying for all those things and more. You see, Tata, the foundations of our democracy have never been shakier, the credibility of our justice system never more suspect, the institutions of state never more compromised and our public culture never more hateful as it is under your successor, Thabo Mbeki.

He has single-handedly taken this country to its most dangerous and most perilous moment. He has become a god unto himself, accountable to nobody in particular but himself. He fires, suspends and punishes those who stand in his way.

Everywhere I go people are shaking their heads in disbelief. 'What has gone wrong with this man?' they ask. I will not presume to comment on the legalities of the cases and the dismissals of high-level ANC cadres such as Jacob Zuma, Nozizwe Madlala-Routledge, Billy Masetlha, Vusi Pikoli, and Makhanya.

These are just the state's most public victims. That is what dictatorial regimes do – they isolate individuals and punish them in public in order to demonstrate that they will not tolerate dissent.

You know from your experience, Tata, that power knows no limits. Stalin showed us that not even the most loyal comrades were beyond the gulag. Power jails, power silences, power banishes and power ultimately kills those who are a threat to it. Power is conscious of itself but power is most dangerous when it is unconscious of its actions or when its actions take on a certain automacity.

The reflexive instinct to punish takes over all faculties – public perceptions and consequences be damned.

For a while, there have been rumours that the wolves are circling around Makhanya. I don't think there is a journalist more hated by Mbeki's regime than Makhanya. This is because he has dared to expose the depravity at the heart of Mbeki's government.

Now we hear that Makhanya and Maker's cellphones have been tapped. When news broke that the SABC had a blacklist of certain commentators, I said any state that blacklists its citizens is only a step away from assassinating them.

Someone called me the other day under the guise of a journalist, seeking commentary about the leadership succession race in the ANC.

But I could immediately sense that I was talking into a tape. Maybe I am being paranoid. How could I not be paranoid when there are allegations of links between the highest offices in our land and the criminal underworld?

The very things that were done to us – the reflexive instinct to punish through imprisonment – have become the order of the day in this land at its birth. To paraphrase the scholar Achille Mbembe, we have forgotten that this democracy was born at the edge of the grave.

I read Justice Malala's painful plea for ordinary South Africans to stand up and express their outrage. But it is his conclusion that scared me so much: 'When, one day, we open our eyes and our mouths, our children will not have a country to live in. This country will be a Zimbabwe because we allowed Mbeki and his cronies to rape it.'

Those of us who can run will, of course, run, if we can get out before the wolves get to us. Another writer, Jacob Dlamini, described Mbeki as 'one of the pettiest presidents South Africa is likely to ever know'. And this is based on the view that Mbeki uses state institutions to persecute anyone who mildly disagrees with him.

In such a short space of time, since you stepped down from the presidency, the state itself has become indistinguishable from the individual.

This is a disgrace for a country that was held aloft as the beacon of freedom, democracy and justice just a mere decade ago. How did we fall so quickly from grace?

Where are the good men and women of the ANC? How could they allow their senses to be deadened this way? How could they connive in the dismemberment of the very project everyone gave up so much for?

How could people, who were so brave under apartheid, just cower under one man? What is it that they know that we do not know?

I am writing this letter, Tata, to say that you are our last hope, our only chance.

You cannot watch silently while your successor deliberately pulls apart everything you and your departed comrades so carefully put together.

Your voice would reverberate across this land, across this continent and across the world. Your voice, Tata, could help avert evils that are certainly going to be visited on the people of this country by a power-mad bunch in the Union Buildings.

Your voice could pull this country from certain ruination. Your voice could save our lives.

Notes

Introduction

1. Benjamin Pogrund, *How Can Man Die Better?* (Johannesburg: Jonathan Ball, 2004).
2. Steve Biko, *I Write What I Like* (Johannesburg: Picador Africa, 2006), 52.
3. Biko, *I Write What I Like*, 170.
4. I conducted interviews with all of these individuals.
5. Jonny Steinberg, 'Mbeki's Anxieties around AIDS have Damaged our National Psyche', *Business Day*, 6 November 2006.
6. Letter from the President, *ANC Today*, online newsletter of the ANC, 20–25 May 2007, Vol. 7, No. 20, www.anc.org.za/ancdocs/anctoday/2007/at20.htm.
7. Belinda Bozzoli, 'The Difference of Social Capital and the Mobilizing and Demobilizing Powers of Nationalism: The South African Case', unpublished manuscript, 3. For Bozzoli's elaboration of syncretism see also Belinda Bozzoli, *Theatres of Struggle and the End of Apartheid* (Johannesburg: Wits University Press, 2004).
8. Frank Ortiz, *Cuban Counterpoint: Tobacco and Sugar*, translated by Harriet de Onis (London: Duke University Press, 1995), 98.
9. David Attwell, *Rewriting Modernity: Studies in Black South African Literary History* (Pietermaritzburg: University of KwaZulu-Natal Press, 2005), 19.

Chapter 1

1. C. Wright Mills, *The Sociological Imagination* (New York: Oxford University Press, 1967), 6.
2. Nelson Mandela, *Long Walk To Freedom* (London: Little, Brown, and Company, 1994), 577.
3. Mandela, *Long Walk To Freedom*, 597.
4. For in-depth discussion of this period see Noel Mostert, *Frontiers: The Epic of South Africa's Creation and the Tragedy of the Xhosa People* (London: Jonathan Cape, 1992).
5. Karl Polanyi, *The Great Transformation: The Political and Economic Origins of Our Time* (Boston: Beacon Press, 1944).
6. Mostert, *Frontiers*, 210.
7. Sandile Ngidi, 'Interview with Ntongela Masilela', unpublished manuscript (2000), 63.
8. Catherine Higgs, *The Ghost of Equality: The Public Lives of DDT Jabavu of South Africa, 1885–1959* (Athens, OH: Ohio University Press, 1996).
9. Bheki Peterson, *Of Missionaries, Prophets and Intellectuals* (Johannesburg: Wits University Press, 2000), 65.
10. For a discussion of the wars of resistance or the so-called frontier wars, see Mostert, *Frontiers*.
11. Donovan Williams, *Umfundisi: A Biography of Tiyo Soga, 1829–1871* (Lovedale: Lovedale Press, 1978).
12. Tiyo Soga, *King William's Town Gazette* and *Kaffrarian Banner*, 11 May 1865. The response initially comes under the pseudonym 'Defensor – a Reply'.
13. Williams, *Umfundisi*.
14. From John Chalmers's biography of Soga, *Tiyo Soga, A Page of South African Mission Work* (Edinburgh: Andrew Elliot, 1877), 430. Chalmers's condescending, paternalistic attitude to Soga is self-evident in the title of the biography.
15. Attwell, *Rewriting Modernity*, 46.
16. Originally published in isiXhosa in *Isigidimi SamaXhosa* on 1 June 1882. Hoho is where the Rharhabe paramount chief Sandile died in 1878.
17. Ntongela Masilela, 'Transmission Lines of the New African Movement', Seminar, Public Intellectual Life Project, Wits University, 5 April 2006.
18. For a brilliant discussion of these debates see Ngũgĩ wa Thiong'o, Steve Biko Memorial Lecture, 12 September 2003.
19. Gianna Pomata, 'A Common Heritage: The Historical Memory of Populism in Europe and the United States', in Harry C. Boyte and Frank Riesman, *The New Populism* (Philadelphia: Temple University Press, 1986).
20. Lewis Nkosi, 'Negritude: New and Old Perspectives', in Lindy Stiebel and Liz Gunner, *Still Beating the Drum: Critical Perspectives on Lewis Nkosi* (Johannesburg: Wits University Press, 2006), 284.
21. I asked Barney Pityana to write this as part of my research on Steve Biko's biography.
22. Aime Cesaire, quoted in Kwame Anthony Appiah and Henry Louis Gates Jr, *Africana: The Encyclopedia of the African and African American Experience* (New York: Basic Civitas Books, 1999).
23. Biko, *I Write What I Like*, 52.
24. Biko, *I Write What I Like*, 115–16.

25. Nine leaders of SASO and the BPC were put on trial under the Terrorism Act for inciting student unrest on black campuses. This occurred in the wake of them welcoming the FRELIMO government in Mozambique in September 1974. All were eventually convicted and sent to Robben Island.
26. Biko, *I Write What I Like*, 147.
27. Biko, *I Write What I Like*, 148.
28. Biko, *I Write What I Like*, 26.
29. Biko, *I Write What I Like*, 26.
30. For a history of Rubusana, see Songezo Ngqongqo, 'Mpilo Walter Benson Rubusana, 1858–1910: The Making of the New Elite in the Eastern Cape', Master's dissertation in history from the University of Fort Hare, 1996.
31. T.D. Mweli Skota, *African Who's Who: An Illustrated Classified Register and National Biographical Dictionary of the Africans in the Transvaal*, 3rd edition of the *African Yearly Register* (Johannesburg: Frier and Munro, 1966).
32. Brian Willan (ed.), *Sol Plaatje's Selected Writings* (Johannesburg: Wits University Press, 1996).
33. Skota, *African Who's Who*.
34. Deidre D. Hansen, speech given at Heritage Day celebrations of the Department of Education, Culture and Sport, Bisho, Eastern Cape, 24 September 1996; Deidre D. Hansen, *The Life and Work of Benjamin Tyamzashe: A Contemporary Xhosa Composer* (Grahamstown: Rhodes University, 1968).
35. Hansen, *The Life and Work of Benjamin Tyamzashe*.
36. Luyanda Msumza, research project on Ginsberg history, unpublished manuscript.
37. This confirms that the earliest experiments with urban segregation did not start only in 1948 but go back to the late nineteenth and early twentieth centuries under the British.
38. Mangcu and Mjamba were the Booker T. Washington and W.E.B. du Bois of our township. Mangcu greatly believed in self-help as the path to black progress, and Mjamba thought that was not possible without a resolution of the political problems affecting black people first.
39. To be sure, Mangcu and Mjamba took over from earlier figures such as Gqaliwe, Zaula, Gushman and Gcilishe. The difference is only that Mangcu and Mjamba were better educated.
40. When Steve Biko was banned and restricted to Ginsberg Township in 1973 the core leadership of the movement shifted to King William's Town. People such as Peter Jones, Mamphela Ramphele, Thenjiwe Mthintso and Malusi Mpumlwana came to live in King William's Town.
41. Peter Jones's detailed account of the beatings is contained in Donald Woods, *Biko* (London: Henry Holt and Company, 1978).
42. See Tom Lodge's authoritative history of the ANC, *Black Politics in South Africa since 1945* (London: Longman, 1983).
43. I am currently working on a manuscript on the history of the black student leadership at Wits in the 1980s. The book contains interviews with some of these leaders and provides interesting insights into the making of a new generation of South Africa's leaders.

44. John Stuart Mill in Carole Pateman, *Participation and Democratic Theory: Structural Analysis in the Social Sciences* (Cambridge: Cambridge University Press, 1973).

Chapter 2

1. Anthony Sampson, *Mandela: The Authorised Biography* (Johannesburg: Jonathan Ball, 1999), 504
2. Gunnar Myrdal, *An American Dilemma: The Negro Problem and Modern Democracy* (New York: Harper and Brothers, 1944).
3. Eric Foner, *The Story of American Freedom* (New York: WW Norton, 1998).
4. Benedict Anderson, 'On the Goodness of Nations', Public Intellectual Life Project, Wits University, 13 September 2006.
5. Shashi Tharoor, *India: From Midnight to the Millennium* (New York: Arcade Publishing, 1997); Sunil Khilnani, *The Idea of India* (New York: Farrar, Straus and Giroux, 1997).
6. Xolela Mangcu, 'Seeking Common National Values', *Mail & Guardian*, 5–11 June 1998.
7. Suren Pillay, 'Intellectuals Dance to a Different Drum', *Mail & Guardian*, 12–19 June 1998.
8. Isaiah Berlin, 'The Bent Twig: On the Rise of Nationalism', in Henry Hardy (ed.), *The Crooked Timber of Humanity: Chapters in the History of Ideas* (London: John Murray, 1990), 246.
9. Eric Hobsbawm, *Nations and Nationalism since 1780: Programme, Myth, Reality* (Cambridge: Cambridge University Press: 1992).
10. Karima Brown, 'The Hour of Barrell's Heresy Comes Round at Last', *Business Day*, 23 October 2007.
11. Thabo Mbeki, Oliver Tambo Memorial Lecture, Wits University, 11 August 2000.
12. Personal communication with Mothobi Mutloatse
13. Xolela Mangcu, 'The Thought Police Ignore our History of Moral Reasoning', *Business Day*, 13 May 2001.
14. Ivor Chipkin, *Do South Africans Really Exist: Nationalism, Democracy and the Identity of 'the People'* (Johannesburg: Wits University Press, 2007), 6–9.
15. Sandile Memela, 'Black Brainpower', *Mail & Guardian*, 5–11 May 2006.
16. Christine Qunta, 'When Blacks are Made to Turn on their own Race', *The Star*, 25 July 2007.
17. Ronald Suresh Roberts, *Fit to Govern: The Native Intelligence of Thabo Mbeki* (Johannesburg: STE Publishers, 2007), Acknowledgements.
18. Thami Mazwai, 'Stop Unashamed Nitpicking', *The Star*, 17 July 2007.
19. Xolela Mangcu, 'Dali Mpofu: What the Paradoxes of One Man Say about our Nation', *Business Day*, 26 October 2006.
20. Michael Walzer, 'The Civil Society Argument', in Chantal Mouffe (ed.), *Dimensions of Radical Democracy: Pluralism, Citizenship, Community* (London: Verso, 1992), 89–107.
21. Thandika Mkandawire, *African Intellectuals: Rethinking Politics, Language, Gender and Development* (London: Zed Books, 2006).
22. Mkandawire, *African Intellectuals*, 23–24.
23. Mwalimu Julius Nyerere, speech at Bellagio, Italy, October 1997.

Chapter 3

1. James Myburgh, 'Here is the Evidence of Mbeki's Denialism', Politicsweb, 12 July 2007, www.politicsweb.co.za.
2. John Iliffe, *The African AIDS Epidemic: A History* (London and Cape Town: James Currey and Double Storey, 2006).
3. Nicoli Nattrass, *Mortal Combat: AIDS Denialism and the Struggle for Antiretrovirals in South Africa* (Pietermaritzburg: University of KwaZulu-Natal Press, 2007), 42. For Mbeki's actual statement see, Thabo Mbeki, 'ANC has No Financial Stake in Virodene', *Mayibuye*, March, www.anc.org.za/ancdocs/pubs/mayibuye/mayi9801. html#contents.
4. Nattrass, *Mortal Combat*, 43.
5. Nattrass, *Mortal Combat*, 57–59.
6. Nattrass, *Mortal Combat*, 58.
7. Nattrass, *Mortal Combat*, 59–60.
8. Peter Mokaba, 'Castro Hlongwane, Caravans, Cats, Geese, Foot and Mouth and Statistics: HIV/AIDS and the Struggle for the Humanisation of the African', March 2002. Available at www.virusmyth.net/aids/data/ancdoc.htm.
9. Mkandawire, *African Intellectuals*, 24.
10. Xolela Mangcu, 'Loyal Cadre Slips up as Country Dies of Haemorrhage', *Business Day*, 31 March 2002.
11. The rebuke of Mandela for breaking ranks reportedly happened at the National Executive Committee meeting of the ANC of 15–17 March 2002.
12. Xolela Mangcu, 'We Must Take the Initiative when our Leaders Fail us on AIDS', *Business Day*, 12 September 2001.
13. Thabo Mbeki, speech at the opening of the Thirteenth International HIV/AIDS Conference, Durban, South Africa, 9 July 2000. Available at www.virusmyth. net/ aids/news/durbspmbeki.htm.
14. *Sunday Times*, 9 July 2000.
15. For a time-line of Mbeki's HIV/AIDS denialism see Myburgh, Politicsweb contribution.
16. *Washington Post*, 25 September 2003.
17. Stephen Lewis, speech at the Sixteenth International AIDS Conference, Toronto, Canada, 18 August 2006. Available at www.whrnet.org/docs/perspective-lewis-0608. html.
18. Michael Ignatieff, 'Getting Iraq Wrong', *New York Times*, 5 August 2007.
19. Isaiah Berlin, *A Sense of Reality: Studies in Ideas and their History* (New York: Farrer, Straus and Giroux, 1996).
20. Ignatieff, 'Getting Iraq Wrong'.
21. Peter Bruce, 'The Thick End of the Wedge', *Business Day*, 22 January 2007.
22. Justice Malala, 'Time to Come Home', *Sowetan*, 22 January 2007.
23. Quoted in Nattrass, *Mortal Combat*, 39.
24. Nattrass, *Mortal Combat*, 75.
25. Thabo Mbeki, letter to African leaders, 3 April 2000. Available at www.virusmyth. net/aids/news/lettermbeki.htm.
26. Thabo Mbeki, Z.K. Matthews Memorial Lecture, University of Fort Hare, 12 October 2001.

27. Mandisa Mbali, 'The Treatment Action Campaign and the History of Rights-Based, Patient-Driven HIV/AIDS Activism in South Africa', Research Report No. 29, Centre for Civil Society, University of KwaZulu-Natal, Durban, 2005, 1–23.
28. Nattrass, *Mortal Combat*, 97.
29. Roberts, *Fit to Govern*.
30. Rhoda Kadalie, *Business Day*, 14 December 2006.

Chapter 4
1. Wole Soyinka described Mugabe as a monster at an address to the Cape Town Press Club in July 2005.
2. Xolela Mangcu, 'For our Collusion with Mugabe, Black South Africa should Feel Ashamed', *Business Day*, 12 July 2007.
3. D. Weiner, S. Moyo, B. Munslow and P. O'Keefe, 'Land Use and Agricultural Productivity in Zimbabwe', *Journal of Modern African Studies*, 23(2), 1985, 251–85.
4. Bill Kinsey, 'Zimbabwe's Land Reform Programme: Under-Investment in Post-Conflict Transformation', *World Development Report*, No. 32, Issue 10, October 2004: 1669–96.
5. Ibbo Mandaza, Introduction to Edgar Tekere's biography, *Edgar '2Boy' Zivanai Tekere: A Lifetime of Struggle* (Harare: SAPES Books, 2007).
6. Kinsey, 'Zimbabwe's Land Reform Programme'.
7. Kinsey, 'Zimbabwe's Land Reform Programme'.
8. Horace Campbell, *Reclaiming Zimbabwe: Exhaustion of the Patriarchal Model of Liberation* (Cape Town: David Philip, 2003), 99.
9. Campbell, *Reclaiming Zimbabwe*, 102.
10. Campbell, *Reclaiming Zimbabwe*, 102.
11. 'The Unleashing of Violence: A Report on the Violence in Zimbabwe as of May 15 2000', Report compiled by the Zimbabwean Human Rights NGO Forum, 16 May 2000.
12. *New African*, May 2007, No. 462, 18.
13. For an excellent discussion of Mugabe's atrocities see *Gukurahundi in Zimbabwe: A Report into the Disturbances in Matabeleland and the Midlands, 1980–1988* (Johannesburg: Jacana Media, 2007).
14. Jonathan Moyo, cited in 'The Unleashing of Violence', Zimbabwean Human Rights NGO Forum Report.
15. Campbell, *Reclaiming Zimbabwe*, 146.
16. Nkosazana Dlamini-Zuma, 'We Will Never Condem Zimbabwe', media briefing to the National Press Club, Pretoria, 3 March 2003.
17. *New African*, May 2007, No. 462.
18. Berlin, *The Bent Twig*, 251.
19. Malusi Gigaba, 'Common Liberals Avoid the Roots of the Problem', ANC Discussion Document, *ANC Today*, Vol. 4, No. 47, 26 November 2004–2 December 2004.
20. Jeremy Cronin, interview with Helena Sheehan, Cape Town, 24 January 2002.
21. For Nzimande's paper see *Bua Komanisi*, Vol. 5, No. 1, May 2006 special edition. Mbeki's response to Nzimande took place at the ANC NEC meeting of 7 October 2006. Mbeki's response on SABC radio took place on 9 October 2006.

22. Xolela Mangcu, 'Despot's Cynical Disregard for the Integrity of his own People', *Business Day*, 17 March 2002.
23. Campbell, *Reclaiming Zimbabwe*, 104.
24. Patrick Bond, *Talk Left, Walk Right: South Africa's Frustrated Global Reforms* (Pietermaritzburg: University of KwaZulu-Natal Press, 2006).
25. Henry Louis Gates Jr and Cornel West, *The Future of the Race* (New York: Vintage Books, 1993).
26. 'SA Arms Deal the Opening Act in the Greek Tragedy of the ANC', *The Weekender*, 27 January 2007.

Chapter 5
1. Paul Kleppner, *Chicago Divided: The Making of a Black Mayor* (DeKalb, IL: Northern Illinois University Press, 1985), 28.
2. All of these descriptions can be found in my Ph.D. dissertation, 'Harold Washington and the Cultural Transformation of Local Government in Chicago (1983–1987)' (Cornell University, Ithaca, New York, January 1997).
3. Pierre Clavel and Wim Wiewel, *Harold Washington and the Neighborhoods: Progressive City Government in Chicago 1983–1987* (Princeton, NJ: Princeton University Press, 1991).
4. De Lille later resigned from the PAC to form the Independent Democrats.
5. Xolela Mangcu, 'Lies have Become the Truth in the Corridors of Power', *Business Day*, 10 July 2007.
6. Msimelelo Njwabane, 'Sexwale: Arms Deal All about Kickbacks, not Defending SA', *The Witness*, 18 September 2007.
7. Thabo Mbeki, *ANC Today*, Vol. 3 No. 21, 30 May 2003. Available at www.anc.org.za/ancdocs/anctoday/2003/text/at21.txt.
8. Xolela Mangcu, 'Mbeki's Actions Give Conspiracy Theorists Plenty to Chew on', *Business Day*, 23 June 2005.
9. Xolela Mangcu, 'When your World Turns into a B-Movie, Roll with the Punches', *Business Day*, 1 September 2005.
10. Raymond Suttner, paper given at the Wits Institute for Social and Economic Research, quoted in the *Sunday Times*, 12 August 2007.
11. Ernesto Laclau, *On Populist Reason* (New York: Verso, 2005).
12. *Financial Mail*, 'Jackie Selebi Should Go or be Fired', 24 November 2006.
13. *Financial Mail*, 19 January 2007.
14. Jean-François Bayart, Stephen Ellis and Béatrice Hibou, *The Criminalization of the State in Africa* (Oxford and Bloomington: James Currey and Indiana University Press, 1999).
15. Xolela Mangcu, 'Race plus Nationalism plus State Power Always Add up to Tragedy', *Business Day*, 22 February 2007.

Chapter 6
1. Dan O'Meara, *Forty Lost Years: The Apartheid State and the Politics of the National Party, 1948–1994* (Johannesburg and Athens, OH: Ravan Press and Ohio University Press, 1996).

2. Njabulo Ndebele, 'Iph' Indlela: Charting the Way Forward', First Steve Biko Memorial Lecture, 12 September 2000, University of Cape Town.
3. Ron Walters, *White Nationalism, Black Interests: Conservative Public Policy and the African American Community* (Detroit, MI: Wayne State University Press, 2003).
4. Xolela Mangcu, 'Good Apples Give Cover to Bad Ones while the Tree Rots', *Sunday Independent*, 11 December 2000.
5. Xolela Mangcu, ' "Our Whites" Absolve themselves of Responsibility at their Own Risk', *Business Day*, 2 August 2007.
6. Walters, *White Nationalism, Black Interests*.
7. Benjamin Barber, *A Passion for Democracy* (Princeton, NJ: Princeton University Press, 1998), 14.
8. Xolela Mangcu, 'Tony Leon: Brilliant Strategist, Poor Leader', *Business Day*, 4 December 2006.
9. Carl Niehaus, 'White Racists Raise Your Hands, None', *City Press*, 1 October 2000.
10. Xolela Mangcu, 'SA se Wit Morele Leierskap is Nêrens Merkbare Faktor Nie', *Rapport*, 1 August 1999. The Afrikaans title can be roughly translated to 'South Africa's White Moral Leadership is not a Noticeable Factor Anywhere'.
11. *Business Day*, 17 September 2000.
12. Ndebele, 'Iph' Indlela'.
13. Xolela Mangcu, 'Denial can be Experienced as a Form of Attack', *Business Day*, 17 September 2000.
14. Biko, *I Write What I Like*, 108.

Chapter 7

1. Milan Kundera, *The Book of Laughter and Forgetting*, translated by Michael Henry Heim (New York: Alfred A. Knopf, 1980), 4.
2. Desmond Tutu, Nelson Mandela Lecture, 23 November 2004.
3. Ernest Renan, 'What is a Nation?', speech delivered at Sorbonne, Paris, 11 March 1882, 19.
4. Achille Mbembe, *On the Postcolony: Studies on the History of Society and Culture* (Berkley, CA: University of California Press, 2001), 16.
5. O'Meara, *Forty Lost Years*, 7.
6. Walzer, 'The Civil Society Argument'.
7. Harry Boyte, The John Dewey Lecture, University of Minnesota, April 2007.
8. Mbembe, *On the Postcolony*, 15.
9. Es'kia Mphahlele, *The African Image* (London: Faber and Faber, 1962), 42.
10. Ngũgĩ wa Thiong'o, Stewart-McMillan Lecture, Harvard University, 2006.
11. Peter Evans, *Embedded Autonomy: States and Industrial Transformation* (Princeton, NJ: Princeton University Press, 1995).
12. William Gumede, *Thabo Mbeki and the Battle for the Soul of the ANC* (London: Zed Books, 2007).
13. Evans, *Embedded Autonomy*, 241.
14. ANC, 'Consolidated Report on Sectoral Strategies', ANC National General Council, 29 June–3 July 2005, www.anc.org.za/ancdocs/ngcouncils/2005/consolidated_report.html.

15. ANC, 'Consolidated Report'.
16. Pallo Jordan, *Mail & Guardian*, 16–22 November 2007.

Chapter 8
1. Gates Jr and West, *The Future of the Race*; W.E.B. du Bois, *Writings* (New York: Library of America, 1986), 842, 861.
2. Saki Macozoma, 'Conversations on Leadership', Platform for Public Deliberation, Wits University Senate Room, 1 November 2007.
3. Mark Gevisser, *The Dream Deferred: Thabo Mbeki* (Cape Town: Jonathan Ball Publishers, 2007).
4. Thabo Mbeki, 'Oliver Tambo: A Great Giant Who Strode the Globe Like a Colossus', in Z. Pallo Jordan (ed.), *Oliver Tambo Remembered* (Johannesburg: Macmillan, 2007), xviii–xix.
5. Garry Wills, *Certain Trumpets: The Call of Leaders* (New York: Simon and Schuster, 1994), 23.
6. Ronald Heifetz, *Leadership without Easy Answers* (Cambridge, MA: Harvard University Press, 1991).
7. Sampson, *Mandela: The Authorised Biography*, 469.
8. Nelson Mandela, 'Statement after Voting in South Africa's First Democratic Election', www.anc.org.za/ancdocs/history/mandela/1994/sp940427.html.
9. O'Meara, *Forty Lost Years*, 414.
10. Thabo Mbeki, interview on *Newshour* with Charlayne Hunter-Gault, 24 July 1996.
11. Xolela Mangcu, 'Can the President Fulfil his Tryst with Destiny?', *Business Day*, 20 June 1999.
12. Barney Mthombothi, 'Salt in the Wound', *Financial Mail*, 2 February 2007.
13. *Mail & Guardian*, 2–8 February 2007.
14. *The Weekender*, 3–4 February 2007.
15. Abe Zaleznik, 'Managers and Leaders: Are They Different?', *Harvard Business Review*, May–June 1977: 67–78.
16. Xolela Mangcu, 'Cryptic Mbeki Runs Risk of Losing Touch with the Common People', *Business Day,* 12 February 2004.
17. Bheki Khumalo, 'Mangcu's Song', *Business Day*, 19 February 2004.
18. Smuts Ngonyama, 'Mangcu Betrays his Insecurities', *Business Day*, 2 March 2004.
19. Njabulo Ndebele, 'Not Deserved', *Business Day*, 24 February 2004.
20. Heifetz, *Leadership without Easy Answers*.
21. Heifetz, *Leadership without Easy Answers*, 268.
22. Wills, *Certain Trumpets*, 168.
23. Barber, *Passion for Democracy*, 97.
24. Barber, *Passion for Democracy*, 99.
25. Xolela Mangcu, 'Ten Reasons why Thabo Mbeki Should Reject Calls for a Third Term', *Business Day*, 7 December 2006.
26. Xolela Mangcu, 'South Africa: Mbeki's Pattern of Kingly Contempt', *Business Day*, 27 September 2007.
27. COSATU, 'COSATU Respond to the President's Letter', 10 December 2006, www. cosatu. org.za/press/2006/dec/press3.htm.

28. Xolela Mangcu, 'Mbeki an Aberration in History of Black Morality', *Sunday Times*, 26 August 2007.

Chapter 9

1. This is drawn from the 1965 directive by Amilcar Cabral, leader of the African Party for the Independence of Guinea-Bissau and Cape Verde: 'Tell no lies; claim no easy victories.'
2. Mondli Makhanya, 'Prosecutors Walk a Tightrope with Decision on when to Charge Zuma', *Sunday Times*, 24 November 2007.
3. Ayi Kwei Armah, *The Beautyful Ones are not yet Born* (London: Heinemann, 1968), 62.
4. Xolela Mangcu, 'This Country is Way Ahead of Both of them. But if you Put a Gun to my Head, I would have to go with Zuma', *Sunday Times*, 9 December 2007.
5. Xolela Mangcu, 'Four Questions about Zuma's Ability to Lead this Country', *Business Day*, 11 March 2005.
6. Jacob Zuma addressing Heritage Day celebrations in KwaDukuza, KwaZulu-Natal, 25 September 2006. Zuma later retracted his comments.
7. Frederick van Zyl Slabbert in 'Minds vs Hearts', *Sunday Times* panel discussion on the role of public intellectuals, *Sunday Times*, 2 December 2007.
8. Gevisser, *Dream Deferred*, 60.
9. Gevisser, *Dream Deferred*, 6.
10. Gevisser, *Dream Deferred*, 5.
11. Gevisser, *Dream Deferred*, 17
12. Gevisser, *Dream Deferred*, 71.
13. Gevisser, *Dream Deferred*, 62.
14. Gevisser, *Dream Deferred*, 16.
15. Wills, *Certain Trumpets*, 23.
16. Benedict Anderson, 'On the Goodness of Nations', Public Intellectual Life Project, Wits University, 13 September 2006.
17. Wills, *Certain Trumpets*, 37.
18. Pauline Morris, 'Zuma Ties', Letters to the Editor, *Business Day*, 6 December 2007.
19. *Financial Mail*, 31 November 2007.
20. Anton Harber, 'Lesson for Media in Zuma's Big Splash', *Business Day*, 5 December 2007.
21. Wills, *Certain Trumpets*, 26.
22. Renée Bonorchis, 'Spokesman Doubles Mbeki's Troubles', *Business Day*, 6 December 2007.
23. Laclau, *On Populist Reason*, 14; Peter Worsley, 'The Concept of Populism', in Ghita Ionescu and Ernest Gellner (eds.), *Populism: Its Meaning and National Characteristics* (London: Macmillan, 1969).
24. Harry C. Boyte and Frank Riessman (eds.), *The New Populism: The Politics of Empowerment* (Philadelphia: Temple University Press, 1986), 305.
25. Laclau, *On Populist Reason*, 123.

26. Xolela Mangcu, 'Populism Gets Short End of the Stick Again', *Business Day*, 6 December 2007.
27. Richard Sennett, *The Fall of Public Man* (New York: Knopf, 1977); William Whyte, *The Organization Man* (New York: Simon and Schuster, 1956).
28. For Njabulo Ndebele's discussion of 'spectacle', see Njabulo Ndebele, *Rediscovery of the Ordinary: Essays on South African Literature and Culture* (Pietermaritzburg: University of KwaZulu-Natal Press, 2006).
29. Steven Friedman cited in 'South Africa's Ruling Party Ousts Mbeki', *New York Times*, 19 December 2007, A11.
30. Angie Motshekga, 'The Leader of the Ordinary People', *The Weekender*, 8–9 December 2007.
31. Richard Neustadt, *Presidential Power and the Modern Presidents: The Politics of Leadership* (New York: Free Press, 1990), 248.
32. O'Meara, *Forty Lost Years*, 49.
33. O'Meara, *Forty Lost Years*, 50.
34. O'Meara, *Forty Lost Years*, 50.
35. Andrew Feinstein, *After the Party: A Personal and Political Journey inside the ANC* (Cape Town: Jonathan Ball, 2007), 176.
36. See Arthur M. Schlesinger, Jr, *The Imperial Presidency* (Boston: Houghton Mifflin Company, 2004). Schlesinger used this term to describe the growth in size and power of the presidency in the United States from Roosevelt to Richard Nixon – the similarities with Mbeki's presidency are striking.
37. For Sexwale's comments, see www.public-conversations.org.za. Zuma called for the protection of the judiciary and parliament against executive interference and for HIV/AIDS and crime to be treated as national emergencies at the International Human Rights Day celebrations at the Kara Institute in Johannesburg, 10 December 2007.
38. Xolela Mangcu, 'South Africa on the Threshold Once More', *Sunday Times*, 22 December 2007.

References

Appiah, Kwame Anthony. 2005. *The Ethics of Identity*. Princeton, NJ: Princeton University Press.

Appiah, Kwame Anthony and Henry Louis Gates Jr. 1999. *Africana: The Encyclopedia of the African and African American Experience*. New York: Basic Civitas Books.

Armah, Ayi Kwei. 1968. *The Beautyful Ones are not yet Born*. London: Heinemann.

Attwell, David. 2005. *Rewriting Modernity: Studies in Black South African Literary History*. Pietermaritzburg: University of KwaZulu-Natal Press.

Barber, Benjamin. 1998. *A Passion for Democracy*. Princeton, NJ: Princeton University Press.

Bayart, Jean-François, Stephen Ellis and Béatrice Hibou. 1999. *The Criminalization of the State in Africa*. Oxford and Bloomington: James Currey and Indiana University Press.

Berlin, Isaiah. 1990. 'The Bent Twig: On the Rise of Nationalism'. In Henry Hardy (ed.), *The Crooked Timber of Humanity: Chapters in the History of Ideas*. London: John Murray.

———. 1996. *A Sense of Reality: Studies in Ideas and their History*. New York: Farrar, Straus and Giroux.

Biko, Steve. 2006. *I Write What I Like*. Johannesburg: Picador Africa.

Bond, Patrick. 2006. *Talk Left, Walk Right: South Africa's Frustrated Global Reforms*. Pietermaritzburg: University of KwaZulu-Natal Press.

Boyte, Harry C. and Frank Riessman (eds.). 1986. *The New Populism: The Politics of Empowerment*. Philadelphia: Temple University Press.

Bozzoli, Belinda. 2004. *Theatres of Struggle and the End of Apartheid*. Johannesburg: Wits University Press.

Campbell, Horace. 2003. *Reclaiming Zimbabwe: Exhaustion of the Patriarchal Model of Liberation*. Cape Town: David Philip.

Chalmers, John. 1877. *Tiyo Soga, A Page of South African Mission Work*. Edinburgh: Andrew Elliot.

Chipkin, Ivor. 2007. *Do South Africans Really Exist: Nationalism, Democracy and the Identity of 'the People'*. Johannesburg: Wits University Press.

Clavel, Pierre and Wim Wiewel. 1991. *Harold Washington and the Neighborhoods: Progressive City Government in Chicago 1983–1987*. Princeton, NJ: Princeton University Press.

Du Bois, W.E.B. 1986. *Writings*. New York: Library of America.

Evans, Peter. 1995. *Embedded Autonomy: States and Industrial Transformation*. Princeton, NJ: Princeton University Press.

Feinstein, Andrew. 2007. *After the Party: A Personal and Political Journey inside the ANC*. Cape Town: Jonathan Ball.

Foner, Eric. 1998. *The Story of American Freedom*. New York: WW Norton.

Gates, Henry Louis, Jr and Cornel West. 1993. *The Future of the Race*. New York: Vintage Books.

Gevisser, Mark. 2007. *The Dream Deferred: Thabo Mbeki*. Cape Town: Jonathan Ball Publishers.

Gukurahundi in Zimbabwe: A Report into the Disturbances in Matabeleland and the Midlands, 1980–1988. 2007. Johannesburg: Jacana Media.

Gumede, William. 2007. *Thabo Mbeki and the Battle for the Soul of the ANC*. London: Zed Books.

Hansen, Deidre D. 1968. *The Life and Work of Benjamin Tyamzashe: A Contemporary Xhosa Composer*. Grahamstown: Rhodes University.

Heifetz, Ronald. 1991. *Leadership without Easy Answers*. Cambridge, MA: Harvard University Press.

Higgs, Catherine. 1996. *The Ghost of Equality: The Public Lives of DDT Jabavu of South Africa, 1885–1959*. Athens, OH: Ohio University Press.

Hobsbawm, Eric. 1992. *Nations and Nationalism since 1780: Programme, Myth, Reality*. Cambridge: Cambridge University Press.

Iliffe, John. 2006. *The African AIDS Epidemic: A History*. London and Cape Town: James Currey and Double Storey.

Khilnani, Sunil. 1997. *The Idea of India*. New York: Farrar, Straus and Giroux.

Kinsey, Bill. 2004. 'Zimbabwe's Land Reform Programme: Under-Investment in Post-Conflict Transformation'. *World Development Report*, No. 32, Issue 10, October: 1669–96.

Kleppner, Paul. 1985. *Chicago Divided: The Making of a Black Mayor*. DeKalb, IL: Northern Illinois University Press.

Kundera, Milan. 1980. *The Book of Laughter and Forgetting*, translated by Michael Henry Heim. New York: Alfred A. Knopf.

Laclau, Ernesto. 2005. *On Populist Reason*. New York: Verso.

Lodge, Tom. 1983. *Black Politics in South Africa since 1945*. London: Longman.

Mandaza, Ibbo. 2007. Introduction to Edgar Tekere's biography, *Edgar '2Boy' Zivanai Tekere: A Lifetime of Struggle*. Harare: SAPES Books.

Mandela, Nelson. 1994. *Long Walk To Freedom*. London: Little, Brown, and Company.

Mangcu, Xolela. 1997. 'Harold Washington and the Cultural Transformation of Local Government in Chicago (1983–1987)'. Ph.D. dissertation, Cornell University, Ithaca, New York.

Mbali, Mandisa. 2005. 'The Treatment Action Campaign and the History of Rights-Based, Patient-Driven HIV/AIDS Activism in South Africa'. Research Report No. 29, Centre for Civil Society, University of KwaZulu-Natal, Durban, 1–23.

Mbeki, Thabo. 2007. 'Oliver Tambo: A Great Giant Who Strode the Globe Like a Colossus'. In Z. Pallo Jordan (ed.), *Oliver Tambo Remembered*. Johannesburg: Macmillan.

Mbembe, Achille. 2001. *On the Postcolony: Studies on the History of Society and Culture*. Berkley, CA: University of California Press.

Mills, C. Wright. 1967. *The Sociological Imagination*. New York: Oxford University Press.

Mkandawire, Thandika. 2006. *African Intellectuals: Rethinking Politics, Language, Gender and Development*. London: Zed Books.

Mostert, Noel. 1992. *Frontiers: The Epic of South Africa's Creation and the Tragedy of the Xhosa People*. London: Jonathan Cape.

Mphahlele, Es'kia. 1962. *The African Image*. London: Faber and Faber.

Myrdal, Gunnar. 1944. *An American Dilemma: The Negro Problem and Modern Democracy*. New York: Harper and Brothers.

Nattrass, Nicoli. 2007. *Mortal Combat: AIDS Denialism and the Struggle for Antiretrovirals in South Africa*. Pietermaritzburg: University of KwaZulu-Natal Press.

Ndebele, Njabulo. 2006. *Rediscovery of the Ordinary: Essays on South African Literature and Culture*. Pietermaritzburg: University of KwaZulu-Natal Press.

Neustadt, Richard. 1990. *Presidential Power and the Modern Presidents: The Politics of Leadership*. New York: Free Press.

Ngqongqo, Songezo. 1996. 'Mpilo Walter Benson Rubusana, 1858–1910: The Making of the New Elite in the Eastern Cape'. Master's dissertation, University of Fort Hare.

Nkosi, Lewis. 2006. 'Negritude: New and Old Perspectives'. In Lindy Stiebel and Liz Gunner, *Still Beating the Drum: Critical Perspectives on Lewis Nkosi*. Johannesburg: Wits University Press.

O'Meara, Dan. 1996. *Forty Lost Years: The Apartheid State and the Politics of the National Party, 1948–1994*. Johannesburg and Athens, OH: Ravan Press and Ohio University Press.

Ortiz, Frank. 1995. *Cuban Counterpoint: Tobacco and Sugar*, translated by Harriet de Onis. London: Duke University Press.

Pateman, Carole. 1973. *Participation and Democratic Theory: Structural Analysis in the Social Sciences*. Cambridge: Cambridge University Press.

Peterson, Bheki. 2000. *Of Missionaries, Prophets and Intellectuals*. Johannesburg: Wits University Press.

Pogrund, Benjamin. 2004. *How Can Man Die Better?* Johannesburg: Jonathan Ball.

Polanyi, Karl. 1944. *The Great Transformation: The Political and Economic Origins of Our Time*. Boston: Beacon Press.

Pomata, Gianna. 1986. 'A Common Heritage: The Historical Memory of Populism in Europe and the United States'. In Harry C. Boyte and Frank Riesman, *The New Populism*. Philadelphia: Temple University Press.

Roberts, Ronald Suresh. 2007. *Fit to Govern: The Native Intelligence of Thabo Mbeki*. Johannesburg: STE Publishers.

Sampson, Anthony. 1999. *Mandela: The Authorised Biography*. Johannesburg: Jonathan Ball.

Schlesinger, Arthur M., Jr. 2004. *The Imperial Presidency*. Boston: Houghton Mifflin Company.

Sennett, Richard. 1977. *The Fall of Public Man*. New York: Knopf.

Skota, T.D. Mweli. 1966. *African Who's Who: An Illustrated Classified Register and National Biographical Dictionary of the Africans in the Transvaal*. Third edition of the *African Yearly Register*. Johannesburg: Frier and Munro.

Tharoor, Shashi. 1997. *India: From Midnight to the Millennium*. New York: Arcade Publishing.

'The Unleashing of Violence: A Report on the Violence in Zimbabwe as of May 15 2000'. Report compiled by the Zimbabwean Human Rights NGO Forum, 16 May 2000.

Walters, Ron. 2003. *White Nationalism, Black Interests: Conservative Public Policy and the African American Community*. Detroit, MI: Wayne State University Press.

Walzer, Michael. 1992. 'The Civil Society Argument'. In Chantal Mouffe (ed.), *Dimensions of Radical Democracy: Pluralism, Citizenship, Community*. London: Verso.

Weiner, D., S. Moyo, B. Munslow and P. O'Keefe. 1985. 'Land Use and Agricultural Productivity in Zimbabwe'. *Journal of Modern African Studies* 23(2): 251–85.

Whyte, William. 1956. *The Organization Man*. New York: Simon and Schuster.

Willan, Brian (ed.). 1996. *Sol Plaatje's Selected Writings*. Johannesburg: Wits University Press.

Williams, Donovan. 1978. *Umfundisi: A Biography of Tiyo Soga, 1829–1871*. Lovedale: Lovedale Press.

Wills, Garry. 1994. *Certain Trumpets: The Call of Leaders*. New York: Simon and Schuster.

Woods, Donald. 1978. *Biko*. London: Henry Holt and Company.

Worsley, Peter. 1969. 'The Concept of Populism'. In Ghita Ionescu and Ernest Gellner (eds.), *Populism: Its Meanings and National Characteristics*. London: Macmillan.

Index

Robben Island 8, 89, 188n.25
Roberts, Ronald Suresh 42–43, 63
Rodney, Walter 15
Roosevelt, Franklin Delano 59, 142,
  159, 164–65, 166, 167–68
Rousseau, Jean Jacques 34, 109
Rubicon 102
Rubusana, W.B. 13, 14, 18–19

Said, Edward 37
Sampson, Anthony 34
Sandile, *King* 18
Sartre, Jean Paul 15
Scorpions 87
Sebe, Lennox 27
Seepe, Sipho 39
Selebi, Jackie 96, 147, 155
Seme, Pixley ka Isaka 13
Senghor, Leopold Sadar 15, 79
Sennett, Richard 172
Sexwale, Tokyo 87, 146, 148, 180–82,
  196n.37
Shaik, Mo 90
Shaik, Schabir 89–90, 93, 149, 156, 160
Shaw, William 8
Sheehan, Helena 77
Shisana, Olive 46
Shubane, Khehla 30
Simon, Herbert 141
Sisulu, Walter 67
Sisulu, Zwelakhe 45
Skota, T.D. Mweli 19
Skweyiya, Zola 64
Smith, Harry 8
Smith, Ian 70
Smuts, Jan 145
Sobukwe, Robert 3–4, 24, 34, 79
Socrates 141–42
Soga, Tiyo xiii, 10–13, 17, 19
Soggot, David 16
South African Broadcasting Corporation
  (SABC) 44, 158
South African Communist Party 5, 77
South African Native National Congress
  13

South African Students' Organisation
  (SASO) 16, 106
Southern African Development
  Community (SADC) 75–76
Soyinka, Wole 67
Spain 179
Squires, *Judge* Hilary 94, 149
Stalin, Joseph 184
Steinberg, Jonny 4
Stevenson, Adlai 166
Strijdom, J.G. 175
Stubbs, Aelred 4
Stutterheim Experiment (1989) 32
Suttner, Raymond 95
Suzman, Helen 112
syncretism 121 *see also* racial syncretism

'Talented Tenth' 131–32
Tambo, Oliver 24, 39, 132, 154
Tanzania 120, 138
Terkel, Studs 84
Tharoor, Shashi 35
Thetard, Alain 89, 93
Thiong'o, Ngũgĩ wa 39, 123
transculturation 5
Treatment Action Campaign (TAC) 55,
  62–63, 118, 120
tribalism 165
Tripartite Alliance 5, 77, 146, 150, 161,
  180
Truth and Reconciliation Commission
  (TRC) 101, 105, 135
Tshabalala-Msimang, Manto 57, 63–64,
  151
Tshatshu, Dyani 22
Tshwete, Steve 24–25, 148
Tsvangirai, Morgan 73–74
Tutu, *Archbishop* Desmond 55, 102, 111,
  118, 148, 154
Tyamzashe, Benjamin 20–21
Tyamzashe, Gwayi 14, 18–19
Tyamzashe, Henry 19–20
Tyamzashe, Mantondo 21
Tyamzashe, Mthobi 25
Tyamzashe, Noteya 18